FROM

HEAVEN TO EARTH

SPIRIT TO FLESH

LIVING SOUL TO HUMANKIND

FROM

HEAVEN TO EARTH

SPIRIT TO FLESH

LIVING SOUL TO HUMANKIND

The Number 666

The Antichrist The False Prophet
The Two Witnesses of Christ
REVEALED

JEAN EUDES FRANKLIN

ARPress
ILLUMINATING IDEAS,
EMPOWERING VOICES

Contents

This book is comprised of three interrelated parts:

ARPress
45 Dan Road Suite 5
Canton MA 02021
Hotline: 1(888) 821-0229
Fax: 1(508) 545-7580

Ordering Information:
Quantity sales. Special discounts are available on quantity purchases by corporations, associations, and others. For details, contact the publisher at the address above.

Printed in the United States of America.

ISBN-13:   Paperback   979-8-89330-410-7
                eBook   979-8-89330-411-4
                Hardback   979-8-89330-412-1

Library of Congress Control Number: 2024900540

Table Of Contents

The Indivisible Glory of God
God is a SOLOIST
The Sixth Seal and the Wrath of God

Dedication

This book is lovingly dedicated to all people, all nations, and all religions around the world who know or perhaps don't know yet that what we see is not all there is to it, and better yet, what we see is nothing compared to what really is.

Acknowledgments

My deepest thanks go to my wife, Marie Charlotte, for the wonderful words of encouragement and the long nights she stayed up with me as the best motivation I could ask for.

I also owe many thanks to my daughters Marsha and Tasha, who, for very long hours, never got tired of being at the computer whenever I needed them.

To my son Charles, I want to express my profound gratitude for all the chores he covered on my behalf around the house and all the errands he ran in my place to allow me the necessary time, which was vital in the creation of this book.

Lastly, to my older sons, Ben-Hur (Junior) and Carstin, and to my oldest daughter, Jennifer, who are flying with their own wings in this vast complex world, I want to say from the deepest part of my heart, "God bless you guys"!

Special Gratitude

Deepest gratitude is offered to RESURRECTION LIFE Family
Worship Center 405 Ixoria Ave in
Fort-Pierce, Florida Apostle **Trevor Banks** And
His wife, Pastor **Martha Banks**
for

their influence in peak spiritual values and shaping my view of the
divine truth.

Special Gratitude

I also must mention two other people whom I could never thank enough for their constant persuasion of getting baptized after knowing what I was going through.

Pastor **Pierre Paul Joseph,** a great friend from Port Saint Lucie, Florida,

and

His ex-associate, Pastor Gaspard Benjamin
Thank you, guys!

Resources Used For My Quotations

Biblical quotations in this book are from four different versions of scripture in both English and French, and I can assure you that was the most wonderful experience, being able to compare different versions of scriptures.

The versions that were used implicitly are: La Sainte Bible

Version Louis Second Société Biblique de Genève, Suisse (1978)

The NIV Study Bible

Kenneth Barker Zondervan Publishing House (1995)

New World Translation

New World Bible Translation Committee

Watchtower Bible and Tract Society of New York, USA (1984)

The Holy Bible

King James Version Giant Print Reference Edition (1990)

A Note From The Author

Since my childhood, I would incessantly find myself at the center of unexplainable events, strange dreams, and other supernatural phenomena. As I got older and the perambulation of these strange occurrences has evolved overwhelmingly, I advertently concluded that the development of a systematic approach was deemed necessary in order to make sense of these peculiar mysteries. Subsequently and peremptorily, I took cognizance of having been approached unwillingly and undesirably by the transcendent world and understood clearly to have come within range of the supernatural.

These spiritual invasions at one point became so predominant that I was compelled to share some of these experiences with a couple of pastors and other practicing Christians I know in hope for answers, but the perplexities continued with no rational explanation until I was about fifty years old.

During my fiftieth anniversary, following a period of being terribly frightened, having been exposed to so many unusual episodes that the exuberant spectrum, if it were published, would ensue me to be declared a victim of some sort of mental disorders or simply from delusions or hallucinations.

For instance, it was about noon on a beautiful sunny day when the Holy Spirit came upon me while I was driving a fully loaded tractor trailer in the Fort Lauderdale area. The truck was instantly airborne all the way to my destination. When I looked at the other vehicles on the road and the pedestrians along the way, nobody seemed to have noticed anything, yet I just sat at the wheel with both legs tucked against the seat as the truck continued on its way, tilting left and right and making all the necessary turns. Once arrived, I will admit and confess that I made my delivery perplexedly, but the Lord Jesus Christ was at the center of my glory the entire time.

The Lord Jesus Christ baptized me with the Holy Spirit which initiated a completely new relationship with God that also brought with it outstanding wisdom and knowledge. I have been visited numerous times both tangibly and covertly, and I can assure you heartbreakingly that they are neither UFOs (unidentified flying objects) nor (unidentified freaking objects) for that matter. We are dealing with angels and demons, and they are everywhere, disguised as regular looking people. I have seen them Caucasian, black and everything in between. They would approach me on the road, at supermarkets, at gas stations, at the junk yard, on the highways, and what's even more interesting, they drive regular cars and trucks, as well as motorcycles. Simply unbelievable! Unless it is given to you to recognize them, they just go about their business unrecognized by the general public.

After having gone through all these experiences, I can tell you with tremendous conviction that this world is not what we think it is and humankind, from the average person to the most honored stature: "Kings, Queens, Presidents, Prime Ministers, Religious Leaders", despite the arrayal of technology and the arsenal of weaponry, is nothing but a deriding joke in the sight of these deranged invisible forces, even in their visible human appearances.

These encounters (the evil ones) have culminated in regretful estrangement as they have literally tried to kill me because of what I know, but to no avail. They have even tried to abduct me while I was on I-95 southbound in Martin County, Florida, but what a safe haven we have in the resurrection power of the Lord Jesus Christ as I found myself repeating continuously with trembling lips and tearful eyes as I was gradually regaining my senses; "Thank you Jesus for the blood; thank you Jesus for the cross", and strangely enough I could not stop crying and mumbling repetitiously these very words for a good moment. Then I realized I was still on the highway but miles away.

After multiple delusive attempts on different occasions by these entities, Satan himself made his appearance in a final alluring effort with all sorts of delusions while I was shopping at this famous store on Saint Lucie West Boulevard in Port Saint Lucie, Florida, to simply realize that even his own manifestation was fruitless in the presence of Christ in me I didn't even know I carry, and he immediately took flight.

You see, like the mystery surrounding Samson in *Judges 13* after he was born, my post-birth immediate existence had gone through a strange episode subsequent to an unwonted vision my mother had in which she was commanded a bunch of "do's and don'ts" she must follow concerning me. "Your son will be protected from all evil", she was cheered by her encounter.

I must admit I never understood and neither my mother, the purpose behind her experience, until these encounters became a reality in my life with seemingly a specific agenda, (the evil ones) to stop me from propagating my knowledge of the truth.

I now understand that the Lord Jesus Christ had allowed me to witness firsthand these phenomena to develop in me a deeper understanding of the spiritual reality, as my spiritual evolution was being molded and shaped by the Lord and Savior himself.

I consequently became overwhelmed with a fierce anger and an intense hatred for sin and the Devil, as I was evidently empowered to live a life with consistent obedience to the word of God and developed an unusual avidity for the things of the spirit while transcending all religious creeds centered on a reclusive theological system of interpreting scriptures that pervades the culture.

Amazingly I discovered that humankind is a "spirit being" in transit, skillfully maneuvered momentarily through this physical temple.

At first, I was confused not knowing what to do with these experiences, but later came this growing feeling that these spiritual episodes or revelations, some of which will be displayed in this book if they are relevant, might be of some interest and utility to both the Christian community and others in the search of the unvarnished truth.

I must confess it was never my intention to write a book about these revelations, but when I couldn't find anybody to listen to my testimonies and to take them to heart; I developed an unusual but consoling habit of talking to myself in desperate solitude. Every time "me, myself and I" would discuss each revelation received, I would jot down the meaning and its spiritual significance. As one revelation led to another and the testimonies so successive, I had tallied up before I knew it hundreds of pages of manuscript which today gave birth to this great book that I hope you will enjoy the blessings and the truth it brings from the Lord of the heavens and the earth.

Granting that your heart and spirit hunger for the things of God, these next pages will embark you on a spiritual journey that will surely open your eyes and reinforce what you may already know about the beginning (Genesis) and the end (Revelation), breaking physical barriers and entering a dimension of God never known before to humankind, less a chosen few, but has been kept secret by God Himself for reasons only known to Him.

Except now God has decided to reveal these heavenly things concerning us and thereby provides a spiritual encroachment that allows us to stealthily know who this man Jesus, whom all people admit walked this earth two thousand years ago, really is.

It's time that we turned our attention from the erroneous world view of God that has emerged due to a lack of knowledge, carefully planned and assiduously proliferated by the enemy (Satan) to keep the deity of Jesus unknown or somewhat mythicized and to prolong the disintegration of the body of Christ to the extent that each denomination reverts to its own reality as if God were the author of confusion, and thereby making it impossible to be wholly as one body in the service of God with demonstrations of power. **Remarkable shrewdness of the Devil!**

Everything you will read in this book is biblically grounded, but the Word of God must be read with the spirit of little children, as being poor both conventionally and spiritually no matter how old and what degrees or faculties one may possess, but with eager desires to learn. Yet what I personally find interesting in the understanding of the Bible is the fact that there might be a verse in Genesis for which in order to unveil its complete spiritual meaning you might have to go to the book of Revelation to find the mate or the complement verse. But only the Author of the Bible, the Holy Spirit, can unlock the inherent allegories and give the appropriate interpretation.

Although everything concerning creation, redemption, and salvation is within the pages of the Bible, some of the mysteries are sealed and reserved to be unleashed solely at appropriate specific times and will only be revealed, according to the wisdom of God, to and through his true prophets.

This great wisdom of God is a hidden mystery that neither Satan nor any of his demons knew about, which God had predestined for the glory of humankind before time began. The issue here is rather complex in the natural because humanity must understand the works of God from before the foundation of the world and appreciate it for what it represents in this given context of present reality where apostasy reigns.

The Apostle Paul says in *1 Corinthians 2:8* that if Satan and his squadrons knew and understood this wisdom, they would not have crucified the Lord of glory. The prophet Daniel, who had remarkable end-time revelation by an angel, was told in *Daniel 12:4-13* to close up and seal some of the end-time mysteries imparted to him, which obviously gives evidence of the metaphorical dimension of his writings.

According to *Daniel 12,* the angel said to Daniel, "Many will be purified and made spotless," but the wicked will continue to be wicked, and none of the wicked will understand the meaning of these words, for they will be revealed only to those who are wise but not those who are wise from the wisdom of this world, because God will bring the wisdom of this world to nothing. For such wisdom is not only foolishness to God according to *1 Corinthians 3:19* but also earthly, non-spiritual, and demonic. *(James 3:15)*

Daniel said in *verse 8,* "My Lord, I hear you but I do not understand. What will the outcome of all this be?" The Lord replied, "Go your way Daniel, you will rest, but at the end of the world you will rise to receive your allotted inheritance."

The apostle John takes the mystery of God even one step further when he declares in *John 20:30* and *John 21:25* that many other miracles, signs, and wonders were performed by Jesus in the presence of his disciples, which are not recorded in the Bible, and the apostle assured that if every one of them were written down, the whole world would not have room for the books that would be written.

It may be that God chose to leave some aspect of the spiritual eschatology open in order to reveal himself and his mystery to his chosen few through a personal relationship.

Before I go any deeper, I must avow a couple of things:

- **I am not a pastor**

- **I am not a theologian**

- **I am not a Bible scholar**

- **I never studied the Bible in any school or in any church settings.**

I first came in contact with my very first bible not too long ago as a gift from a close friend who knew these spiritual ordeals I was facing. But don't think for one minute that I underestimate the patency of universal mockery when God is using a "nothingness" Like me, an uneducated anonymous, someone who is not even in ministry, a poor man with no importance whatsoever whose origin goes back to a worldwide despised country, Haiti, as a vessel to bring such great and crucial understanding of the word of God and end-time prophecies to a confused, fearful and distrust culture.

But wait, don't curse me out yet. Did not God say to Isaiah? "I will be found by those who did not seek me, and I will reveal myself to those who did not ask for me," *(Romans 10:20).*

When God became man, Jesus did exactly that. He did not go to the temple in the search of "Old Testament scholars" or "Doctors of the law" to become his disciples. In fact, when Jesus was twelve, he met with these specialists of the "Law" but nothing deserving commendation came out of that meeting. Among the chosen twelve "Apostles" were men who were not only poor but who also had no educational background whatsoever.

In the scripture when one reads about the "Pharisees and Sadducees", the first thought that comes to mind is "Nobility" as we tend to associate them with the "highest class of citizens" of that day. But the sad truth is that both of these religious groups were rebuked by Jesus because they relied so greatly on their traditional rules and practices in lieu of the sacred truth of the scripture. The problem was that their customary beliefs and practices simply turned out to be nothing more than traditional observances with no supernatural significance, which Jesus himself confirmed of having no spiritual foundation.

Objectively, the contrasts became more evident when the Apostle Paul, unmatched in his theological radicalization and his zeal for the monotheistic nature of God and who was himself a prominent member of the religious eminency, declared that everything he had learned or practiced was garbage compared to the surpassing excellence of knowing Christ whose blood washed away all sins.

Let me borrow this next statement from the Apostle Paul which I solemnly declare to be also true for me. It is found in *Galatians 1:20*: *"I assure you before God that what I am writing you is no lie. This message was not received nor taught by any man. It was received by revelation from the Lord Jesus Christ. (Galatians 1:11-12)*

Today, two thousand years later, even with the clarity of the "New Testament" teachings, the "Church" still falls short of the spiritual realities of the "Word of God." I know some may condone and in fact will condone my audacious proclamations.

But part of the challenge is when the depths of the interpretation included in this book become evident, it would be preposterous not to admit there is only "one" bible scholar and his name is Jesus Christ, who alone can bring out such spiritual truths as described herein.

Spiritual realities as a legacy seem to have been lost, but as a decisive generation of the end-times we need to get pragmatic and seriously reconsider the related perspective in order to take fully informed decisions in line with the scripture and manage our lives as serenely and thoughtfully as possible.

Evidently, I will admit that if it were based on human restrictive orthodox academic standards, I would not have any religious qualifications to speak with any spiritual authority on this complex theological subject that has left some of the most prominent Bible scholars and some of the greatest theologians in disarray.

"Oh, the depth of the riches of the wisdom and knowledge of God! How unsearchable his judgments and his ways beyond finding out?" *(Romans 11:33).*

You see! Anybody who has been through seminary and obtained a pastoral degree has been taught how to study the Bible and explain its physical historicity as well as its moral and ethical principles in a very organized manner, which is good for the body and perhaps somewhat for the physical soul but not enough for the spirit.

Assertively, the key to the revelation of spiritual truth is not one's theological academic background or achievement, but to know who this man Jesus really is and to devote total obedience to his Word. Only then will the spiritual prevalence of the historical events be made known, as infinity becomes exceptionally accessible.

Our goal through these pages is to reveal a greater truth by explaining what it all means in the spirit, which is by far more valuable for the "living soul" or "the spirit", setting you free indeed.

Meanwhile, even though the world is desperately on the margin of spiritual subsistence and despite the legacy of resentment against the deity and the Lordship of Christ, (even amidst certain Christian communities), the last verse of the only book that offers humanity eternal life through an atoning blood sacrifice for sinners in need of grace thankfully and mercifully reads:

"The grace of our Lord Jesus Christ be with you all Amen." *(Revelation 22:21)*

The Apostle John, from the end of the world looking back, sadly declares in *Revelation 12:9* that, "Satan has deceived the entire world", which (Satan being the father of lies) literally means that his lies have thoroughly replaced the truth and fully conquered the world of science, politics and religions, instigating a worldwide forsaking of God through a defective knowledge of Christ whose cross has been mocked. But yet at the spiritual level Christ is the Lord, the Almighty God, the Creator of heavens and earth and the Savior of all mankind.

This persuasively gives prominence to the spiritual and the supernatural such as in the example of John in *Revelation 4:2* translated in the spirit by Christ to the end of the world (on the Lord's Day) as a witness of the true nature of the "Savior".

Accordingly, we propose in this book to carry you in that spirit dimension where you can come to truly know who Jesus is in the spirit, and then go back to the very first verse of the Bible and paraphrase it in the following manner: "In the beginning, Jesus created the heavens and the earth."

When and only when you can bring yourself to truly believe that God the Father, the Creator of heavens and earth, is Jesus incarnate, will your spirit be in readiness to receive the riches of the Spirit of God that is only given immeasurably to true worshipers.

Revelation 19:13-14 tells us that Jesus is the Word of God, and according to the scriptures, the Bible is the Word of God. Therefore, the Bible is Jesus translated in manuscript as both the object and the subject matter of this great revelation. To him be the glory forever, "for from him and through him and to him are all things! Amen." (Romans 11:36)

Bon appétit,
Jean Eudes Franklin

PART I

Introduction

When there are countless other respectable literatures about God and religion with well-supplied principles for guidance for a peaceful temporal physical life, why this book? Well, first because humans are more than mere physical creatures; second, because so much that is misleading has been taught and published about Jesus and his deity around the world, deceiving people from all religious backgrounds, subtracting from or adding to the Word of God, manipulating the message of the gospel to suit a secular need or purpose; and third, because sadly enough some of us continue to be deceived in believing that this life is all there is and therefore express more faith in secular publications, written or referenced by people we know or bygone historians, than to put our trust in the Word of God, which is the Spirit of God that guarantees an everlasting life with the Creator.

Today, as in the days of the prophet *Jeremiah (5:31)*, "the blind leads the blind and Prophets preach lies and rule by their own authority; and my people love it this way, said the Lord." Our unwillingness to come to terms with the truth of the scripture which is the necessary basis for understanding and knowing the true nature and character of God is primarily the root of our many social, political, economic and religious problems

Throughout history, science, philosophy, and certain religions have appropriated a certain elite that has been able to compound these three entities in the assumption they can know all things. In cases of unexplainable occurrences, such as divine miracles, signs and wonders, or the deity of Christ, adapted theories are developed, razing all spiritual vindication to suit their worldly agenda. People with big titles before or after their names have written numerous literatures based on false and bogus ascriptions, but a great ravisher in the natural to both science and religion.

Today, people with all types of religious beliefs continue to be misled by those ancient literatures and philosophies about the nature of God and particularly with regard to the deity of our Lord Jesus Christ. The scripture presents a very precise view of God pertaining to his oneness and fostering any imaginary expansion into three distinct beings is an affront to the monotheistic God.

The solemn truth is that God operates in a very desultory fashion. Without total obedience to his word, God mysteriously abides in such highly unfathomable and impenetrable dimensions as to confound those who love the wisdom of this world and to keep them from attaining the greater wisdom which is like the wind. Briefly put, it is not surprising that God is impossible to ever understand in this side of heaven, less his chosen few.

As disconcerting as this may sound, the Apostle Paul in *Colossians 2:8-11* warns us not to be captive through hollow and deceptive philosophy, which is based on human traditions and the basic principles of this world rather than on Christ in whom dwells the fullness of Deity, the Father, and the Holy Spirit in bodily form.

As an initiative challenge, let me tickle your spirit to see if you can believe beyond the natural where most people painfully accommodate themselves, unaware of the spiritual wonders that lie beyond. The New Testament presents Jesus as "the son of Abraham," "the son of David," "the son of Mary," and "the Son of God" *(Matthew 1:1–16* and *Luke 3:23–38).*

What do you think? Are any of these true about Jesus?

True/False

Jesus is the son of Abraham   _____

Jesus is the son of David   _____

Jesus is the son of Mary   _____

Jesus is the Son of God   _____

All of these proclamations are true in the natural. But looking at a higher truth and from the mouth of Jesus himself, I want to set the stage right off the bat by solemnly declaring that in the spirit this man called Jesus, whom all religions from all walks of life admit walked this earth at one time in history, is not the son of Abraham, not the son of David, not the son of Mary and Joseph, and it's most certainly not blasphemy to assert that in the spirit, Jesus is not the Son of God, as we will later see.

If you answered "True" to any of the above questions, you're in need of a milky pacifier to compensate for the lack of your spiritual satiation, because spiritual adequacy will fail you.

In fact, since the death of the "Apostles", no one has come out boldly about Jesus being the Creator and God of the universe. Instead, in keeping with the flow, inspirational tales about his deity have been supposedly nurtured to a certain degree. But the irony is that, instead of serving the true purpose of his incarnation, this adeptness in fact degraded it.

In stark contrast to this negative widespread belief, a heightened emphasis of his deity is given in the next few passages.

- **"Truly, truly before Abraham was I am." "How can Jesus be the son of Abraham?"** *(John 8:58)*

3

- "David, filled with the Holy Spirit, called Me Lord, how can I be the son of David?" *(Matthew 22:45)*

- "Mary, the mother of Jesus, and her cousin Elisabeth, both filled with the Holy Spirit, refer to Jesus in the womb as their Lord and Savior." How can Jesus be the son of Mary? *(Luke 1:39–55)*

- "Mary, the mother of Jesus and the other women with her, filled with joy after seeing the empty tomb and suddenly meeting with Jesus, bowed as they clasped the feet of Jesus and worshiped Him." Therefore, Jesus cannot be the son of Mary. *(Matthew 28:8-9)*

- Philip said to Jesus, "Lord, show us the Father." Jesus answered: "I am the Father." *(John 14:8–9)*

The Deity of Christ

The Bible claims in *Luke 10:22* that no one knows who Jesus is except the Father, and no one knows who the Father is except Jesus and he to whom Jesus will reveal him. This mystery has a serious effect on how we perceive God. Everyone may believe in God, but not everyone has the same concept of the God Almighty, whose greatest commandment, as we read in *Mark 12:29,* pertains to the following:

"Hear O Israel, the Lord our God is ONE LORD"

In essence, after this defiant evidence of the spiritual over the natural we just read in the adjacent preceding pages, one must begin to see the real focus of the word of God, which is definitely centered on Christ. It would be a grave mistake to forsake the spiritual dimension of worship as commended by the Apostle John, *(John 4:24)* and revealed throughout the scripture if one were to avert any shortcomings.

In short, let me suggest a few assertions that I believe would be of crucial significance to understanding and interpreting the word of God at its spiritual level.

- **God, although sinless, was the first to have been affected by sin from before the foundation of the world.**

- **The scope of the scripture extends from eternity to eternity, encompassing time.**

- God gracefully and emphatically exposed the two creation accounts in Genesis to reinforce the vital necessity of the cross for the possibility of spiritual emendation:

1- The spiritual, sinless dimension of the creation of humankind in the Garden of Eden, the Paradise of God, which is in third heaven.

2- The ex-post-facto account involving the physical creation as a result of sin; the six-day account of Genesis and the transmigration of humankind to the earth.

- The word of God is not bound by time or dimensions of life and therefore should not be enclosed or limited inside a specific context.

- The word of God from Genesis to Revelation, no matter how mysterious it may seem or sound, is defined elsewhere in the Bible. But only God can reveal it.

- For any truth to be truly true, it must hold universally.

- When God speaks, his word is one of his manifest operations and must be thoroughly considered in its various implications. A conclusion at first sight may be primarily historical but will engender a deeper understanding of the spiritual truth it conveys if one were to go beyond the historical data into a higher realm where truth is at its utmost.

- Crucial answers that will make the biblical experience concerning the nature of God complete cannot be found, unless the spirituality of God as the sole source of revelation in our mind is clear and coherent.

- The inveteracy of the nature of God, which is set apart implicitly throughout the Holy Scripture, will be fathomed necessarily through having recourse to the origin of biblical data and some facet of foresight, in relation to the immanency of God through times.

Stated another way, an equilibrium must be established between the two concepts (spiritual and physical) if one were to avoid any misinterpretation of facts, while bearing in mind that the spiritual interpretation always has predominance.

Jesus made it clear in *John (3:12)* **that there are two dimensions to life.**

1. A spirit dimension,

2. An earthly dimension.

So therefore, the setting should be as followed:

1. One interpretation directed to the physical world.

2. One interpretation associated with the spirit realm.

Also, one must recognize that (5) five entities are literally or figuratively involved as actors concerning all matters of interpretations.

1. **God** (*in his three known dimensional existences*)

2. **Humans** (*as souls, spirits, or flesh*)

3. **Angels** (*holy or satanic*)

4. **Heaven** (*visible or invisible*)

5. **Earth** (*physical or metaphysical*)

Every expression is either directed to or is symbolic of one or more of these five actors. Also, be aware that the words "nations" and "trees" are interchangeably used for "angels" and "men" depending on the context, but "nations" at times would as well stand for literal countries.

Most importantly however, one must never lose sight of the utmost fact that Jesus is the principal object and subject of the entire scripture. In fact, Jesus, revealing his origin, says in *John 3 verse 13*, "No one has ever gone into heaven except the 'One' who came down from heaven, the Son of Man", referring to the 'Highest Heaven' where the Throne of God is, Heaven being comprised of many dimensions according to *John 14:2*.

Concerning the deity of Christ precisely, let me echo this infallible statement found in *Isaiah 45:5*, which is also the foundation for this book, *"Apart from me there is no God"*, giving evidence of the oneness of God unequivocally portrayed throughout the Bible, reverberating to the whole world that Jesus and the Father and the Holy Spirit *"is"* **One**.

In *Hosea 4:6* we are told that God's people are destroyed for lack of knowledge, which knowledge resides and can only be cultivated through the Lord Jesus Christ according to the Apostle Paul, who teaches in *Colossians 2:3* that Jesus is the great mystery of God in whom are hidden all the treasures of wisdom with all sorts of knowledge.

"All things were made by Jesus and for Jesus, things in heaven and on earth, visible and invisible, whether thrones, powers, rulers, or authorities."

Throughout the New Testament we read that Jesus is the Light of the world. But in our days such a low wattage has been assigned to his Light that those who do not know Jesus are in total darkness, and the ones who happen to know Him are kept in a dimmed environment.

Yet the prophet Isaiah in chapter 9:6 refers to the man Jesus as follows:

- **"Unto us a Child is born"**

- **"Unto us a Son is given"**

- **"His name shall be called Wonderful Counselor"**

- **"His name shall be called The Mighty God"**

- **"His name shall be called The Everlasting Father"**

- **"His name shall be called The Prince of Peace"**

A simple dissection of *Isaiah 9:6* **vanquishes all philosophies hostile to the deity of Christ.**

- A child is born, or a son is given. Everyone will agree this is in reference to Jesus in the flesh as the Son of Man born through the Virgin Mary.

- When it comes to Jesus being the Wonderful Counselor or the Mighty God, we read in John 14:26 that the Counselor is the Holy Spirit.

- Everlasting Father and Mighty God are titles used interchangeably to describe God the Father, the very Creator of the heavens and the earth.

The truth is that, based on *Isaiah 9:6,* Jesus is at the same time the Father, the Son, and the Holy Spirit. In fact, *1 John 5:7-9* teaches that there are three that bear witness in Heaven, the Father, the Son, and the Holy Spirit: And the **"Three"** are **"One"**. Much the same in the physical world, Jesus was born to bear witness in the earth when He came by water and blood: And these **"Three"**, according to *1 John 5:9,* also agree as **"One"**.

I know this statement probably makes some of you the "Nicodemus" of our days by proclaiming: *"How can these things be"?* But obviously this is a mystery to the flesh or to our limited carnal mind. Unfortunately to compensate for this knowledge deficiency, certain Bible scholars, teachers, and other theologians have adopted an expletive theory to satisfy their limited understanding of the infinite God. A notion that is well spread among evangelicals, called "the Trinity", where God the father is the most powerful, God the Son with a little less power, and frankly I do not even know where the Holy Spirit fits within that man-made power structure.

But this ironical concept of the nature of God is an emanation of the kingdom of darkness, so well-polished as to deceive with a clever and an indistinct interjection of a polytheistic mentality, making the pluralization of God a sad reality within the evangelicals. Christians at all levels are deceived and fall into that trap.

I am not good at math, but I know "three" are more than one and therefore plural; even if it's three of the same things. Three bananas are more than one banana, three apples are more than one apple, and three Gods are more than one God; whether it is "God the Father," "God the Son," or "God the Holy Spirit," generally described by our church leaders as the First person, the Second person, and the Third person respectively. The etymology has sadly not only resulted from bad theology but also from a significant lack of understanding of the scriptures and of the power of God.

The condescension of the Creator to our natural human dimension for our own sake *(men being spiritually retarded)* to identify with all men and to be known as a personal God, does not in any way give us the right to extemporarily separate the monotheistic God, and worst, distinguish and assign different attributes to each "Component" about "Whom" the scripture, *(which does not promote this tripartition),* supplies rather a heightened emphasis on a congenerous existence. Our focus in this post-natal generation of our Lord and Savior is to align ourselves with the teachings of the New Testament which truly satisfy the fundamentals of the new covenant between God and his people.

In the Old Testament, God manifested his presence or his power in a variety of ways through a diversity of self-representations.

- In *Genesis 1:2 we see Him* as the **Spirit of God hovering over the waters.**

- In *Genesis 3:8* as the voice of the Lord God.

- In *Genesis 15:1* as the Word of God talking to Abraham.

- In *Genesis 16:7-11* we see God as the angel of the Lord

- In *Genesis 18:1* God came down to talk to Abraham as "a Man"

- In *Genesis 21:17* we see God as the angel of God with Hagar.

- In *Genesis 26:2-24* God physically appeared twice to Isaac as a man

- In *Genesis 32:24* God is a man wrestling with Jacob.

I find this peculiarity of the unison of our patriarchal ancestors concerning the signification of God very interesting. And what I find even more astonishing is the fact they never doubted for one minute that they were reckoning with God the Father, the Almighty, the very Creator of heavens and earth, even though God not only would take different physical aspects in his many apparitions and would sometimes mingle them with incongruous demands and still that would not deter them from the faith they held as a solid rock in the monotheistic nature of a single true **GOD** of the universe.

- Adam and Eve knew that the voice they heard in the garden was God the Father.

- Abraham knew that the Word of God who spoke to him in that vision was God the Father.

- Hagar knew that the angel of the Lord who appeared to her was God the Father.

- When the angel of God came to Abraham as a man and gave him the promise, Abraham knew that was God the Father.

- When Jacob wrestled with that man for his blessing, he knew that was God the Father.

- When the Lord physically appeared to Isaac, he knew that was God the Father.

- When the angel of the Lord spoke to Moses in the fire out of the midst of the bush, Moses knew that was God the Father.

With that kind of faith, it is no wonder that God calls himself, "The God of Abraham, the God of Isaac, and the God of Jacob." And

God said, "This is my name forever, the name by which I am to be remembered from generation to generation."

Most theologians agree that the angel of the Lord in the Old Testament is the Pre-incarnate Christ! But we have been ineptly told— heightening the inequality of the Godhead—that Christ is the second person, making him divinely less significant. But the Apostle Paul, who had the privilege of going to Heaven and seeing what no other man has, in complete corroboration of the credence of all the Old Testament prophets that the "angel of God" is "God the Father," says in *Acts 27:23* that God appeared to him in the form of an angel.

Now for those who like to butcher God into three, after reading the following words used by the Apostle Paul in characterizing the angel that appeared to him, ask yourself: "Is Paul referring to God or Jesus?" Because in the "King James" Version these are his words in context verbatim:

"The angel of God whose I am and whom I serve appeared to me."

I don't know what your answer will be, but Paul already gave his in *Ephesians 3:1* when he specifically proclaims that he belongs to Christ as his prisoner, and in *Colossians 3:23,* Paul says that it is the Lord Jesus Christ whom he serves.

Therefore the **"angel of God"** that appeared to Paul, to whom Paul belongs and whom only he serves is none other than the Lord Jesus Christ himself. But that's not all. Moses, Joshua, Abraham, Isaac, Jacob, and Hagar, just to name a few, all had encountered the angel of God and called him the "Almighty God" or "God the Father." That is precisely why Jesus says in *John 14:9,* "He who has seen me has seen the Father."

The Apostle Paul in his divine perspicacity, knowing the potential for misinterpretation of this uttermost principle, asserts in *Ephesians 4:6* this ultimate truth, "There is only one God and Father of all," in corroboration with Malachi 2:10, where we were already taught in the Old Testament that we were created by one God, who is Father of all.

This whole notion of Trinity, denaturing the Almighty God, is a total delusion. If Jesus is the Son of God, this certainly means that at one point in celestial history Jesus did not exist.

Therefore when God the Father supposedly gave birth to Jesus **(whenever that was)** God the Father, who has no beginning and who is forever on his throne in Heaven, consequently would make Heaven precursory to the existence of Christ, hence making Heaven impossible to have been created by Christ, and in which case would make God through his sacred word a preposterous liar, when God clearly proclaims that the heavens and the earth and all things therein, visible and invisible were created by Christ and for Christ. *(Colossians 1:16)*

I could go on and on with this to show you how ludicrous this notion of Trinity is when the Bible is clear that thrones, heavens, powers, dominions, principalities and all that is in the earth, were made by the Lord Jesus Christ, and "without him nothing was made that has been made". *(John 1:3)*

I am well aware of the fact that in *Genesis 1:26* God said, "Let us make man." And I will admit with you that you are not totally wrong in thinking that "us" here refers to more than one entity. I am also very much aware that Jesus is presented in the New Testament as the "Son of God." Jesus even commands we be baptized in the name of the Father, of the Son, and of the Holy Spirit.

To many, these aspects of the Gospel can be in some cases very confusing, pushing some Church leaders to adapt to current world views, distorting the fundamental of the message, questioning the infallibility of the scripture, and most importantly, rejecting the deity of Christ, the only God through whom men are redeemed and reconciled to God.

God is a supernatural being, and I think the problem lies in our indeterminacy of the full potency of the ideology. God is spirit, and this is the very essence that is misunderstood. And frankly not too many people understand what that means.

In the Old Testament we have seen God as a pillar of fire, we have seen God as a pillar of cloud, we have seen God as a rock, and so forth, yet none of the patriarchs ever expressed any doubt those elements in fact represented the Almighty Creator of the universe. Yet today some of us are still crucifying Jesus who is God incarnate, the visible "Kingdom of God" because he says when you see Him you see God.

The Trinity, which is at the core of today's teaching in Christianity, I will admit, is a good-feeling doctrine. Despicably, despite this distortion of the Gospel, most people think they are so close to God because they can separate or differentiate between the Father, the Son, and the Holy Spirit. The Devil is a liar.

Studies have shown that separation or divorce is a real threat to social stability, dividing families to the point of making strong relationships difficult to achieve. This makes the very essence of being united misunderstood and detrimental. The same mischievousness holds true for the unity of God's people, making the miscegenation of the church impossible but most importantly at the ultimate level where the unity or the oneness of God in the spirit is of the greatest significance.

In *Matthew 19:6* Jesus, in reply to a question regarding marriage and divorce, inserted the "highest spiritual principle" regarding the oneness of God in the following manner: "What God has joined together, let no man separate".

Between me and you, all hypocrisies aside, we know he is not talking about marriage between a man and a woman when divorce was not only permissible by Moses, but Jesus himself in *Matthew 5:31-32* allows for divorce on the basis of adultery. God is not the author of confusion and would never contradict his word. Let it be clear once and for all that all marriages are not from God and believe it or not, the ones that are from God will be kept united "till death tear them apart".

But Jesus, knowing the potential for misinterpretation and wanting to make it clear that he is not talking about a union between a man and a woman but rather the unity of God, concluded in verse 11 with this affirmation: **"Not everyone can understand this passage, but only those to whom it has been given"**.

Even though the context was marriage and divorce between a man and a woman, Jesus took it beyond the natural into the spirit realm referring to the oneness of God that no one should separate. But again, only those to whom it has been given can understand it.

The grave danger of the creed of the Trinity is the subconscious alienation of Jesus and the Holy Spirit on the bus of salvation, leaving the bus with no driver at the steering wheel. And while we are all singing "Hallelujah," Satan comes and takes the wheel and gets all the glory. Because Satan's main objective is for Jesus to remain unknown or feeble in our lives.

None of us truly knows God and can never know him fully in this life. For no one can totally understand what he or she cannot see. That is why Thomas was filled with unbelief and lost all hope when Jesus died. Because he knew that no man could go through what Jesus went through, be nailed on a cross and put to death and buried in a sealed tomb, to then walk out of there three days later like nothing had happened. For the same reason, the other apostles and disciples were still a bit skeptical even though they had been told that Jesus had resurrected. But Thomas upon seeing the resurrected Christ fell immediately on his face at his feet and worshiped him because he knew Jesus had to be God. And then the amazing happened, the truth was revealed when Saint Thomas yelled, **"My Lord and My God."**

Let me jump ahead of myself a little bit. This is exciting! Do you know that in the book of Revelation, the 11th chapter and the 16th verse, Saint John tells us that when the seventh angel sounded his trumpet, there were twenty- four elders sitting on their thrones before the throne of God? They fell on their faces and worshiped God just like Thomas did, saying: "We give thanks to you, Lord God Almighty, the one who is and who was, because you have taken your great power and have begun to reign."

The scripture teaches clearly that "God is". The only time God ever was, was when God came down to the earth and the Holy angels with him and lived as a man for about thirty-three years and took on the name of Jesus for the sake of humanity.

These thirty-three years of Jesus in the earth seem to be the equivalent of **"about"** half an hour in celestial time. We are told in *Revelation 8:1* that there was a total silence in heaven for **"about"** half an hour. This spiritual imagery is obviously in reference to the time Jesus physically spent in the earth representing the fullness of God, from his birth to his ascension back to heaven.

In other words, while Jesus was in the earth, the Father and the Holy Spirit **"was"** in the earth in him, as we are told by the Apostle Paul in *Colossians 2:9,* leaving the literal throne of God in heaven empty so to speak with no one to receive honor and glory as angels would normally sing incessantly "Holy, Holy, Holy" before the throne. It was total silence at the throne in heaven for the entire time Jesus was in the earth.

It is evident that more was at issue than could be understood by any being, because the inconspicuousness of God's perspective was not only enigmatic to the contemporaries of Jesus, but the very concept remains questionable today. However, we are not to blame ourselves for our ignorance or false notions, because even the angels of God themselves, according to *1 Peter 1:12,* did not fully understand the mystery of the revelation of Jesus Christ and remained astonished as they looked into the deep secret surrounding it, while of course broadening their horizons in regard to the Creator's mysterious love for humankind.

No wonder Saint Thomas, after seeing the nail prints, was convinced that the resurrected Christ was no longer the same Jesus he was acquainted with before the cross. He knew that he was in fact in the presence of the God Almighty, the Creator of the universe and immediately fell on his face at his feet and worshiped the "Man" and called Him by his true appellation, **"My Lord and my God."**

I think this is worth repeating. But this time I will use *Revelation 4:8-11,* where you have the four living creatures who are the highest angels known in heaven, higher than the Cherubim and the Seraphim, joined by the twenty- four elders sitting on their respective thrones, and together they are giving glory, honor, and thanks to God, who sits on his throne and saying day and night: "Holy, Holy, Holy is the Lord God Almighty, who was, and is, and is to come."

Undeniably, there is an impressive connection between this passage and the Lord Jesus Christ. Because Jesus Christ **"the son Man"** is the only God about whom we can talk in the past tense. In *Revelation 1:8* Jesus himself out of his own mouth says that he is the Alpha and Omega, the beginning and the end, who is, and who was, the Almighty. Very curiously, these fundamentals are the exact characteristics of the "One" sitting on the throne in heaven receiving honor and glory.

Apostle Paul in 1 Corinthians 12:4 teaches that:

- There are different kinds of gifts, but one Spirit.

- There are different kinds of service, but one Lord.

- There are different kinds of working, but one God.

The Bible is one book written by a single author (the Holy Spirit) using an assortment of prophetic stenographers through the ages and in different generations but put together into a marvelous whole. The Word of God, although systematic, can be truly understood only in the spirit. It is a unified book, coherent, and consistent, which answers rationally any inquiries or enigma according to the degree of your faith but is at the same time beyond the understanding of even the finest of minds possessed by any human in the natural.

Part of the challenge of "Divine Reality" mysteriously concerns the works of God. As the required work of God changes, a new medium, mutatis- mutandis, is brought into play as a distinct personality, yet related to and generated by the same God.

It is interesting to read one of the highlights of the book of Luke in connection with the apparition of the angel Gabriel to Virgin Mary relating to the conversation that took place between them, or better yet, the declaration of the angel during the interlocution emphasizing the deity and the true nature of Christ which the entire world, for the sake of their souls, should earnestly take upon themselves to imbue with the greatest sense of responsibility.

Amazingly, the angel Gabriel made mention of seven holy titles for the Creator of heavens and earth to Mary in the course of that momentary dialogue.

1- **God**

2- **The Lord**

3- **The Holy One**

4- **The Most High**

5- **The Lord God**

6- **The Holy Spirit or the Power of God**

7- **The Son of God**

We know the Bible uses many more titles for God throughout its content, but I thought it was extremely important to note how the angel Gabriel himself brought into play these different appellations to illustrate the unity of God despite the diversity of operations.

Hebrews 1:1 teaches that in the past, God spoke to our forefathers through the prophets in various ways, but in these last days, He has spoken to us by his Son, who is the radiance of his glory and the exact representation of his being, and also through whom the universe was made and who sustains all things visible and invisible by the power of his word.

The apostle Paul teaches in Hebrews 11:3 that all things visible emanate from or have their origin in the invisible. His intrinsic thoroughness provides incredible background, full of clues that, when examined carefully, one cannot but be led to believe that everything visible is truly an emanation leading back to divinity.

The Apostle Paul describes a "spirit" dimension that remains a mystery to most. But this supernatural, invisible world of spirits is both extensively and explicitly known to many leaders around the world, and it is comprised of creatures of power, namely angels and demons. However, in fear of mockery or losing their credibility, spiritual leaders prefer to completely ignore the subject, making the true face of Satan, who is an objective being, a fantasy.

To understand the relevance of this issue, the less you make Jesus in your life, guess who is bouncing on the heavy side of the two-sided scale of all conflicting notions in your life. Satan! You guessed it correctly.

It is evident that the steadfastness of Apostle Paul in saying that there are different kinds of working but the same God is free of any ambiguity and gives genuine awareness that we are dealing with a God who takes on many forms. Amazingly, when we go to *Hebrews 13:8* to read that Jesus Christ is the same yesterday, today, and forever, is beyond all temporal intellectual exercises.

Jesus in the flesh is referred to as the Son of God or the Son of Man because logically all men, of course, must have a line of descent either biologically or at least genealogically. These remarks are simply for the purpose of establishing his place of origin in contrast to the apparition of the Antichrist, whose origin will be a mystery to the unwise. Furthermore, both Jesus and the Bible are the embodiment of the Holy Spirit of God. With this in mind, it is not possible to experience or even explore these certitudes in the natural if we want to deepen our spiritual understanding of the works of God.

As you can see, uncovering the truth and understanding the relevance thereof is the central itinerary of the pages of this book. We are examining the very core of the Bible and offering you a spiritual delicatessen that Jesus Christ from ages past has prepared for the remedy of our souls, bringing to light in a very simplistic way certain spiritual truths susceptible to potentiate the most profane mind not only to come to know Jesus as Savior but to profess that our Lord Jesus Christ is the very God and the only true God of this world.

The apostle Paul in *1 Corinthians 2:9-14* teaches that "no eye has seen, no ear has heard, no mind has conceived what God has prepared for those who love him". But the man without the Spirit of God does not accept the things that come from God, for they are foolishness to him, because they are spiritually discerned.

The greatest **"foolishness"** that is taught in the scripture which remains one of the greatest mysteries for all humanity is the **"ONENESS"** of God.

- **Isaiah 43:10, "Before Me no god was formed nor will there be one after me."**

- **Malachi 2:10, "Did not One God create us?"**

- **1 Corinthians 8:4, "There is no God but One."**

- **1 Timothy 2:5, "For there is one God."**

- **Mark 12:32, "There is one God and there is none other but He."**

The inscrutability of the oneness of God is obnoxious to the pagan mind of the intellect, and to express the unravelment of the infinite profundity of God, the Bible says in *Isaiah 55:8,* "My thoughts are not your thoughts, neither are your ways my ways. As the heavens are higher than the earth; so are my ways higher than your ways and my thoughts than your thoughts."

Your accordance to this profound declaration in *Isaiah 55:8* is the key that will humble your flesh and bring you under complete submission to the word of God for a perfect alignment of your spirit with the Holy Spirit, enabling you to receive the things of the spirit of God, doing away with false, incomplete, and dangerous theological interpretations that are just hunches. It's supernatural.

Remember, the biblical setting is that the Word of God is Jesus Christ in the print, and that involves a double connotation that requires a dual application with one aspect symbolizing the spiritual dimension and the other representing the physical, which is an illustration in human terms.

The Bible teaches that Jesus, the Son of Man, is God in the flesh, and in *John 5:19* we read that Jesus only does what he sees the Father do. In other words, whatever the Father did in heaven in the spirit, Jesus replicates it in the earth in the physical.

To further put it another way, whatever works our Lord Jesus as a Man did in the earth in the physical realm is a derivative of what is already done in heaven by the Father. Furthermore, we are also told that Jesus only speaks what he hears the Father say.

Now to bring these analogues closer to home, we will say that everything that was done or said by the Spirit in the Old Testament from Genesis to Malachi, Jesus either performed it as a Man in the earth or it will be carried out before or after He returns the second time in the book of Revelation.

All of these approaches will help deepen your knowledge of the truth as the Apostle Paul confirms the Lordship of Christ in *Colossians 1:15* by saying that Jesus is the image of the invisible God, and we're told in *John 6:62* that Jesus ascended back to heaven where He was before.

The truth underlying the last detail should send chills to one's pragmatism with uncommon propensity to portend the subsummation of the preexistence of Jesus in heaven before He was in Mary's womb. This perspective alone is humanly unfathomable, and this is why most people adhere to the admonition of the deity of Christ, rejecting the ideology of the cross and the resurrection and thereby his propitiatory love, rather than submit to his rhetorical teachings.

In *John 14:21-23*, Jesus says, "Whoever has my commands and obeys them, he is the one who loves me. He who loves me will be loved by my Father and I too will love him and show myself to him." Then Judas (not Judas Iscariot) said, "But, Lord why do you intend to show yourself to us and not to the world?" And Jesus replied, "If anyone loves me, he will obey my teaching. My Father will love him and we (my father and I) will come to him and make our home with him."

Take notice that I emphasized the word "we," understood to be in this case the Father and the Son as mentioned by Jesus. The Holy Spirit is omitted here by Jesus because the spirit of the Father and the spirit of the Son are one and the same, giving evidence of the Holy Spirit himself.

In *Acts 16:6-8,* the Apostle Paul gives us a clear confirmation of this with the following account: "Paul and his companions traveled throughout the region of Phrygia and Galatia, they were kept by the Holy Spirit from preaching the word in the province of Asia. When they came to the border of Mysia, they tried to enter Bithynia, but the Spirit of Jesus would not allow them to. So, they passed by Mysia and went down to Troas."

As you can see, the Holy Spirit and the spirit of Jesus are one and the same. *Romans 8:9-10* uses the names "Spirit," "Spirit of God," "Spirit of Christ," and "Christ" interchangeably to indicate that Jesus and the Holy Spirit once again are one and the same.

In *Luke 8:38-39,* we read about the man from whom the demons had gone out and who begged to go with Jesus, but Jesus sent him away, saying, "Return home and tell how much God has done for you." So, the man went away and told all over town how much Jesus has done for him.

Whether you realize it or not, Jesus has unequivocally made explicit what we Christians perceive as implicit, the equivalency of God the Father and himself. This mysterious relationship is clarified by the Apostle Paul in *Colossians 2:9* teaching that in the humanity of Jesus dwells the fullness of the deity, giving evidence of the very essence of God being present in totality in Jesus from before his conception in Mary's womb to the pronouncement on the cross of the following statement: "It is finished".

The Apostle Peter tells us in *2 Peter 3:16* that Paul writes some things that are hard to understand, which ignorant and unstable people distort as they do the other scriptures to their own destruction, and in verse 18, the Bible exhorts us to grow in the grace and knowledge of our Lord and Savior Jesus Christ, who is to be glorified both now and forever.

How does one grow in the knowledge of Christ? Well! 1 John 2:3 offer us a starting point, which reads like this: "We know that we have come to know him if we obey his commands. The man who says I know him but does not do what the commands is a liar, and the truth is not in him. But if anyone obeys his word, the love of God is truly made complete in him."

The Bible offers a panoply of exposé pertaining to the nature of Jesus Christ through a panorama of events from Genesis to Revelation, unveiling the mystery of God that can only be under- stood through pertinacious intimacy with Christ and therefore coming to terms with the "New Covenant" teachings.

The Apostle Paul teaches that when you obey the word of Jesus Christ and receive him as Lord and Savior, no one can take you captive through hollow and deceptive philosophy that is based on human tradition and the basic principles of this world. For in the humanity of Christ dwells the fullness of the Deity in bodily form.

According to *Luke 10:22,* Jesus astonished his disciples with the following statement, which still keeps even today's Christians totally perplexed; it reads like this: "No one knows who Jesus is except the Father, and no one knows who the Father is except Jesus and anyone [that includes you and me] to whom Jesus wishes to reveal him." In other words, you could be the greatest Bible scholar, or a specialist in ancient theological writings, but if Jesus Christ does not resolve to make himself known to you, you will never uncover who He really is, let alone believe his true identity.

Perhaps you'll agree with me that this is one of the most challenging statements made by Jesus in the New Testament. Furthermore, turning to his disciples, He said privately about him- self, "Blessed are the eyes that see what you see. For I tell you that many prophets and kings wanted to see what you see [referring to himself] but did not see it and to hear what you hear but did not hear it."

Wow! What a statement! This clearly demonstrates that Jesus is more than the verbal description portrayed of Him in the New Testament. Although Jesus was given to remain anonymous, with this affirmation he surely puts his story and history into perspective.

Dumbfounded by this fact, subsequent historians desultorily scatter through their maleficence the immanency of Christ and the true significance of the title "Son of God," which is a mere designation symbolizing the condescension of God to our human level of spiritual poverty for the sole purpose of redeeming the souls of humankind.

At the Sermon on the Mount one of the declarations of blessedness made known by Jesus is: "Blessed are the poor in spirit, for theirs is the kingdom of heaven," making reference to those who are misled and kept ignorantly in the prevaricatory belief of Jesus as the Son of the virgin Mary in the likeness of sinful flesh, rather than the preternatural entity whose significance is far beyond his physical appropriation, thus having conspicuously descended from the highest heaven in a body like ours to make the impartation of his Holy Spirit a human reality to his followers.

The Apostle Paul tells us in *Romans 8:3* that the flesh is sinful and weak because God has condemned sin in the flesh so that the righteousness of the law might be fulfilled in us who walk not after the flesh but after the spirit. There is absolutely no power in the flesh. But Jesus in spite of this fact still chose to submit himself to this abject humiliation of becoming man, like one of us, emptying himself of his glory and of his Alpha and Omega prerogatives, and adhering to a self-imposed penalty through a momentary suspension for about half an hour of his eternal, infinite existence as God to experience death in order to take dominion over the same and to save his people from that destitute disgrace. Through Him we can live a life of peace and be spiritually minded by virtue of the true power that resides in his risen name who is

24

now the Holy Spirit, who lives forever. (**2 Corinthians 3:17, Hebrews 7:24, Romans 8:26-34**).

According to Luke 24:36, when Jesus appeared to his disciples after his resurrection, they were startled and frightened, thinking they saw a ghost, but Jesus said to them, "Peace be with you, why are you troubled, and do doubts rise in your minds? Look at my hands and my feet. It is I, touch me and see. A ghost or a spirit does not have flesh and bones as you see I have."

After that, Jesus ate in their presence and said to them, "This is what I told you while I was still with you: Everything must be fulfilled that is written about me in the Law of Moses and the prophets and the psalms. Then the amazing happened. He opened their minds so that they could understand the scriptures. Then Jesus led them out to the vicinity of Bethany, He lifted up his hands, and blessed them. While He was blessing them, He left them and was taken up into heaven, where He was before. (See *John 6:62*)

Jesus being God is a hard theology for the carnal mind to affirm, because God being "One" translates inevitably to the conclusion that the same Jesus who was born of the Virgin Mary, crucified, and resurrected is also God the Father and God the Holy Spirit at the same time. But I tell you, laying hold of this ultimate spiritual truth will make you the recipient of unprecedented spiritual revelations that Jesus gives only through the Holy Spirit to anyone who obeys his teaching *(John 14:15-25)*. Jesus says in *John 8:31,* "If you hold to my teaching, you are really my disciples and you will know the truth and the truth will set you free."

Unfortunately, the church has rejected either willfully or ignorantly the full deity of Christ and failed to attain the necessary physical and spiritual unity for the ultimate divine reunification with God, which can only be fulfilled in and through Christ as our rescuer.

Despite this emphasis, we have greatly been deceived into believing that spiritual unity exists or can be achieved in the Church despite its multiplicity. Or without physical unity or fellowship with one another, spiritual unity will remain a vain wish. We must first believe in the man Jesus, who He is, who He was, and why He came, and as we have fellowship with him, through him we can truly say we have fellowship with one another.

The Apostle Paul in *Ephesians 2:18* teaches that through Christ we have access to the Father by one spirit, and in Christ the whole building is joined together to become a holy temple in the Lord *(Ephesians 4:1)*. So therefore, only in and through Christ are we built together until we all reach unity and maturity in the faith and attain the whole measure of the fullness of Christ suitable for the dwelling of the spirit of God, following the example of the multitude in the aggregate who had believed the testimony of Peter and John in Acts 4 and consequently exhibited one heart and soul to the point that no one would no longer consider the things he possessed as his own, but had all things in common *(Acts 4:32)*.

Impressively, this level of spirituality is out of this world. The apostle Paul teaches in 2 Corinthians 3:17 that Jesus Christ is now the spirit, and the emphasis is that there is one body, one spirit, one Lord, one faith, one baptism, and one God and Father of all, who is over all and through all and in all *(2 Corinthians 3:17, Ephesians 4:4)*.

In fact, this spiritual conception taught by the Apostle Paul is not suggesting that Jesus is *"a"* spirit, which in reality would mean that Jesus is one spirit among others. But he instead makes it very clear that Jesus is *"the"* Spirit, indicating, by using the definite article *"the,"* the singularity, the uniqueness, and undoubtedly the adjective *"One".*

The crucial truth that should inhabit humanity is that Jesus should no longer be regarded after the flesh, Him being the source of all life. And though everyone is not ready to admit it, there is a biblical agreement that points to this ultimate truth.

Certainly, the Bible teaches that the Holy Spirit is the source of life. But God through the prophet Job broadens our horizon by giving a preliminary decantation of the meaning of the word "us" mentioned in

Genesis when God said, "Let us make man in our image." (Again, I am going ahead of myself a little bit.)

Accordingly, in *Job 33:4* we read, "The Spirit of God has made us, and the breath of the Almighty gives us life." Obviously, those who deny the deity of Christ will see no relevance to Jesus whatsoever in this passage because the two entities mentioned here by Job are the Holy Spirit and the Almighty God. But what they won't admit is the very fact that *Revelation 3:1* proclaims that Jesus aggregates the Seven Spirits of God, which undeniably signifies that the man Jesus is the true personification of the Holy Spirit. As for the "Almighty" mentioned by Job from whom came life, need I say that in *Revelation 1:8* we're told that Jesus is the Alpha and the Omega who is and who was and who is to come, the Almighty?

The dominant universal divine "Title" of the Creator of the universe is "God" whom all religions agree to be monotheistic in nature because the word of God clearly teaches there is only "One True God". But king Solomon, the wisest man known in all the earth, to whom God appeared and with whom he had a dialogue says in *2 Chronicles 6:1* and *6:18* that God who is Spirit was to take on a sinful nature and to come and dwell in darkness with mankind upon the earth.

From this perspective, the visible result of king Solomon's prophecy is undeniably the coming of Christ in the earth who came by water and blood in a sinful body *(1 John 5:6)*, having made to be sin for us, that we might become God's righteousness by means of "Him" *(2 Corinthians 5:21)*.

Moreover, according to the Apostles Paul and John, who have a deep knowledge of who Christ is in the Spirit, sum it up this way.

- **"Jesus is before all things and all things are held together in him"** *(Colossians 1:15-20)*.

- **"In the beginning was Jesus, and Jesus was with God, and Jesus was God. All things in heaven and in the earth were made by him and in him was life"** *(John 1:1-4)*.

What is beyond understanding and strikingly amazing and I am sure we will all marvel at it, is the fact that, according to the Old Testament, some of the names God attributed to himself had not been revealed until the arising of a connection between the work that is divinely required of God and which variant of the nature of God that is appropriate for that purpose.

Consider the following setting: During a face-to-face conversation between God and Moses in Exodus 6:3, God said to Moses, **"I am the Lord. I appeared to Abraham, to Isaac, and to Jacob as** *'The God Almighty',* **but they did not know me by my name** *'The Lord'"*. As you can see, each work of God is an expression of his multifarious nature and must be expressly understood in relation to his "Monotheistic character".

All things considered, neither Job nor any other prophets in the Old Testament knew God by the name of Jesus or knew Jesus by name. When it was revealed to them that God would come down to live among his people, Moses called him a "Prophet," Isaiah said of him that a "Son" is given, and the name closest to God they could come up with was "Immanuel," which means "God with us."

The eventual coming of the Savior to the earth was hilarious, but obviously none of the prophets knew Jesus by name, because God simply had not yet revealed his name as Jesus until it became evident the redemption era was at hand, and accordingly, God through the angel Gabriel made known in the fullness of time his congruous name for the apparent purpose of rescuing humankind.

Perspectively, the Apostle Paul, who had the honor of going to heaven and back, is not at all argumentative in his opinion of Christ when he affirms that Christ is the bodily form of the fullness of God *(Colossians 2:9).*

In the beginning we see God speaking a word, and things would spring into existence. Likewise, although the physical methods employed by Jesus to perform his deeds are infinitely diverse, one undeniable consistency is that nothing was done that was not preceded by a verbal articulation.

In other words, there was always a pronouncement of a word proceeding out of Jesus mouth before any physical or visible action to take place.

Upholding his teaching and making this experience complete by way of illustration, Jesus affirms, **"My words are Spirit and Life"**, initiating some very challenging and astonishing procedures, and leaving the crowd sometimes confused and uneasy with the miracles, signs and wonders that would follow.

A great example of that is in the healing of the four blind men found in *Matthew 9:29, Marc 8:23, Marc 10:46,* and *John 9:6.*

- **For the first blind person, Jesus simply touched his eyes and said, "Be healed according to your faith."**

- **For the second, Jesus using his hand applied "spit" in the man's eyes and healed him.**

- **For the third, Jesus just spoke a word and commanded he be healed.**

- **For the fourth, Jesus "spat" on the ground and made a little mud with his saliva and the man was healed upon the application of the mud.**

As one can see, different physical methods were used by Jesus in the performance of these four accomplishments, but his words or his commands, although invisible, are radiant *(Psalm 19:8)*, triggering the Holy Spirit into action for the fulfillment of the desired purpose.

In the case of the second or the third Jesus did not use audible or familiar human words commanding them to be healed. Instead, He "spit", to let us know that more is at issue than common ritual, but the protocol remains.

Now anyone who is not in the Spirit will be at a lost and not fully grasp this solid basis for understanding the general principles guiding the scripture, *"that the Word is the Spirit"*.

Psalm 33:6-9 says, "By the Word of God were the heavens made, their starry host by the breath of his mouth. For He spoke, and it came to be, He commanded, and it stood firm." The Bible teaches that there is

"One Spirit". If the Word is the Spirit and Jesus is the "Word", *tacitly Jesus is the spirit.*

Jesus himself refers to the acknowledgment of the indivisibility of the word and the Holy Spirit as having abundant faith. The story is about a centurion who had a sick servant about to die which is found in Luke 7:6-10 and reads like this: "Jesus was not far from the house when the centurion sent friends to say to him, Lord, don't trouble yourself, for I do not deserve to have you come under my roof. That is why I did not even consider myself worthy to come to you. But say the word and my servant will be healed. For I myself am a man under authority with soldiers under me. I tell this one go and he goes; I tell this one come and he comes. I say to my servant, do this and he does it".

When Jesus heard this, he was amazed at the words of the centurion, and turning to the crowd following him, he said, "I tell you, I have not found such great faith even in Israel."

In our days, pluralistic theology obliged, every denomination has developed its own particular faith in which they proudly elate, as if the acquisition of a particular doctrinal wisdom, based on its own standard and obtained through its respective training institution, had sufficient spiritual substance to proudly propel itself above another.

The Apostle Paul in *1 Corinthians 3:18* warns us of this worldly wisdom, which is foolishness in God's sight. This wisdom according to *1 Timothy 1:3- 7* and *1 Timothy 6:3-5* promotes controversies rather than God's work, which is the faith of Christ and the faith in Christ. But sadly, some have wandered away and turned to meaningless talk as they can no longer put up with sound doctrine, but instead, to suit their own desires, they have and will heap to themselves doctors and teachers to say what their itching ears want to hear. They will turn away from the truth and turn aside to myths.

The Apostle Paul continues to say that the truth will be taken away from those who desire to be teachers of the Gospel and think that godliness is a means to financial gain. They will be false teachers who do not know what they are talking about and when they speak whatever they so confidently affirm will be fallacious.

This is a very serious statement from God concerning the teachers of the word of God of these last days. Fortunately, the Apostle Paul made a comforting statement in *1 Corinthians 4:20* on the basis of this particular subject, concluding that "the kingdom of God is not a matter of talk but of power" and the power is in the blood. Unless there is a strong emphasis on the blood of Christ shared on the cross, we are simply dust that will be easily eaten by the snake.

Jesus, teaching about him being the bread of life in *John 6:53,* said to the crowd, "I tell you the truth, unless you eat the flesh of the Son of Man and drink his blood, you have no life in you." On hearing this, many of his disciples said, "This is hard teaching; who can accept this?" Many of them turned back and no longer followed him. Jesus then turned to the twelve and asked, "You do not want to leave too, do you?" Peter answered him, "Lord, to whom we shall go? You have the words of eternal life. We believe and know that you are the Christ, the Son of the living God."

When you compare *Isaiah 61:1-2* and *Luke 4: 18-19,* God only promised one "thing" to his people to free them from captivity. This supernatural contraption gives evidence according to Acts 1:4-5 which corroboratively proclaims that the gift God the Father promised is the "Holy Spirit" who was born as "Christ" in whose life rests all eternal hope.

At Jacob's well the Samaritan woman said to Jesus, "I know the "Messiah" is coming, the one who is called 'Christ', to explain everything to us". To this Jesus answered and declared, "I who speak to you am the Christ", the Messiah whom God had promised.

Those who had a moment's glimpse beyond the natural perspective of Jesus into his divine glory on the mountain of transfiguration are not at all confused about the "Lordship" of Christ, his "Deity", and his true appellation.

By the way, among other names and titles pertaining to Jesus, He is called:

- **God** (*Romans 9:5*)

- **The Light** (*John 8:12*)

- **The Rock** (*1 Corinthians. 10:4*)

- **The Lord God** (*John 20:28*)

- **The Holy One of God** (*Luke 4:34*)

- **The Christ** (*John 4:25*)

Inherent in those names is the fulfillment of his mission on earth and in this universe: creation, sustainment, and redemption. However, to have a complete view of who Jesus was and is, we will examine some other appellations or designations that are titles God self-appropriated as needed at different times and for specific missions throughout the history of the world.

To begin with, the name "Jesus" is God self-allotted name for the specific purpose of redeeming humankind and this universe. Jesus said that he is spirit before he was man. In *John 6:53,* Jesus talks about his flesh and blood as nutriment for salvation and eternal life, which was considered hard teaching by the Jews and some of his disciples. Upon teaching this, He said to them, "Does this offend you? What if you see the Son of Man ascend to where he was before?"

No one can deny that this establishes the heavenly pre-existence of Jesus prior to his incarnation. The Bible teaches that Jesus came down from heaven to be born of Mary as a man. *John 4:24* says that God is spirit. *Ephesians 4:4* acknowledges that there is only one spirit. As I have already argued, if Jesus is spirit before he was man, and there is only one spirit, it's no wonder the Apostle Paul in *2 Corinthians 3:17-18* repeats it twice that Jesus is "The Holy Spirit."

Now if this is still hard to swallow, let us dig even deeper. The Bible tells us that Jesus is God *(Romans 9:5)*. If Jesus is God, he cannot be attributed ancestries neither in the flesh nor in the spirit. God cannot descend from anything. The prophet *Isaiah (43:10)* puts it very clearly that God said, "Before me no God was formed, nor will there be one after me."

You may not agree with me, but I know there is one thing God cannot do. God cannot create another God. God is the Alpha and Omega, the first and the last, the beginning and the end. To have been created logically would denote the existence of a starting point. Hebrews 13:8 tells us that Jesus is the same yesterday, today, and forever, meaning that He is eternal. Therefore, it is impossible for Jesus to have been created.

Colossians 1:15 tells us that Jesus is the image of the invisible God, the first born of all creation. For by him all things were created: things in heaven and on earth, visible and invisible, whether thrones or powers or rulers or authorities. All things were created by him and for him. Jesus is before all things, and in him all things hold together. He is the head of the body, the Church. He is the beginning and the first born from among the dead, so that in everything he might have the supremacy. For God was pleased to have all his fullness dwell in him and through him to reconcile to himself all things, whether things on earth or things in heaven, by making peace through his blood, shed on the cross.

We just read that Jesus is the firstborn of all creation, and in other places the Bible tells us that Jesus is God. So, which one is it? To answer this rather ambiguous question, we're going to trace Jesus back as far as the Holy Spirit will take us and identify where and when Jesus first came on the scene.

What is known, and Luke is absolute about it, is that everything and all things that were written in the Old Testament, in the Law of Moses, the prophets and the Psalms are about Jesus, and they have found or will find, whatever the case may be, their fulfillment in him.

Before we proceed, let's pay a visit to the father of our faith, Abraham in Genesis 22:8, and examine the answer he gave Isaac pertaining to the lamb for the burnt offering. Abraham said, "God Himself will provide the lamb for the burnt offering." Anybody who has a minimum understanding of grammar knows that a group of words that express a complete thought is a complete sentence. Now let's rewrite Abraham's answer omitting the word "Himself" and see if the sentence loses its meaning or if the thought behind Abraham's expression was incomplete or perhaps why the word "Himself" was added to it.

"God himself will provide the lamb for the burnt offering." Any specialist will tell you this is a perfect and complete sentence. Why then the use of the pronoun "Himself" in that sentence? What was Abraham conveying? The only logical conclusion is that the insertion of the word "Himself" was already a hint that Abraham offered us as children of the faith that the lamb would be God Himself.

We know from *Revelation 19:14* that one of the names used by Jesus in his pre-humanity is the "Word of God." Elsewhere we saw him as the "angel of God" or the "angel of the Lord." The Apostle Paul in *Hebrews 6:13* tells us that the Word of God is God the Father Himself. Let's look at it. When God made the promise to Abraham, since there was no one greater for him to swear by, he swore by Himself.

Do you agree that the appellation "God" mentioned here by the Apostle Paul in *Hebrews 6:13* is in reference to God the Father Himself, because there is none greater? Presuming your answer is yes; let's go pay another visit to our father Abraham in *Genesis 22:10-12*. The story goes like this. When Abraham reached out his hands and took the knife to slay Isaac, "the angel of the Lord" called out to him from heaven, "Abraham, Abraham, do not lay hand on the boy. Now I know that you fear God because you have not withheld from "Me" your son, your only son." In *verse 15* of *Genesis 22,* the angel of the Lord called to Abraham from heaven a second time and said, **"I swear by myself"**, *"The Word of God",* I will surely bless you and make your descendants as numerous as the stars in the sky and as the sand on the seashore."

In effect, the **"angel of the Lord"** made it clear to Abraham that there was no one higher than Him by whom he could swear. If this doesn't send chills down your spine, I don't know what will. I can therefore confidently say that the "angel of the Lord" calling from heaven and talking to Abraham is none other than God the Father Himself.

Furthermore, when you correlate *Hebrews 6:13,* which says it was God the Father Himself who said this to Abraham, with *Genesis 22:10-15,* which says that it was the angel of the Lord who said this to Abraham, you cannot but come to the irrefutable conclusion that *"the angel of the Lord and God the Father are the same person".*

There is more, let us now go to *Exodus 32:9-13* on the Mount Sinai where God the Father gave Moses the two tablets of the testimony and said to him, "I have seen these people and they are a stiff-necked people. Now leave me alone so that my anger may burn against them and destroy them". But Moses sought the favor of the Lord *"his God"* and said, "Turn from your fierce anger O' Lord, relent and do not bring disaster on your people. **Remember your servants Abraham, Isaac and Israel** *"to whom you swore by your own self"* that you will make their descendants as numerous as the stars."

There you have it again, on the one hand we see God the Father being referred to by Moses as the Lord God who had sworn by his own self, making them one and the same, and on the other hand when we go to *Genesis 22,* the one mentioned by Moses who swore by his own self to Abraham was the angel of the Lord.

A quick comparison of the facts, from the explanation of the relationship between the "Almighty God" and "the angel of the Lord," adding to it the connection between "the angel of the Lord" and Jesus Christ himself, conveys the most logical deduction that **this man called Jesus is truly "the Ancient of days."**

Accepting these sentiments, the first reaction is to set out to understand the interactions of those various existential self-attributes, the variance in the names and apparitions for God presented by the prophets, but yet perfectly congruent in establishing synonymy and exhibiting God the Father Himself.

In *Genesis 31:3* we see Jacob in a conversation with God, and the Bible again refers to God as the "Lord". We also see in verse 11 that God is being addressed as **the angel of God** as compared in preceding paragraphs as **the angel of the Lord**. In *Genesis 31:13* we behold the angel of God talking to Jacob and saying, "I am the God of Bethel where you anointed a pillar and where you made a vow to "Me".

The Bible in *Genesis 28:18-20* identifies the anointment of the pillar and where the vow was made by Jacob to the Lord. The angel of God as mentioned in *Genesis 31:11-13* said to Jacob, "I am the Lord, the God of your father Abraham and the God of Isaac." This time we notice instead of "angel of the Lord," the appellation of the angel of God is used in *Genesis 31:11* to equate God the Father as revealed in *Genesis 22:10* and *15* and *Genesis 28:13*.

It is evident there is unequivocally a biblical consensus on the co-equality of the multi-composite descriptions seemingly deigned of God. Undoubtedly each deiform had specific purposes, such as putting divine orders affecting the physical world into effect. But what is astonishing is the fact that every prophet regarded each decrement as God the Father himself.

There is still even more, in Acts 7:30 and beyond, we read that **"the angel of the Lord"** appeared in the midst of the burning bush to Moses, and as Moses drew near, **"the Voice of the Lord"** was heard saying, "I am the God of your fathers, the God of Abraham, the God of Isaac and the God of Jacob." But that's not all! Way back in the Garden of Eden, as we read in *Genesis 3:10,* after Adam and Eve sinned and became aware that they were naked; they heard **"the Voice of the Lord"** walking in the Garden and hid themselves behind the trees.

So, you see, **"the voice of the Lord,"** which is **"the angel of the Lord,"** which in turn is **"Jesus Christ"**, goes way back in the Garden of Eden. Unfortunately, most teachers only swim on the surface and ignore the deeper and more important concepts that deal with the fundamentals of spiritual truths. Despite this abundance of self-evident truths in the "New Testament" relative to Christ and his pre-incarnation appearances in the Old Testament, the questions: "is Christ the son of

David? Therefore man" or "is Christ the son of God? Therefore God, are still emblematic today.

The answers to these questions are found in the writings of the Apostle Paul when he teaches in *Hebrews 13:8* that Jesus is the same yesterday, today, and forever. All hypocrisy aside, we know these majestic words are self-evident and that Jesus Christ is eternal. Yesterday and forever are expressions symbolizing eternity past and eternity future and therefore can only be attributed to the everlasting Father.

Matthew begins his gospel with a genealogy of Jesus as follows: "Jesus the son David, the son of Abraham all the way down to Joseph the husband of Mary of whom was born Jesus as a man". *Matthew 1:22* tells us that all this took place in order to fulfill what the Lord had said through the prophet: "The virgin will be with child and will give birth to a son and they will call him Immanuel, meaning God with us or God incarnate," which the Apostle John corroborates in *John 1:1* and *John 1:14* when he clearly teaches that Jesus, who is the Creator of all things, was God before he took on flesh.

It is true that in both Matthew and Luke's genealogy of Jesus Christ, he is presented as being the "son of David, the son of Abraham." But there is a higher truth found in *Romans 9:5* that dissipates all doubts about Jesus being God in probably one of the clearest statements found in the Bible. The Apostle Paul declares, "Though in the flesh the human ancestry of Christ can be traced from the patriarchs *(Abraham, Isaac, Jacob through David, and so forth), Jesus is God over all forever praised! Amen.*"

Now if you are still a little skeptic about this spiritual truth, let's see what Jesus himself had to say about this issue. The story can be read in *John 8:52* and following. The Jews said to Jesus: "Abraham our father died and so did the prophets, yet you say that if anyone keeps your word, he will never taste death. Are you greater than our father Abraham? Who do you think you are?" In verse 56 Jesus replied, "Your father Abraham rejoiced at the thought of seeing my day; he saw it and was glad."

The Jews said to Jesus, "You are not yet fifty years old, and you have seen Abraham?" Jesus answered and said, "Before Abraham was born, **I am".**

All things considered, In the Spirit, Jesus has never been and is no longer the Son of God. Therefore, it is not surprising that Jesus makes it very clear in *Matthew 22:41, Marc 12:35,* and *Luke 20:41* that he is not the Son of David as portrayed in the Bible.

If Jesus is not the son of David, he is most certainly not the son of Mary, as we saw earlier. And if Jesus is not the son of Mary, he is most certainly not the Son of God. I know that some Christians are ready to stone me for this latter remark. But the truth is: "if God is the Savior, it must conversely mean that the Savior himself is God."

God proclaims in *Isaiah 43:11* and *44:6,* "I am the Lord your God, the Holy One of Israel your Savior, the King of Israel and his Redeemer. I am the First and I am the Last. There is no other God besides me." And so, it was, while the Pharisees were gathered in the temple, Jesus asked them, **"Whose son is the Christ?"**

"*The son of David,*" they replied.

Jesus said to them, "How it is that David speaking by the Holy Spirit calls him 'Lord' in the book of Psalms?" The Lord said to my Lord, referring to the Christ:

"Sit at my right hand

Until I make your enemies

A 'footstool' for your feet. "

Then Jesus added, "If David calls him Lord, how is it that the Christ is the son of David? If King David calls Jesus 'Lord,' how then can Jesus be his son?" *(Luke 20:44).*

You will agree with me that if Jesus is not the son of David as a natural progeny of Mary and Joseph, who themselves were direct descendants of David, it's more than obvious there is a lot more to this fact than meets the eye. It's no wonder the name "Jesus" is a great mystery to many.

In fact, the book of Judges in *chapter 13:17-18* reports that when Manoah, the father of Samson, asked the **angel of the Lord** who appeared to him: "What is your name?" the angel replied, "Why do you ask my name? My name is beyond understanding".

This esoteric answer given by the angel to Manoah is not at all surprising. Certainly, these are not the words of an ordinary angel, for no one beside God the Father, the Creator himself, can proclaim such affirmation.

The indeterminable of the creation, redemption, and salvation power of Jesus Christ stretches from eternity pass, oozing through him becoming the light in *Genesis 1:3* and culminating with Him being the Alpha and Omega in the book of Revelation.

PART II
The Book Of Genesis

An author once said, "The goal of any writer is to bring to his reader's attention his thoughts, his views and beliefs concerning certain issues and events."

Certainly, if you are going to write about something, it first must have existed somewhere, either tangibly or imaginatively, which generally implies the preexistence of the experience before any ideas or thoughts can be formed.

Based on the contents of the Bible, God is no different. Knowing and declaring the end from the beginning *(Isaiah 46:10),* God writes the truth of his Word to include events that took place in the invisible world before the physical creation, as well as current episodes and also matters afar as part of biblical prophecy that must take place in the far future.

As we will see in the paragraphs that follow, the heavens and the earth were created simultaneously but the earth was not put into use to receive humankind until after the Fall of Adam and Eve (humankind in general) whose sin, having put a ceiling on their lifespan, resulted in God having to create physical time and space, which was the new environment necessary to sustain the new kind of life, the physical body, about to be transmigrated to the earth in conformity to the word spoken by God to Adam in *Genesis 2:17,* but most importantly according to the "grace given us in Christ Jesus before the beginning of time or before the world began" *(2 Timothy 1:9)* "The day that you eat from the tree of the knowledge of good and evil you will surely die," thus setting out a time frame from the beginning of the physical creation to the end of the same, reaching out its full allotment in seven thousand years, each thousand year corresponding to one of the twenty-four-hour days, when God spoke this physical universe into existence.

To be bluntly honest, everything about this physical universe is evil. But what could have persuaded a Holy God to create such an embarrassment? Let's find out!

"As when juice is still found in a cluster of grapes and people say, 'Don't destroy it, because there is yet some good in it,' likewise I will do on behalf of my people; I will not destroy them all. My chosen people will inherit my mountains" *(Isaiah 65:8)*. This statement concerns God's Book of Life written before the foundation of the world *(Exodus 32:31-32)*. But those who forsake me will be killed by the sword and will all bend down for the slaughter. *(Isaiah 65:12)*

In complementarity to all that have been said since the beginning of *Isaiah 65* concerning judgment and salvation, God said in *verse 17,* as if to render all this possible, "I will create new heavens and a new earth and the former things will not be remembered, nor will they come to mind."

These new heavens (plural) and this new earth are not to be confused with the new heaven (singular) in *Revelation 21* out of which the New Jerusalem will come down, as if God had forgotten to create something that needed to be created during the creation process. Such continuative creation mind-set simply suggests a remedial afterthought which is totally contrary to the nature of God, as portrayed in the scripture, who knows the end from the beginning.

Jesus said, "In my Father's house are many mansions, I will go and prepare a place for you." As it is expressly stated, Jesus will prepare what's already there, but all creation ended six thousand years ago during the six days of "Genesis" which culminated on the seventh day with God rested from all his creation work.

So, when God says in *Isaiah 65* that he will create new heavens and a new earth, God is speaking from a dimension outside of time and space, even before time began, as he surely resolved and promised himself not to keep silent or overlook the sin and the wickedness of his people. "I will pay them back in full," says the Lord. Because they burned sacrifices on the mountains and defied me on the hills, I will measure into their laps the full payment for their deeds.

In retrospect, something else became remarkably evident when one thinks of it. The fact that God because of "John 3:16" decided to spare momentarily Lucifer in his remonstration that lead to war in heaven in order to give mankind a second chance in the earth.

These new heavens and the new earth mentioned in Isaiah 65 are the exact ones mentioned in *Genesis 1:1,* **"In the beginning God created the heavens and the earth"** and they clearly have the twofold missions expressed by God throughout the chapter of *Isaiah 65:*

1- To exacerbate God's judgment on the ungodly.

2- To facilitate God's redemption for his chosen ones.

However, the single most significant element I don't want anybody to miss is that God is referring to a people that have defiled him before the physical inception of the heavens and the earth in Genesis 1. Isaiah 65 teaches that the defilement of the people caused God to create the new heavens and the new earth. I know this is mind-boggling, but as we move along, all clouds will dissipate.

As taught in Genesis, the physical universe was supernaturally put into place, but because of the tremendous love of God for his people, not wanting any to perish, light did not overtake darkness in the beginning, as evidence of God's patience toward those who love 'Him" and whom "He" loves, giving them six thousand years to repent, each in his own time and for his own sin, but after that, final judgment and total destruction will come.

Corinthians 15:26 tells us that death is the last enemy that will be destroyed when Jesus returns, which by inference signifies that the enemies are many, and also that death is a spirit, a fallen angel who is presented as one of the riders of the pale horse in *Revelation 6:8* when Christ opens the fourth seal.

In *Revelation 20:10* we are told that the Devil who is described in *Revelation 20:2* as the dragon, the ancient serpent, or Satan, who is Lucifer, is the last spirit or the last entity that will be destroyed at the end of the millennium. Therefore, it is evident that Satan or Lucifer undoubtedly personifies the spirit of death.

So, when Adam and Eve hearkened to the vileness of the serpent in the Garden, they took on a new garment and mysteriously entered a new dimension, totally overshadowed by the spirit of death, under the reign of Satan.

Jesus said in *Luke 10:18* that he watched Satan fall like lighting from heaven. In fact, after sin was found in Satan and his ensuing subornation of Adam and Eve in the Garden, he was declared unworthy to be part of the heavenly host. Consequently, war broke out in heaven, and after losing to Michael the archangel, (one of the chief princes), Satan and his angels with him were hurled down to the earth. *(Revelation 12:7-9)*

These spiritual phenomena occurred before all physical existence on the earth, which is not only confirmed by the Apostle Paul in *Hebrews 11:3,* where he declares that what is seen was made out of what was invisible, but also to some extent explains why darkness preceded light in the physical realm. For Satan and his demons with him were banished to darkness until the year of their punishment, when total disaster will be upon them, as we read in *Jeremiah 23:12*. Saint Jude in the New Testament says it this way, "The angels who sinned against God are kept in darkness, bound with everlasting chains for the judgment of the great day", which is scheduled to take place in the earth on the last day.

In other words, Satan and the angels under his command were vehemently kicked out of heaven to the earth, awaiting everlasting destruction, once redemption is complete, in a cumulus that will be ordered by God at the onset of the millennium.

Amazingly, our association with Satan in the garden, man being an eternal creature, led to a meticulous resolution of God to trans- mute man to the earth, as dead souls. The transmigration involved giving man a physical body, which is sin compatible, and placing him in this purgatory dimension, the earth, reserved as a temporary place of penal servitude for penitent souls, which is in force at physical birth, not after physical death, as some are promoting.

Job 14 and *15* tell us that God changed our countenance and sent us away *(verse 20),* and that our physical existence is of a few days and full of trouble. Man born of woman is created impure, and God predetermined the number of his days. Man springs up like a flower and withers away. Like a fleeting shadow, he does not endure. Yet God will bring man before Him for judgment. Who can bring what is pure from the impure? No one! But God will cover over our sins. Wow! What a verse!

In short, I know the shallows will disagree, but whether we realize it or not, the earth was created as a physical mechanism to allocate and encompass sin and through which mankind may be purified, which will culminate with the planet being lit with the eternal fire out of the mouth of Christ with no subterfuge, turning it into the eternal hell at the end of his thousand-year reign.

For we read in *2 Peter 3:5-16* that the same Word that spoke the universe into existence has reserved the present heavens and the earth for fire that will come out of his mouth on the day of judgment to destroy all ungodly men, "whose worm in their dead bodies will never die, nor will their fire ever be quenched, and they will be loathsome to all mankind" *(Isaiah 66:24).* But also, in keeping with his promise, we are looking forward to new heavens and a new earth, wherein dwells righteousness.

As an abridgement in meaning, if any lessons are learned from this, "Heaven" is synonymous to "Paradise," and the "Earth" is the equivalent of "Hell." Put boldly, the first verse of the Bible should be read as follows, "In the beginning God created the Heavens and Hell", in awe and total reverence of God. "For our God is a consuming fire"

(Hebrews 12:29). The earth is simply a nickname for hell," but don't take my word for it. Let's see what the Bible says.

After sin was found in Satan and his angels, they were cast out of Heaven and they fell onto the earth, having been delivered into chains of darkness and reserved unto judgment day *(Luke 10:18* and *Revelation 12:13)*.

But Peter, establishing the synonymity between the earth and hell, was more specific when he conclusively states in *2 Peter 2:4* that after sin was found in Satan and his angels, they were cast down to hell, bound in chains of darkness until judgment day.

After all is said and done and the New Jerusalem, which is the new earth, makes its appearance, do you ever wonder what will be of the present earth and the people that are left behind? Well! Think about that.

Saint Luke refers to the location where they fell to as "earth," but the same location in question is referred to by *2 Peter* as "hell." Very interesting!

Interestingly enough, if one sets out to understand the Rapture, it corroborates the idea of the earth being hell for the simple fact that it will transpire in the complete removal of both the dead in Christ and those living for Christ, far away from the earth before God, as we read in *Revelation 20:10,* strikes the eternal match and sets fire to the earth, burning all that remain with flames that will never be quenched.

If one were to analyze closely the relevance of the earth as a temporary experiment for hell, it's easy to see the connection through the rather surprising conclusion that we read in *Genesis 1:2* when it is evident that darkness preceded Light in the earth, which corroborates the fall of Satan and his host of demons to the earth prior to the transmutation of humankind into the world, giving evidence to the proclamation of Jesus that hell was created for Satan and his angels.

Despite the unavailing power of Satan against God's plan for mankind, he and the rest of the fallen angels are nevertheless to this day spirit beings and therefore outside of time and space. Furthermore, they do not need the air that we breathe, the light of the sun, the moon, or the stars, which constitute the indispensable elements for physical life.

They are invisible creatures representing sin, death, and darkness. All the more reason their presence was signified in *Genesis 1:2* before any physical elements were put in place by God.

Without any subtleties, *Luke 4:5-7* teaches that the kingdoms of this world were given to Satan to do as he will. The terms of the inherent convention are found in the parable of the tenants told by Jesus in *Mark 12,* the tenants being Satan and his host of demons, the servants being the prophets, and the son is Jesus himself. Thank God the contract is temporary as *verse 9* gives evidence of the vineyard being taken away from Satan forever. In that same sentence we also read that all the tenants are killed by the owner of the vineyard.

Another very significant point to consider when we follow the daily sequence of creation of the physical earth is that man was created on the sixth day posterior to the existence of trees, the sea creatures, the birds, and all land creatures.

The beginning of the book of Genesis is a faithful description of how the physical dimension was put in place, and accordingly, the very first verse of the Bible reads, "In the beginning God created the heavens and the earth."

There are three important elements to retain in this first statement of the Bible.

1- **The word beginning.**

2- **The appellation of God.**

3- **The two objects in question: Heavens and Earth.**

The word beginning simply describes the starting point of something, which is time. It extends, as a matter of course from an inherent inception to its cohesive completion as described in *Matthew 24:14,* marking the end of such time, which also conveys that the earth and these lower heavens that are part of this physical universe are temporal and will come to an end the same way they began by the same Word who spoke to them into existence *(Matthew 24:35* and *2 Peter 3:11-13).*

However, of that sort of time which has a beginning and an ending, God is transcendental, as we are told in *Psalm 113:5-6* that God's glory is above the heavens from where he rules the entire universe, both the visible and the invisible, sitting enthroned on high stooping down to look on the heavens and the earth.

There is a mind-blowing truth that will remove some of the husk associated with the first chapter of the Bible and will bring forth the richness of this first revelation of God, which is foundational to the understanding of the rest of the Bible. Perhaps this is the first time some people will come in the knowledge of it.

There is a corporate belief and there is a hidden truth, not that the truth is a mystery, but the reality is that for fear of seeming nonsensical or even foolish, our leaders have chosen to ignore the first creation at the spiritual level, where Adam's engenderment preceded all other creations, perhaps considered somewhat trifling by many, but of the utmost significance to understanding the sacrifice of the cross.

In other words, Adam's creation involved a mystical symbiosis, and this is true for the entire human race. The truth is there was a spiritual creation that preceded this physical existence as we know it, that, although very dissimilar from each other, guaranties the perennation of mankind through different dimensions of life (**pre-physical, death and beyond**).

Simply put, Adam and Eve and all of us had a pre-physical existence and were very much alive as distinct beings before we were transmuted in this physical, visible realm. I know this is mind-boggling, but the Bible is clear that man was created twice. Or simply put, we (**humankind**) are in our second dimensional existence as physical beings.

Interestingly enough, God used some very intriguing adjectives to describe the earth when he said that it was formless, empty, and totally void of dust, thereby giving us the necessary material for our spirit to make an informed resolution in total conformity with undoubtedly the most profound reality that we had a pre-physical existence. And besides, the obvious absence of tangible elements that are part of the physical creation simply indicates that the earth was clearly and unequivocally spiritual.

All of these approaches as taught in *Hebrews 11:3* is simply to tell us that spirituality is an extractable substance capable of evoking matter, which enables God to maneuver the physical dimension of the universe as a consequence of our spiritual death in the Garden of Eden. In other words, what is seen was made out of what is unseen. The physical came from the spiritual which makes the visible definitely an emanation of the invisible. This is the word of God, and most will probably acquiesce to this biblical principle.

But if I confirm exactly what the Bible teaches that man was created twice in the beginning, many of you will probably laugh your hair off your head, because the generally accepted view of creation is limited to its physical aspect, forgetting that God is Spirit and dismissing the sacred truth that we were created in his image and likeness, and sadly belittling the spiritual dimension of the "Garden of Eden" which simply not of this natural universe. There is no question that the bible is full of metaphors. But it is the duty of those in charge of the flock to bring to light these figurative languages which definitely lie beyond our natural senses. But unfortunately, the teachers of the word of God propagates less than adequate spiritual truths that the people of God need to know in order to understand and appreciate the sacrifice of the "cross".

The truth is the Bible does teach that humankind underwent an existential transmutation resulting in the physical formation in the womb, which is the first of a total of three intrinsic transformations before reentering the kingdom of Heaven.

1- **From the spiritual state as a living soul to the dead state having been physically transmigrated into the womb.**

2- **From our dead state as in our physical appearance, the body of death, to the born-again dimension as believers in Christ.**

3- **From our born-again nature to our final Christ-like transmutation with incorruptible bodies as a prerequisite for reentering heaven.**

For this reason, the Bible is explicit about the two dimensions of creation in Genesis that people unfortunately just read over, missing the subtle pervasiveness and the devastating power of sin and evil. This inadvertence simply ostracized the sacrifice of the cross, which took a long four thousand years to come and reverse the trend.

The panorama of the two accounts of creation presented in *Genesis 1* and *2* is described as follows:

1- **A spiritual dimension prior to sin as living souls.**

2- **A physical dimension as we know it today as a result of sin.**

The LIVING SOUL

The spiritual account of the earth is given to us by God beginning in *Genesis 2:4* going back generations, not in terms of physical years, but in terms of unspecified ethereal existence. You will notice that all the elements and their necessary interactions that would be indispensable for sustaining human life in the earth are nonexistent, such as the sun, the moon, the stars, the air, the birds, the livestock, and all other creatures that would move along the ground. Neither were there any trees, plants, nor grass in the earth.

Furthermore, and best of all, in *verse 5* God says that he did not create these things yet in the earth because there was no man to take care of them; these elements a priori clearly being the ensuing of the existence of man.

Again, this is very important to grasp. *Genesis 2:4* states that before any shrub appeared on the earth and any plant of the field sprung up, a mist would come up from the earth to water the ground. And God proceeded in *Genesis 2:7* to form the first man of the plant-less, treeless dust of the ground and breathed into his nostrils the breath of life, and the man became a living soul.

Then we read in *Genesis 2:9* that after God created the first man, Adam, from the ground, "God made all kinds of trees grow from the ground". This is a pivotal statement, probably one of the most significant pieces of information found in the scripture about humanity straightforwardly affirming and confirming the creation of all races associated with humankind in the earth. This great mystery of different races of people that even science struggles with is clearly given here in *Genesis 2:9,* though very succinctly, but the verse supplies the necessary ingredients that will certainly help in the enlightenment of *Ezekiel 31* when the "Trees" of the Garden of Eden were transmigrated to the earth. These metaphors and their explicit relationships to both men and angels in the Garden are definite indications of the indigenous substance shared by them in conjunction with their makeup as spirit beings, but humankind with an addendum ingredient called the soul, which can be redeemed.

It's not without reason the Apostle Paul refers to God in *Hebrews 12:9* as "the Father of Spirits." You will also notice that during our spiritual existence throughout the sinless era in the Garden of Eden, there were no days and nights mentioned, because the sun, the moon, and the stars, which are signs to indicate seasons, days, and years in the physical realm did not exist and had not yet any reason to. Neither do we see the familiar adjective "wild" being associated with any of the animals as irrefutable evidence of a conjoint and peaceful environment that existed in that dimension. But the most important dynamic of the original, spiritual creation to keep in mind is that man was created first, and then the trees, the rivers, the plants, and the animals followed.

Interestingly enough, even though we are still in the ideal sin- less era in the Garden of Eden, the pressure of the responsibilities given to Adam seemed to have affected his emotional stability and somewhat created the need for companionship.

Let it be clear that it was not to couple in sexual union to procreate. Not only spirits cannot have children, but sex did also not come into play until after sin in the physical world.

Nevertheless, Adam, who needed a helpmate, found no suitable helper among his animal friends. Obviously, this was not a concern for God as he thoughtfully managed the process of creating yet another human being while totally maintaining the cohesiveness of the blood or the soul that Adam was made of. This quest ensued God in *Genesis 2:21* to cause the man to fall into a deep sleep, and God took one of his ribs and made a woman out of the rib and brought her to the man and the man called his female version, "woman."

I don't want anybody to miss this. During the spiritual creation of man and his kingdom, Adam was brought forth before the environment was put in place, and Eve came as a last resort. In other words, between the time Adam was created and the time Eve came to be, the arrayal of the whole creation was completed, and saving the best for last, after Adam was introduced to the entire host of creation and named them, Eve as a ravishing amenity was then created and presented to Adam by God. This is how it took place in the spirit *(Genesis 2:4-25)*.

In contrast, following the intromission of sin, it is worth noticing that the woman will be called "Eve," inuring the inhabitation of their dead bodies, the physical body, which represents sin and the body of death *(Genesis 3:21, Romans 7:24)*. This kicks off the trans- migration of all men and women into this physical world, transiting through the womb, as the name "Eve" by definition clearly suggests in *Genesis 3:20*. Thereby passing from the eternal realm to this physical sphere as human beings.

Accordingly, during the recorded account of the six days of the physical creation, God first put the environment and all the necessary elements in place, and then on the sixth day, the last day, God proceeded with the creation of both the man and the woman almost simultaneously like the birth of twins so to speak *(Genesis 1:27-28, Genesis 3:21)*.

The motive and the difference between the two dimensions are very important to grasp, and the highly estimable essence of the cross will be exerted for the sake of all willing souls. Impressively, *Jeremiah 18* gives us a vivid testimony of the parallel between the two facets involved in the creation of humankind when God sent him to the potter's house to receive one of the greatest revelations concerning the creation of mankind through two distinct dimensions.

To ensure the accuracy of the two worlds revealed to Jeremiah by God, the Prophet begins *verse 4* of *chapter 1* with these words: "The word of the Lord came to me, saying": "Before I formed you in the womb I knew you, before you were born, I set you apart and I appointed you as a prophet to the nations".

The depth of this revelation is the central theme of Genesis and should force us to look beyond the surface to examine carefully this vital information and to develop the appropriate understanding of why God who is a "Spirit Being", "Holy" in character concluded to create this "physical sinful" universe.

Given the universal destination of humanity, Christians at all levels question the abnormality of our existence in the earth and the difficulty of this present life. In order to understand why this world was created, we must discern our origin and how it relates to our present condition. The revelation given to the Prophet Jeremiah pertaining to the Potter's House in his "Workshop" very well clarifies all misconceptions linking to our physical existence or to this physical reality.

The evidence of the analogy is very intriguing. All ambiguities are removed and the reasoning behind the creation of the world is given. The distinction however will not be too obvious for some and may even be quite disconcerting.

The Potter	God
The potter sitting at his wheel and using clay made a pot. The pot he shaped was marred, ruined in potter's hands (*Jeremiah 18:4*).	God using the dust of the earth created mankind as living souls or spirits, and sin came and destroyed them (*Genesis 3:6-7*).
The potter then took the same clay marred and formed it into another pot shaping it as it seemed best to the potter (*Jeremiah 18:4*)	God then took their spirits and clothed them with garments of skin and transmigrated them as Humans to the earth (*Gen 3:21-24*)

Also, in *Romans 9 verses 20-24* we read the following,

- "Who are you O man to talk back to God?"

- "Shall what is formed say to him who formed it, 'Why did you make me like this?'"

- "Does not the potter have the right over the clay to form out of the same lump of clay some pottery for noble purposes and some pottery for common purposes?"

- "What if God choosing to show his wrath and make his power known, has endured with great patience the potteries of wrath made for destruction?"

- "What if God did this to make the riches of his glory known to the potteries of mercy that he prepared in advance for his glory, Jews and Gentiles' alike?"

Again, as a spiritual pottery, prior to sin, the primogeniture of Adam did not only concern the human race, but his existence was also primordial to all other creation. Also true is the fact that Eve was the last to be created, successive to all other creations *(Genesis 2:18-23)*.

As the evidence points out, in regard to the human race, Adam and Eve were the first to be created in either dimension. In the spirit Adam and Eve were the multipliers at the command of God which resulted in the existence of all pre-physical men and women in the Garden prior to sin, and also in the flesh as the multipliable first couple through the inauguration of sex as the means of bringing about through the womb all preexisting men and women from the spirit dimension into this physical world as dead souls. This is what Jesus meant when he said in *John 3:5,* "Unless one is born of water and the Spirit he cannot be saved." As each person is formed in the womb, he or she inherits the intrinsic nature of the first man, Adam, who himself was made of water from which dust came. The earth was formed out of water and water" *(2 Peter 3:5)*, is the essential nature of man.

Born Of Water Vs Born Of The Spirit

To be born of water simply signifies coming through the womb, which gives legal existence in the earth, physically alive but without the spirit of the living God, as compared to fallen angels who fell in the earth as spirit beings but who can also have human physical appearance.

These "men-angels" are kept in darkness and bound with everlasting chains for hell. But Jesus in this assertion is clearly distinguishing between the two categories of men. The ones who came through the womb versus the ones who are simply fallen angels taking on the physique of men, and for whom there is no redemption. This is why as a prerequisite for propitiation and the dwelling of the Holy Spirit one must be born of water or have come into this world the natural way.

To be born of the spirit, as taught in *John 3,* is approbatory to the "born again" notion in place since Abel, the brother of Cain, the first prophet of God to have received the spirit of Christ, which is the life-giving spirit resulting in the new birth that gives access to the kingdom of God.

In other words, no one can be born of the spirit unless he or she came through the womb. Jesus in the simplification of the water birth and the spirit birth to Nicodemus in *John 3:5-6* says, "Flesh gives birth to flesh, but Spirit gives birth to spirit." This expression, "Spirit giving birth to spirits," is another element of great significance that needs to be fully understood as more light is shared on our spiritual existence in the Garden, which is one of the dimensions of heaven, but unfortunately also beholding the presence of Lucifer. *Ezekiel 28* teaches that Lucifer is an angel, a cherub who was created perfect in all of his ways. He was perfect in beauty, perfect in glory, and was made to walk up and down in the midst of fire stones. *Verse 13* tells us that Lucifer was assigned in the Garden of Eden, which we know inhabits the Tree of Life, the garden being the Paradise of God. So, in obvious coherence the scripture rightly says in *Revelation 2:7* that the Tree of Life is in Paradise. What is not obvious to many is how the Tree of Life got in Paradise, when *Genesis 2* clearly states that the Tree of Life was in the Garden of Eden, where Adam and Eve were placed.

The answer is fairly simple. So, let's clear up the confusion once and for all. The scripture teaches that those who are alive and who belong to Christ when he returns will be instantaneously changed to incorruptible bodies and taken up to heaven.

The same principle applied to Adam when he was formed sin- less from the ground and received the spiritual breath of life from God who is spirit. We are told that Adam became a living soul and was taken to the Garden of Eden, the Paradise of God, which is not of this physical world. Certainly, you remember Jesus telling us that in his Father's house there are many mansions, thereby making Heaven conceptually multifarious.

In fact, this is so true that *Genesis 3* tells us that after Adam sinned, he was driven out of the garden *(verse 24)* to work the ground from where he was taken. For we read in *Genesis 3:19* that the consequences of Adam's sin after he was sent forth from the Garden, among other things, are that he will be overtaken by sorrow until he returns to the ground, since from the ground he was taken; for dust he is and to dust he shall return.

Now the Garden of Eden or Paradise is still where it has always been. Neither has the Tree of Life been relocated. It is clear that through Jesus we will regain the right to eat from the "Tree of Life," which is located in the Paradise of God, according to *Revelation 2:7*. However, we humans are the ones that got kicked out of the Garden, and so did the Devil, but the Garden of Eden remains as the Paradise of God.

Just a few more clues to confirm that Paradise or the Garden is not of this physical world and that we have no business to be in our present condition in this physical temple.

The Apostle Paul tells us in *2 Corinthians 12:4* that he was caught up to Paradise but cannot utter what he heard because those things are not permitted to be told. In *2 Corinthians 12:2* the Apostle Paul clearly divulged where Paradise is located, and he said that Paradise is up in the third heaven.

Do you see how coherent the word of God is? And how all these ideas are connected as evidence of an unambiguous revelation, with superlative pomposity, if only mankind were to recognize the utmost truth that Paradise or the Garden of Eden is a place where sinless spirits dwell, and for us to have been there is beyond all understanding.

It is so much so that *Luke 23:43* teaches that Jesus on the cross, about to die, said to the thief being killed next to him on his cross, after the thief recognized Jesus to be God and Savior, "Today you will be with Me in Paradise." But what is sad and also true is that Lucifer before he became Satan, we're told in *Ezekiel 28:12-13,* dwelled during his entire splendor in the Garden of Eden, the Paradise of God.

As you can see, the issue here is not entirely complex and we will irradiate, as it becomes necessary, the return of man to this physical earth as from spirit to flesh or from living soul to humankind, and what the new garment (coats of skin) entails in its most simplistic way.

Apart from that, the single most important element about the beginning of creation is that God (singular) is the Creator. One God, just one God created the heavens and the earth, Isaiah reminds us in chapter 45:18. Also inherent in the very first verse is the spirit of God hovering over the waters, which is another evidence of Jesus being the Holy Spirit.

Corroboratively, this is another irrefutable evidence of Jesus being the Holy Spirit and it is found in *Luke 24:44,* where we are taught that everything written in the Old Testament, starting with Moses, the prophets, and the psalms, will be fulfilled in Jesus or by Jesus in the physical, as the object and the subject of the entire Bible.

Therefore, the contingency of the Holy Spirit hovering over the waters in *Genesis 1* was the equivalent of Jesus hovering over the ocean while the disciples screamed in fear thinking they saw a spirit.

In speaking of spirit, God, after revealing the spiritual nature of the earth in *verse 2* of *Genesis 1,* informs us that despite the formlessness and the emptiness of the earth, the earth was covered with darkness as darkness covered the surface of the deep. But God in his omniscience revealed through the prophet *Isaiah (45:18)* that he did not create the earth to be empty but formed it to be inhabited.

Throughout the Bible, darkness represents the existence of sin, evil, and death, and more precisely, the presence of Satan and his horde of demons. Again, did not our Lord Jesus Christ say in *Luke 10:18* that he saw Satan fall like lightning from heaven to the earth? This certainly implies that before light came in *Genesis 3,* Satan and his demons, who symbolize darkness (sin, evil and death), had already organized and established their invisible kingdom in the earth. Although in the physical sense the earth was still formless and empty, keep in mind that Satan and the fallen angels, a priori being spirits in an invisible kingdom, are not affected by physical elements.

In *verse 3,* God said, "Let there be light," and light appeared. God separated the light from the darkness, calling the light "day" and the darkness "night," and thereby established the two opposite, uncongenial kingdoms of the physical world. The kingdom of darkness presided by Lucifer (Satan) and the kingdom of God represented by the light in the person of Jesus Christ.

John 1:4 declares that in Jesus was "Life" and that life was the "Light" of all mankind. Understanding these basic theological principles is primordial before any spiritual connection of the multifaceted trends prevails. In *Deuteronomy 30:19* the connection is clear when God said, "Today I call heaven and earth as witnesses against you that I have set before you, life and Death, blessings and curses. But hold fast to your God, for the Lord is your 'Life'."

The evidence of the link between "Light" and "Life" points without any doubt to the Lord Jesus Christ as the "Light" we read about in *Genesis 3*, establishing the kingdom of God in the earth in contravention to the darkness which represents the kingdom of Satan that had covered the entire surface of the deep.

To establish the conclusion that the "Light here in *Genesis 3* is in fact the Lord Jesus Christ, consideration must be given to the affirmation of the Apostle Paul in *2 Corinthians 4:6*, where he explains boldly and credibly that when God said, "Let there be light" out of the darkness, the light was in fact the Lord Jesus Christ.

In passing, it is very important to anchor in your mind the vivid distinction between *verse 3* where God Said, "Let there be light" (singular) referring to the first appearance of Jesus in the earth realm as the "Life" giving Spirit representing the kingdom of God in this dead and dark world and *verse 14* where God said, "Let there be lights" (plural) when the sun, the moon, and the stars were created. This distinction carries great weight in the understanding of God and the connection between him and his physical creation.

When the Apostle John in John 1 talks about Jesus being the word, and that the word was in the beginning with God, and the word was God, and the word is the light of the world, and the word became man, no one at this point should have any difficulty believing that John was essentially and precisely referring to Jesus as described in *Genesis 3*, representing the kingdom of light or the kingdom of God.

For the first five days of creation in action, everything that was to be part of the earth was created and came to be by a singular God. Up to this point, I don't think anyone would have any problem with that aspect. The first day, the second day, the third day, the fourth day, and the fifth day, God spoke and the air, the sun, the moon, the seasons, the trees, the water creatures, the land creatures, and the air creatures, all came to be. However, on the sixth day an ambiguity surfaced when

God decided to make a creature called "man," and the most interesting thing happened. Instead of "me" the objective case of "I" in reference to himself, God used the pronoun "us," the objective case of "we" denoting Himself and others in the process of the creation of humankind.

At first glance, this verse is saying that more than one God made man, or simply put, God is more than one. We know this cannot be true, because the word of God is coherent and not self-contradictory. *Malachi 2:10* tells us that ONE God made man and that He is the Father of all. Therefore, the ostensible plurality of God as evidently portrayed here in *Genesis 1:26* is simply establishing once and forever the eternal truth that the light revealed in *Genesis 1:3* that would later take the name of Jesus in the form of a man is not only God but is of the same essence as the Father.

King David tells us in *Psalm 56:13* that the light (the kingdom of God) was created to deliver sinners from darkness and death. All of us may not yet understand the foundation for this absolute truth and the reasoning behind it, but the emphasis in regard to *Genesis 1:3* is without ambiguity that the two kingdoms, light and darkness, were already in the world before anything was ever created. The million-dollar question is why darkness was, which is symbolic of sin and death, found in the earth before man was even created.

Until you understand the significance of what took place in *Genesis 1:1-5* and the mystery behind the creation of man, the crucifixion of Jesus will make no sense whatsoever.

Before we proceed, let me remind you that God is spirit, and everything about him is supernatural. His revelation, although universal, is blurring for many, causing oxymoronic definitions left and right, because it simply cannot be cultivated, and Jesus only gives it to whomever he alone wishes. No particular religious, social, academic, or ethnic cultures have any preeminence in the affairs of God, and there is no respect of persons with God *(Romans 2:11)*.

The Bible teaches in *1 Corinthians 14:33* that God is not the author of confusion. Being spirit, God's word cannot be restricted or understood in a single context. So, anyone can easily imagine who is behind the many disagreements among Christian leaders, giving rise to the proliferation of the church, while claiming the use of the Bible as the basis of their doctrines.

Although the immediate context of a passage can be the basis for its partial and historical interpretation, we must remember that the spiritual principles surrounding any specific passages are timeless and should constitute the predominant guide leading to the knowledge of God's intended truth.

But people, especially in the Western world, have cultivated over time a negative mind-set that has now become an acceptable world view, building into their thinking that the blessings and the mysteries of God are associated with advanced cultures or linked to a certain standard of living. Not realizing that cultural, social, economic, and religious prejudices and stereotypes have taken roots in their subconscious, and as soon as they are faced with unfamiliar experiences outside of their circle of belief, those negative unconscious stereotypes emerge unexpectedly, making it more difficult or even impossible to reconcile or incorporate these differences into some kind of theological coherence so that together we come to a better understanding of the word of God as one people.

Consequently, the Word of God makes the nature of God as a Spirit Being evident in absolute congruousness despite of his heterogeneous makeup in the person of Christ, while he defies comparison with anything known to mankind. Even man, who is an emanation of the spirit for having been created in the image and likeness of God, who is "The Spirit", is a mystery in our own backyard.

Though we totally ignore the makeup of the spirit and the details of his power, we do know, however, that spirits are formless, supernatural beings operating with supernatural powers, unexplainable in their ultimate dimension to the rational mind.

On the surface, no one would decisively refute the idea that man, who is perhaps the most important aspect of God's creation, is created in the image of God. I don't think anyone with common sense would also deny that God can speak things into existence. But the mystery behind man's creation is that man was not spoken into existence like the rest of the creation, but rather, as taught in *Genesis 2:7*, God formed man and man became a "living soul," which is a clear indication that God through one of his manifest operations must have given evidence of his substantiative existence in order for the prophet Isaiah to be true in his affirmation that God is the "Rock" from which man was cut.

In other words, what the prophet Isaiah is declaring is that God is the Rock, and mankind is gravel that came from that Rock, which turns our attention to *Revelation 13:8* to unveil a double intricacy surrounding God's self-slaying from the foundation of the world, and begin to understand, on the one hand, the plurality of God portrayed in Genesis 1:26, and on the other hand, his image and likeness as pertained to the first man, Adam, which of course brings us to another important point. If the heavens cannot contain God in his full spiritual dimension, there is no way any substantive manifestation of God through self-abscission in Jesus Christ can accommodate his full divine potencies.

Therefore, distinguishing between the two concepts and keeping them clearly apart will certainly clarify the spiritual drought endured by the man Jesus, though an abscission of God manifested in the flesh, and bring it in some kind of coherence to justify his incapacitation as a human being to encapsulate within the little mind of the man he became, the manifestation of the full essence of the power and the glory of God. That is why he could say, "My Father is greater than I am."

But the resurrection put an end to that abridgement and reverted Jesus' back to his rightful former condition as "The Spirit", the Almighty God.

Jesus did say on the cross, "It is finished," referring to the redemption work. But God has not averted his glance on humanity. His purposes and self-ascribed operations are not only still in effect, but he continues to revert back and forth in the earth in the form that he chooses as appropriate for any particular environment and still be the God of the universe. There is no variance in God, whether it is his spirit that is in action, whether God is operating through his soul or whether it is his dead body on the cross. God is still the same Almighty God enthroned on high. They each can operate independently of one another as if they were three distinct entities but in complete unfathomable unison.

There is no straightforward answer that fully explains this spiritual complexity. As humans, some of us understand that our genesis precedes the womb, but as far as the interactions between the human spirit, the human soul, and the human body, if we want to be honest, we are in total ignorance.

My spirit would warn me of some danger, my body would suffer the consequences, and my soul would cry. That is all I understand the interconnection. But I wish I had the power to transiently extract each substantiator as an independent entity thrice around a table like God can and engage a plan for an agenda for each of the three distinct entities to follow, and when all is said and done, blend the threefold in a twine and return to the enjoyment of a solitary intimacy as one. With man this is impossible, but with God it's a piece of cake.

In fact, I don't know why some people only limit God to three persons— God can be everywhere at the same time in various forms, eating and drinking with his chosen ones, and his multipartite will still be comprised of his full unified divinity. Now tell me this is not mysteriously supernatural.

So, when God said in *Genesis 1:26,* "Let us make man in our image and in our likeness," don't be so hasty to jump to the popular conclusion there may be more than one God. There aren't! And the word of God is clear that God does not share his Glory with no one. If one of the three that supposedly form the so-called Trinity is of a higher realm or intrinsically has more power than the other two, then the title of the most powerful has the capital "G," and the other two are simply "gods" with lower case g's.

You see, the pluralization of God is a very dangerous assumption that remits the sacrifice and the crucifixion of Jesus to a completely separate domain, rendering almost opaque its life-giving significance. Additionally, cutting off Jesus as the Creator and savior and therefore the God Almighty," this obversely makes God a liar and a coward. A liar, because God the Father clearly said in *Isaiah 43:11-15*, **"I myself am the creator and the savior"**, and a coward, because God would use an entity other than himself as a scapegoat in obvious evidence of his scantiness and put him publicly through such agonizing and shameful predicament on a cross.

Jesus said, "The Father and I are One," "I am in the Father and the Father is in me," and "When you see me you see the Father." So wouldn't you agree that when the Bible states that Jesus was slain before the foundation of the world, it necessarily equates to the Father's self-inflicted slaying to become the Word and therefore the light resulting from the "Let there be light" command in *Genesis 1:3* as a direct result of the effect of sin on God himself causing him to become the needed physical savior and redeemer in the likeness of sinful flesh in the person of Jesus Christ?

So, you see, the separation of God into multiple distinct entities is a grave distortion of the word of God, and whether it is done willfully or from ignorance, it is not played out with impunity. Such mishandling of the scriptures can be very dangerous and will ultimately lead to eternal damnation, eternal destruction, as taught in *2 Peter 3:16*.

The Apostle Paul in *1 timothy 6:11* warns us to flee from all unrighteousness and ungodliness and to take hold of the eternal life to which we are called in Christ before the physical universe, or simply put, before the foundation of the world.

This is not a mystery that is understood by all yet, that people can be regenerated in this life and be transformed into a totally new and different person in perspective of the return of Christ with the promise of the "Kingdom of Heaven"

In fact, the Apostle states in *1 Timothy 3:16*, "Great is the mystery of Godliness," and he proceeds to define it as follows:

- He appeared in a body.

- He was vindicated by the spirit.

- He was seen by angels.

- He was preached among nations.

- He was believed on in the world.

- He ascended into glory.

I hope this is illuminating, but again let's return to Genesis and the creation of man. In *Genesis 1:26*, God said, "Let us make man in our image, in our likeness," and he also said to let "them" rule over the fish of the sea, and so forth. But in the next verse, something of great spiritual significance happened, and it is striking to see how much emphasis God has particularly given to Adam, and it's a connotation not to miss. I believe this verse is one of the most important verses in the Bible pertaining to the nature of God.

It reads as follows: "So God created man in his own image, in the image of God, God created Him" *(Genesis 1:27)*. By using the word or pronoun "him," the objective case of "he," meaning only Adam, God is totally dismissing Eve in this verse, not that she herself is not made in the likeness of God, but there is something exceptionally unique, a subtle distinction noteworthy about the image of God that Adam bore, which reveals the oneness of God concerning the Father, the Son, and the Holy Spirit. It's a remarkable clue that in both processes of creation, spiritual dimension and physical dimension, Eve was the last piece of both creation puzzles, brought forth at the last moment, almost as an afterthought so to speak, to make creation complete and eventually the redemption of mankind possible.

In *Genesis 2:7*, talking exclusively about Adam, the Bible says that God formed the man from the dust of the ground and breathed into his nostril the breath of life, and Adam became a living soul.

Up to this point, Eve had not been created yet. Nevertheless, all livestock, all land creatures, all sea creatures, and all the birds were created and brought to Adam to receive their appropriate names. With all these varietal surroundings, *Genesis 2:18* tells us that Adam was alone, or perhaps lonely after seeing that all creatures were created male and female, and yet he did not have a suitable companion for himself. So, God, not from another dusty substance, or from any outside source, but from within Adam, a fragment from Adam himself, made a woman and brought her to the man Adam.

Now Adam said, "This is bones of my bones and flesh of my flesh, she shall be called woman" *(Genesis 2:23)*. Despite of them being two distinct entities, they (Adam and Eve) were of the same flesh and of the same spirit.

This may sound a bit trivial, but this peculiarity about Adam makes him unique in all of creation. What was so peculiar about Adam that others didn't have? you ask!

Well put on your seat belt as we are about to enter spiritual turbulences. Adam is the only male in all of creation that carried a child in his bosom and was able to give birth so to speak, though cesarean section was a necessary tool, to the mother of all humans, Eve, as she is called in *Genesis 3:20.* Having come from his bosom, Adam referred to Eve in *Genesis 2:23* as bone of his bones and flesh of his flesh. In which case, we all agree retrospectively that Eve came from Adam, having been one with Adam as an intrinsic part of Adam before she was taken out.

Interestingly, in the first chapter of the book of John we read that Jesus came from the bosom of the Father, which certainly means, as in the case of Adam and Eve, that Jesus, was at one time hidden in the Father as one intrinsic entity before becoming the light in Genesis 1 as part of God's plan for humanity.

In *1 Corinthians 3:1* the Apostle Paul refers to Christians who refuse to grow in Christ as infants that cannot digest solid food but should be fed milk. However, the Apostle said when he is among mature Christians; he speaks a message of wisdom that is not of this world and that even the rulers of this physical universe (Satan and his demons) who are coming to nothing knew about.

In *1 Corinthians 2:6-7* the Apostle defines God's secret wisdom as the providence that has been hidden in God and that God des- tined for our glory before time began. None of the rulers of this age was given to know or even descry this divine wisdom, for if they had, they would not have derided and crucified the Lord Jesus Christ, who is the very personification of this great wisdom. In *verse 13* Paul says that these are not words taught us by human wisdom, but words taught by the spirit expressing spiritual truths in spiritual words.

What's even more astonishing is the fact that none of the angels, not even Lucifer, knew of the existence of Christ prior to his birth as a human being *(1 Corinthians 2:6-16)*.

If you are still not convinced that Jesus was hidden in all eternity past inside the Father like Eve was inside Adam as "one", let's go pay a visit to King Solomon, the wisest man who ever lived, and consult his authoritative proclamation in *Proverbs 8:22* and let the King tell us where Jesus came from. You will be amazed when you realize, given the facts, there was no way Jesus could not have been known, even by the angels, unless he was hidden in the Father as "One" from all eternity until the unveiled fragmentization of God manifested in the book of Genesis as the "Light" to create and give life to the world.

This is the Spirit of Christ talking in the book of Proverbs:

- *The Lord brought me forth as the first of his works, the earliest of his achievements of long ago. I was appointed from eternity, from the beginning, before the world began.*

- *When there were no oceans, I was given birth as with labor pains (New World Translation).*

- *Before the mountains were settled in place, before the hills, before the earth was made or its fields or any of the dust of the world, I was given birth.*

- *I was there when he set the heavens in place.*

- *I was there when he established the foundation of the deep, the boundaries of the sea and the foundations of the earth.*

Ephesians 3:9 tells us that Jesus Christ, the mystery of God, for ages past was kept hidden in God, who created all things. *Verse 10* tells us that the reason God had kept Christ Jesus hidden in him until his physical birth was so that through the church, it is made known to Satan and his fallen angels the manifold or diversified wisdom of God. For there are varieties of operations, but yet it is the same God who works all of them *(1 Corinthians 12:6)*.

Before we go back to Genesis, I have an exhortation that might be helpful in understanding the word of God, and it's very simple. "Always keep in mind that with God, you are dealing with extra supernatural."

So, in momentary conclusion on the provenance of Jesus, let me say that before his first appearance in the earth when God said, "Let there be light" in *Genesis 1:3,* Jesus was in the Father as One entity, analogously to the oneness of Adam and Eve prior to the extraction of Eve from Adam. The incredible difference between Eve and Jesus is that it would have been impossible for Eve to reenter Adam and become one with him again, but this is exactly what Jesus will do at the end of his kingdom in the earth.

As a matter of fact, Jesus has already become One spirit with the Father again since the resurrection, based on this excerpt from *John 17,* when Jesus, looking toward heaven, uttered these words before going to the cross, having completed the work he came to do: "I have revealed you Father and brought you glory in the earth by completing the work you gave me. Those you gave me know with certainty that I came from you. Protect them by the power of your name so they may be one as we are One just as you are in me and I am in you."

This calls for great insight, but Paul the Apostle warns that spiritual truths will sound like foolishness to the man without the Spirit of God, for he cannot understand them, because they are spiritually discerned *(1 Corinthians 2: 10-14)*.

This is precisely the great mystery behind the image and the likeness that God and Adam had in common. God the Father, having had Jesus in Him for eternity past and having temporized for the completeness of time, which became complete, executed a self-slaying to bring forth through a mysterious transmutation the Savior and Lord Jesus Christ in alikeness to Adam, who carried Eve inside of him for an unknown length of time and actually gave birth to her, so to speak, through a transplantation of a fragment of his own body for the integral formation of her body as a complete other individual with all the necessary faculties as flesh of his flesh and bone of his bones. This is very mysterious!

As it was, this exceptionally unique image of God Adam characterized was very short-lived for the simple fact that it presupposed a one-time event, which took place in the spirit before sin. The scripture is clear that Adam no longer had the image of God after he was kicked out of the Garden. In Genesis 5 we read that after the death of Abel, Adam had another son, who was in his own image and likeness, and he called him Seth.

Also, very enigmatic are Adam's first two sons, Cain and Abel. Abel was the first true prophet of God *(Luke 11:50-51)*, while Cain was the first representative of Satan in the earth *(1 John 3:12)*. We will study him in future paragraphs.

In *chapter 2* of Genesis, the Bible talks about Adam and how he came to be. Eve had not come into existence yet. In *verse 7* we read that God formed Adam from the dust of the ground and breathed into his nostrils the breath of life, and Adam became a living soul.

The word of God teaches that spirit gives birth to spirit. So, the first thing that should strike you is why God, being spirit according to *John 4:24*, would create his first son, Adam, and label his existential character as simply a "living soul"? Note that this is a dimension many erroneously consider to be less than a spirit. But the answer is found in *1 Samuel 2:35* where God himself declares to have a soul, obviously either inherent in his spirit or in addition to Him being spirit.

Job 36:26 tells us God's nature is beyond the understanding of any human and accordingly the Apostle Paul, shedding a little light regarding the nature of God in *1 Corinthians 2:6-16,* tells us that the soul or the mind of God is full of wisdom and knowledge even beyond the understanding of angels. But we have the mind of Christ from whom the secrets concerning the wisdom and knowledge of God are revealed without measure.

So, Adam, being made a living soul upon receiving the spirit of God at creation has indubitably made him a spirit a priori, but distinctly the beneficiary of the mind of God as a subsuming addendum built into his spirit giving him the ability to act like God, with great wisdom and knowledge without necessarily prior instructions from God.

It's no wonder that this man Adam was the object of great envy by some of the highest and most powerful angels in the heavenly realm.

Luke 3:38 tells us that Adam was the Son of God. The principle of sonship carries with it spiritual weightiness. Adam was created by God to live eternally, which means that Adam had an immutable quality of existence in the likeness of spirit beings. *Luke 24:39* tells us that spirits do not have flesh and bones and in *1 Corinthians 15:50* we read that flesh and blood cannot inherit the kingdom of God. Furthermore *2 Corinthians 4:18* teaches that visible things are temporal, but invisible things are eternal. So, Adam not only could not have had flesh and bones, having been potentially created with everlasting existence, but also the Bible tells us only invisible creatures can live forever, so therefore Adam must have been an invisible being according to our current physical standard.

These biblical analogies are definitely pertinent to the intrinsic spiritual nature of the first man Adam. Not only Adam but Eve herself was directly created by God; therefore, both Adam and Eve were spirits. I know this is a mouth-twisting, jaw-dropping, head- scratching statement. But one important thing to keep in mind is that God is all-powerful. Nothing is left to chance, and nothing takes God by surprise. He foreordains and makes decrees based on his foreknowledge of all that is to come to pass.

Genesis 2:8 talks about a Garden in Eden that God planted with all kinds of trees. In the middle of the Garden were the Tree of Life and the Tree of Knowledge of Good and Evil. There God put the man he had formed from the dust of the earth.

Job 17:16 teaches that dust symbolizes death. We also know from Genesis 3:19 that flesh is also dust. So, sin is flesh, flesh is dust, and dust is death.

Thematically, flesh came as a result of sin, and the Apostle Paul tells us in *Romans 8:3* that the wage of sin is death, as sin has been condemned in the flesh by God *(Romans 6:23)*. Therefore flesh, darkness, and dust are all symbols of death, which is an emanation of sin. The obvious minglement of these substantive properties around the existence of humankind is evidence that the physical man was created as a result of sin.

So, God created Adam and Eve and put them in a paradisiacal environment called the Garden of Eden. But, as I said earlier, in the Garden were two special trees, one that is referred to as the "Tree of Life," which gives and prolongs life indefinitely, and the other one which is called the "Tree of Knowledge of Good and Evil," which produces poisonous fruits that in fact represent the serpent with its lies that kill on contact. You know the rest of the story; they were poisoned by the Serpent after eating the forbidden fruit and became the inhabitation of Satan. In other words, they became demon possessed and no longer were worthy of God's presence.

Despite the Quintessence associated with the creation process, God having brought forth each day and called the inherent elements good, a discordant medium, out of nowhere, suddenly makes "his" appearance. In the immediate context he is presented to us as a "Serpent and a Tree".

But later as the extensiveness of his power and the expediency of his evil agenda become more apparent, he'll be more specifically projected as a "Cedar Tree", to explicate the extent of his irrefragable negative influence over the elements of his immediate environment.

What I find very intriguing is the description given in *Ezekiel 31* and *32* regarding this killer tree, also known as the serpent, both symbolizing this powerful wicked angel called "Lucifer". We know from *Ezekiel 28* that Lucifer is a cherub, which is a very high-ranking angel. But when we read about his countenance and his mission through the *verses of Ezekiel 31* and *32,* it is astonishing that an angel with these kinds of prerogatives could fall into sin and is now reduced to a mere man.

This is all spiritual and very supernatural which can be easily rejected or distorted if your focus is limited primarily upon which that can be explained in the natural by science and philosophy.

According to *Ezekiel 31* Lucifer was once a cedar in Lebanon with beautiful branches overshadowing the forest. **He was the sustaining source of all the trees in the field,** (This is very significant for later) and as we read in verse 6, all the people of the earth lived in his shade.

In other words, Lucifer was the assigned guardian of the Garden of Eden. And believe it or not, according to *Ezekiel 31:4* Lucifer was the sustaining power of all the angels under his command, as it is revealed clearly in *verse 4* that the waters that nourished him around his base as the Cedar Tree are then channeled to all the other trees of the field.

Verse 8 tells us he was so unique that the other cedars in the Garden of Eden could not rival him, neither could the pine trees nor the plane trees compare to his branches. In addition, he was so beautiful that verse 8 concludes that in fact no other trees in the Garden of Eden could match his beauty.

This kind of language is enough to provoke a dyslectic coup and contrecoup, but as we strive to understand what is being taught here, do not be overtaken by the obvious ambiguity and confusion that the word "tree" impressively displays in both *Genesis 2* and *3*.

God being Spirit, our traditional interpretation of Genesis is too simplistic in relation to the supernatural extent displayed of God in the scripture which transcends all human understanding.

When one is worshiping in the spirit, however, the general theme of the scripture becomes so gracefully simplistic that the dynamic of the revelation evolves into a clear, unconfused apprehension that creates a personal, intrinsic revival, like a "tree" in desperate need of water that finally came.

As brainstorming and evocative its usage may seem, the word "tree" as used by God in Genesis 2 and 3 represents four different and very distinct characters.

- *In the sentence, "No other trees in the Garden could match Lucifer's beauty," "trees" stand for the other angels placed under Satan that were assigned in the Garden.*

- *The "Tree of Life" in the middle of the Garden symbolizes the Lord Jesus Christ.*

- *The Tree of Knowledge of Good and Evil represents Satan.*

- *When Adam, upon hearing the Voice of the Lord, hid himself among the "Trees" (plural), a double connotation exists. The word "Trees" here corresponds to humanity explicitly, but mysteriously also wicked spirits.*

Moreover, in *verse 10 of Ezekiel 31* we read that Lucifer became proud because of his height and sinned against the "Most High", and this is when war broke out in Heaven as we read in *verse 11* that God handed him over to the ruler of the "Nations" to be dealt with according to his wickedness. The word "nations" in this context stand for the community of angels, and the ruler of the nations is none other than Michael the Archangel, who is one of the chief princes described in *Daniel 10* and whom John said in *Revelation 12:7-9* cast Lucifer and his angels out of Heaven to the earth.

That's not all, and this is very important. *Ezekiel 31* teaches in *verse 12* that as the Cedar tree was cut down and brought down to the grave *(verse 15)* and his boughs fell on the mountains and in all the valleys and all the ravines of the land, meaning all his angels with him.

When we go to the Old Testament there is a brief but amazing description of the hierarchy of the angelic order given by the prophet *Ezekiel in chapter 6:3* from highest to lowest as follows?

1. **Mountains**

2. **Hills**

3. **Ravines**

4. **Valleys**

So, the reason behind our presence here in this current physical universe will never be fully understood unless the relationship or better yet the interactions between the fallen angels and humankind in the Garden of Eden, not just Adam and Eve, but humanity as a whole, involving sin of which this is the result, are considered in their most detailed nature, as revealed here by the prophet Ezekiel.

Remember we are still in the Garden of Eden, and the prophet is using four dominant symbols **(nations, trees, waters, and beasts)** to describe the multifarious interactions that took place as God stepped in to inoculate the Garden following the contemptuous conspiracy conjoining both men and angels as they relinquished their given right and exert God to propel the next dimension, putting the earth into use to receive our dead souls and the fallen spirits of the angels.

We also read in *Ezekiel 31:12* that as the cedar tree is cut down, all the nations of the earth came out from under his shade and left him. (This is humanity as a whole represented by Adam, when the Voice of the Lord, immediately following the fall, exclaimed with excursion power: "Adam where are you?" sending forth a retrieval command for all humankind from among the "Trees" and from under the shade of the "Cedar Tree" which God is about to cast down to the pit of hell.)

But Ezekiel tells us that all the birds and all the beasts of the field were among his branches as the "cedar tree" fell to the earth. (These are all the angels over whom Lucifer had authority and who delusively deigned in wickedness). The totality of these fallen angels are destined and delivered unto death "in the earth below" among mortal men who will also go down to the pit. *(Ezekiel 31:13-17)*

Verses 15 through *18* contain a mixture of what happened in the Garden and what will take place on the day of the Lord at the end of times. *Verse 15* reads that because of the cedar tree (Lucifer), God clothed Lebanon with gloom and all the trees of the field withered away, referring to the binding of the fallen angels with everlasting darkness.

But now in *verse 16* there is a switch in the meaning of the word "nations" and "trees" **(to be representative of people)** as when Adam hid himself among the trees or as we read here that "all the nations tremble at the sound of the fall of Lucifer when he was brought down to the grave." Remember we're still in the Garden, and immediately following this, God added that "all the Trees of the Garden of Eden that were well watered were consoled in the earth below."

As this last statement clearly suggests, can anyone truly deny that these trees being referred here as coming down from the Garden of Eden to earth the effectively represent humanity? When we know clearly from scripture that all demons or fallen angels, including Lucifer himself, are subject to the same eternal curse from the beginning of time and there certainly is no consolation or even a relenting respite in the earth for any of them. For as the Bible clearly teaches, God will not rescind his final decree of total destruction against them on judgment day. Therefore, these trees that came down to the earth from the Garden of Eden are again none other than humanity in its totality. Very mysterious!

In light of all this, the book of Matthew outlines a couple instances where Jesus clearly states that trees are definitively representative of people. In *Matthew 3:10* Jesus said, "The axe is already at the root of the trees, and every tree that does not produce good fruit will be cut down and thrown into the lake of fire."

Moreover, we read in *Matthew 7:15-20* that Jesus said, "Watch out for false prophets [bad trees] that will come in sheep's clothing, but inwardly they are ferocious wolves. By their fruits you will recognize them. Do people pick grapes from thorn-bushes or figs from thistles?" Every good tree bears good fruit, but a bad tree bears bad fruit. Thus, by their fruit you will recognize them".

Now the "Cedar Tree", which is symbolic of Lucifer, in a foresight expressed by Ezekiel in verses 17 and 18, will finish in total destruction together with those who lived under his shade as his allies among the "Nations". He will go down to hell with them, joining "Those" who will be killed by the sword, when Christ on judgement day sends the ungodly to the eternal lake of fire. (The second death).

Of particular significance, and I don't want anybody to be confused about it, is this profound distinction revealed by God of the two categories of **"People"**, or should I say **"Beings"**, that are going to hell.

1. **Nations** "who" lived under the shade of Lucifer in the Garden of Eden will go to hell conjointly with him. **(The word "Nations" here refer to the "Angels" who were consentient to his evil deeds as his connivers)**

2. **Those,** (Human beings) who will be killed by the sword out the mouth of Christ on judgment day. **(Those to whom it will be told, "Depart from Me I never knew you")**

As a reiteration, still emphasizing the distinct characteristics of the "Cedar Tree", *verse 18* reads that God said to Lucifer, "even though your splendor and majesty cannot be compared to any of the trees in the Garden of Eden, yet you too will be brought down with the trees of Eden to the earth below and in the end, you will lie among the uncircumcised, those killed by the sword.

I hope this seems reasonable enough as an irrefutable foundation for the clarification of this mysterious minglement involving the creation of humankind, the Garden of Eden, and our fascinating interactions with the angels of God, which had a "life and death" effect as a final consequence.

But despite their spiritual deaths, which came as a result of their disobedience of God, Adam and Eve, we're told, still had the potentiality of reaching the tree of life, whose fruit gives everlasting existence. Had it not been for the cherubim and a flaming sword put in place by God to guard the tree of life, they could still have eaten from it and lived forever, obviously without any forgiveness, as sinful creatures or evil spirits, *(Genesis 3:22)*.

I must say I was very intrigued by the fact that no forgiveness was offered by God to the first couple, nor do I see Adam and Eve being penitential for rejecting the Holy Spirit that was in them. But then I realize that God had a much bigger plan than just forgiving Adam and Eve, whose actions made sin complete, and death was not only the inevitable result but a necessary mechanism for the purification of our souls in the Blood of Jesus Christ through the perspective of the flesh as our second and ultimate chance of returning to heaven and reconciling with God.

So, when God banished Adam and Eve from the Garden of Eden in Paradise *(Genesis 3:22)* and transmigrated them to the physical earth to cultivate the ground from which they came from, God did not kill an animal, as some suggest, and made garments or coats of skin and clothed them.

Remember that Adam and Eve were spirits and sinless when they were created, which explains why they were considered naked from a human standpoint and felt no shame. The reason lies in the fact that before sin there was an interesting relationship that existed between God and his people, and the Holy Spirit was the only garment that was needed so that one does not go naked and be shamefully exposed.

Jesus in *Revelation 16:15* says it this way: "Blessed is he who stays awake and keeps his clothes with him, [the Holy Spirit] so that he may not go naked and be shamefully exposed."

Besides, the resurrection of Christ has substantiated the validity of such reality when Jesus came out of the grave naked from a human standpoint, leaving in the tomb the linen he was wrapped in and the burial cloth that had been around his head *(John 20:7)*.

Both *John 20:6-7* and *Luke 24:12* tell us that the clothes Jesus was buried in were left in the tomb. The principle of spiritual garment was reiterated by Jesus in *Luke 24:49* to expose the apostles to the relevance of being clothed in the Spirit, which simply signifies to be cloaked with power from high as the Holy Spirit dwells in you.

Once that Holy Garment was lost in *Genesis 3,* Adam and Eve immediately lost their spiritual estate or the state of righteousness required to enjoy the Holy benefits of Heaven. And God at this point, as the sole life giver and sustainer at all dimensions of life experience, provides the appropriate garment suitable for survival in the new given environment away from his presence.

The physical and temporal earth, as we know it, with its multifarious environmental conditions, was created and reserved as an inhabitable dimension for sinners. As a result, sin having been condemned in the flesh, God, as *Genesis 3:21* teaches, gave Adam and Eve flesh and bones as coats of skin representing their new state of being and thereby created a dead, sinful creature called humankind. We are not self-existent; our physical body is only a mean by which activities of the soul and the spirit are made visible in the earth realm in remembrance of our new sinful character.

The flesh and bones as clothes for dead spirits applies to both men and angels. It is the word of God and a divine principle that all who sin, from whatever dimension of committance, will lose their spiritual inhabitance and be clothed with flesh and bones awaiting final judgment.

Now in *Genesis 4:1* we experience sex for the first time and the engagement of procreations was initiated. But something a bit mystical is also being revealed here by God when he portrays Satan as a progenitor or a Father as we see God in *Genesis 3:15* infusing an antagonistic disposition not only between Eve and Satan, but also between her descendant and his descendant.

At first glance, one would be brought to think that as Eve would have children, grandchildren, and us today, Satan would also bear children and grandchildren, and so on. But that simply is not the case. Satan as ruler or king over the fallen angels has in fact become their sustenance, so to speak, as we saw earlier. Those fallen angels who went along with Satan in his perverseness depend on his evil spirit for self-preservation. But remember the Devil is not self-appointed and therefore not subject to self-aggrandizement. Though Satan is depicted in the Bible as a king, his power derives from God who sustains it or restrains it according to God's purpose.

It is almost impossible to do justice to these revelations in so far as every contingency of our physical life was a priori dealt with by Jesus before the foundation of the earth in the two books of life pertaining to life and death. In Christ, those who will be saved were chosen, having been predestined according to the plan of God who works out everything in conformity with the purpose of his will. *(Ephesians 1:11)*

There is absolutely no fulfillment that matters outside of Christ as He circumscribes humanity from an eternal perspective, revealing:

- **What we were before time began, where we came from and how we got here.**

- **What we will become at the end of the world and where we are going.**

We should also remember as I said before that God's actions in relation to humanity have at least two possible implications.

1. One interpretation is directed to the physical realm and is for our physical well-being on earth.

2. The other interpretation, which is the dominant concept that pleases God the most, extends to the spiritual dimension.

In other words, when you take that same physical context as it applies to God's ultimate purpose for both the universe and our personal lives and are able to transcend the natural routine and understand the inherent spiritual meaning associated with it, a hyper-physical manifestation occurs, overflowing with wonders of true excitement, exhibiting a genuine relationship with the Creator that can only be revealed and attained in the spirit, as God is Spirit and so pleased with his people worshiping him only in spirit and in truth.

Now, let's go back to the descendants of Adam and Eve and those of the evil spirit, commonly known as Satan.

Genesis 2:1 tells us that in six days God created the Heavens and the earth and all their army. If you are not a spiritual person you will miss out on the essence of this passage and thus fall short of the true meaning of our existence on the earth. I think God meant what he said when he said that all the armies of the heavens and all the armies of the earth were created and complete in those six days of creation.

During the physical "six day" creation the armies of the heavens refer to the galaxies, the stars, the planets, the wind, the rain, the clouds, etc., that are part of the physical universe. These are not to be confused with the armies of the Heavens in the spiritual sense which are comprised of different categories of "angels".

This being said, nobody would question my sanity if I said that all the armies of the heavens that would ever exist as invisible beings or the zillions of stars that filled the sky as physical elements that God saw fit were created and complete in one command in either dimension, or not one more was created afterwards. But if I said the same holds true for the existence of all mankind in the Garden of Eden when God made all kind of "trees" grow out of the dust of the ground, *(Genesis 2:9)* I would be sent to be seen by a psychiatrist. But the truth is from Adam the first man to the last person that will be born at the end of the tribulation period, we were all created and complete and had our individual existence in the spirit before we were given this physical temple as sinners.

Assuming you are consentient to the creation of zillions of angels by God just speaking a word, what could have hindered God from multiplying Adam and Eve into multiple billions of human beings? And as sinners, each would pay for his own sin. The soul who sins is the one who will die *(Ezekiel 18:4)*. From a spiritual standpoint "fathers will not be put to death because their sons have sinned, nor will a son be put to death for his father's sin" *(Deuteronomy 24:16)*.

However, as sin has entered humanity resulting in these physical temples, God has decided not to leave the guilty unpunished (sins that are committed in the earth), "visiting the iniquity of fathers on their children and grandchildren as described in the scripture to the third and fourth generations" *(Exodus 34:7)*.

All things considered, It is a good reminder that in heaven there is no procreativity, but conversely, sex, which is the instrument for procreation is earthly and was instituted by God as a repercussion of sin to save mankind, as only those that are naturally born of women, which includes all mankind, will have a second chance to be saved; compared to demons to whom it is given to appear as men, but whom are kept in darkness until the great day of the Lord. Remember that in the spirit before Adam's disobedience, the earth was there hanging in space, formless, and uninhabited. But God in his foreknowledge of the sinful conduct of both men and angels says in *Isaiah 45:18:* "I who fashioned and made the earth and established it, did not create it simply for nothing, I did not create the earth to be empty, but I the Lord formed it to be inhabited. I am the Lord and there is no other."

From being king over the whole creation to this mishmash on earth, how did men fall so low? Adam was king over the Garden of Eden until envy and covetousness against Adam's position were found in Lucifer, whose dream was to institute a coup to overthrow Adam and replace him as king over God's creation. The details concerning the meaning of all this may still be a bit obscure, but one thing is certain, we have endured the horrific consequences for about six thousand years and counting.

PART III
The Book Of Revelation

The book of revelation or the "Apocalypse" encompasses the ultimate decrees of Jesus pronounced in the Garden of Eden against sin and evil and their final outcome. This book of prophecy is nothing more than the final judgment of Jesus the Creator of all life visible and invisible, putting an end to this long evil conspiracy, involving a number of powerful fallen angels and their king, namely Lucifer, commonly known as Satan, that started out in heaven and has been continuing in the earth realm for about six thousand years with limited power even reaching an all-out, both in resources and time attaining swiftly the inevitable, detrimental juncture with Christ for their complete obliteration.

The spoliation of spiritual potency in the pursuit of wisdom and power, initiated in the Garden of Eden subsequent to the cogency of Satan, was apparently engrossing for the congeners, but evidently ended up hounding both men and angels following that complementary sin against the "Word of God". Subsequent to a number of decrees pronounced by God concerning the future of men and these fallen angels, Satan apparently obstreperous, war broke out in Heaven between these fallen angels in league with Satan as their king *(Revelation 9:11)* and Michael the Archangel and his angels.

This war, as purposed by God, did not end in real victory on any side *(Revelation 12:7)*. As an episode of God's plan for salvation, Satan and his angels with him, refusing to be made subservient, were hurled down to the earth retaining their angelic powers, mad as hell, in readiness to strike, but this time at God's people whom they had deceived into sin in the Garden of Eden, and which people sin has reduced to an entity lower than the angels called "human" as a second and only chance to return home in heaven once evil is completely destroyed, man being predestined to die only once after which comes judgment *(Hebrews 9:27)*. Again, this is not referring to physical death as we saw earlier. Many were raised from the dead to die a second time later in life. This is another piece of evidence we are simply strangers passing through the earth, God, proving Satan wrong of his elusive goal.

As we have seen in preceding paragraphs, Satan and his demons were already in the world when Adam and Eve, thus all of us humans, were brought onto this physical realm after having died spiritually as a result of our collective disobedience to the commandment of God in the Garden of Eden, one of many dimensions of the spiritual universe where the Tree of Life is planted and guarded.

Jesus in *Luke 10:18,* four thousand years after Satan and his angels fell on this planet, said that he saw Satan fall like lightning, which undeniably means that Jesus was in heaven four thousand years earlier prior to him being born as a man, witnessing the fall of Satan from Heaven. This perspective evidently brings to mind the question of who is this man Jesus that can speak of things from an indefinite past and declare and predict new things before they spring into being? His authoritative proclamation about yesterday, today, and tomorrow brought a new understanding and a new light to the word "prophecy," which is not simply foretelling the future.

As demonstrated in the Bible, a prophet of God is a vessel of the spirit of God that can speak accurately of things of distant past, as well as things that will not take place for many generations to come.

For example, Moses was born in Exodus but his prayer in Psalm 90 goes back to before creation. As a matter of fact, all the prophets of the Old Testament, as they were filled with the Holy Spirit **(the Spirit of Christ),** spoke about Jesus, the forgiveness and the judgment of sins and the end of the world, which was thousands of years away.

On a negative note, however, expressions such as "judgment of sins" and "the end of the world" are very husky to digest these days by many, which to some extent mar all interest in the exploration of the book of Revelation in which God answers all the end time mysteries, considered generally somewhat covertly written. And we propose to decipher the quiddity herein as faithfully as the Holy Spirit will lead us.

The book of Revelation is first and foremost about the true nature of our Lord Jesus Christ. It gives us an exhaustive description of who Jesus is in the spirit, his ultimate message to the Church, and his final endeavor to redeem humankind as he puts an end to this widespread conspiracy of Satan and his demons.

The span of the information contained herein will take us as far back from before the foundation of the world, to beyond the New Jerusalem, the kingdom of heaven, which is coming down at the end of the thousand-year reign of Christ and his Church.

CHAPTER 1-3

The book of revelation begins with words of "good news" which gracefully incorporates seven beatitudes for the people of God onto salvation:

1- **Blessed is the one who reads the words of this prophecy and blessed are those who hear it and take to heart what is written in it because the time is near** *(Revelation 1:3)*.

2- **Blessed are the dead who die in the Lord from now on; they will rest from their labor, for their deeds will follow them.** *(Revelation 14:13)*.

3- **Blessed is he who stays awake and keeps his clothes with him, so that he may not go naked and be shamefully exposed** *(Revelation 16:15)*.

4- **Blessed are those who are invited to the wedding supper of the Lamb!** *(Revelation 19:9)*.

5- **Blessed and holy are those who have part in the first resurrection. The second death has no power over them, but they will be priests of God and of Christ and will reign with him for a thousand years** *(Revelation 20:6)*.

6- **Blessed is he who keeps the words of the prophecy in this book.** *(Revelation 22:7)*.

7- Blessed are those who wash their robes, that they may have the right to the tree of life and may go through the gates into the city. Outside are the dogs, those who practice magic arts, the sexually immoral, the murderers, the idolaters and everyone who loves and practices falsehood *(Revelation 22:14).*

With this obvious specificity of the seven beatitudes, Jesus is very straightforward and meticulously selective, as it appears that his goal is to bring into the kingdom of heaven those who satisfy these criteria. Twice he reiterates the importance of the book of Revelation as he stresses on the crucial observance of its teaching **(Beatitudes 1 and 6)** by not only reading it but also taking it to heart.

Before the intended focus of the message behind the revelation, the Apostle John begins by unveiling different titles that are applied to the Lord Jesus Christ as he is told by Jesus to write what he sees in a book and send it to each of the seven angels in charge of the seven churches, a mystery in and of itself, to reveal the real world we live in and to help us find new meanings that should improve our "God-given" character and our awareness of the horror awaiting those who do not know Christ.

Allow me to present a summary analysis, giving thought to the single essential message behind all the letters, thus having to do with the synthetic reality of both traditional and contemporary religions of the world. It is obvious that based on the twofold characteristics, both emollient and appalling, explicitly inherent in all seven letters , Jesus is talking from the Creator's standpoint, but at the same time as the sole "Redeemer" and judge of the world, addressing through the Apostle John all religions, Islam, Judaism, Hinduism, Buddhism, Christianity, and all the others, with a universal message that there is an invisible reality swiftly catching up to us, and we are going to have to deal with it one way or the other.

At first glance, three of the seven churches, **(the church in Smyrna, the church in Pergamos, and the church in Thyatira)** are outright declared to be a synagogue of Satan, where Satan has his throne and where the woman Jezebel is teaching and seducing the people of God to commit fornication and to eat things sacrificed unto idols. But Jesus still promises to save them and spare them from the great tribulation to come if they repent of their deeds.

There are, broadly speaking, certain good deeds being practiced by some of the churches, but these benevolences seem to be very insignificant because Jesus holds quite a few unpleasant assertions against them. The church of Laodicea, whatever its equivalent is in today's society, because of its current culture of worshipping God and money concurrently, seems to be in the most trouble. For Jesus threatens to spew her out of his mouth.

To be honest, I think the whole world sadly falls under this last category, regardless of religious affiliation. No wonder Jesus says in *Luke 13:24* that "many" think they are saved but they are not.

So, the question our brothers, the apostles, asked Jesus in *Matthew 19:25* still applies, "Who then can be saved? But the "Gracious Lord" answered, "With men salvation is impossible; but with God all things are possible".

Regardless which stance your religion holds concerning Jesus Christ, these seven letters are reminders to stimulate you to wholesome thinking so you will not be taken off guard as we look forward to a **"New Heaven and a New Earth"** in the presence of the Almighty.

In *2 Peter 3:18* the scripture commands that we grow in the grace and knowledge of the **"Lord and Savior"** Jesus Christ, to whom be glory both now and forever! Amen.

Appellatives Ascribed To The Lord Jesus Christ

The Apostle John begins each of his greetings to the seven churches with a description of Jesus or even better, different titles attributed to Jesus as follows:

- **The one who is and who was and who is to come.**

- **The one who has the seven spirits of God.**

- **The first born from the dead.**

- **The ruler of kings of the earth.**

- **The Almighty.**

- **The Alpha and the Omega.**

- **The First and the Last.**

- **The Living One.**

- **The one who holds the keys of death and Hades.**

- **The one who holds the seven stars in his right hand.**

- **The one who has the sharp double-edged sword.**

- **The Son of God, whose eyes are like blazing fire and whose feet are like burnished bronze.**

- **The one who is holy and true.**

- **The Amen.**

Without thought, the dynamics of this prophecy, which makes it even more inscrutable, is the fact that the Apostle John states in *verse 10 of chapter 1* that he was in the spirit on the Lord's Day.

People in general miss this great revelation and what it means. To give you a reasonable idea what John meant by the expression "Day of the Lord," I suggest you read: *Zechariah 14, Isaiah 2, Isaiah 13, Amos 5:18-20,* and *Obadiah 15,* which will tell you that **"The Lord's Day"** is a day of wrath, a day of judgment, a day of great darkness. But closer to us, the Apostle Paul in *2 Corinthians 1:14* teaches that the "Day of the Lord" is the second coming of Christ to the earth, which certainly will begin with the Rapture, encompassing his thousand-year reign and will definitely culminate with the casting of all ungodly to hell.

The apostle Peter, concerning the Lord's Day, is by far more explicatory when he teaches in *2 Peter 3:7-10* that not only "the day of the Lord" will come like a thief, but it will also be sudden and when we least expect it. It will be a day of judgment, a day of fire and the day of destruction of all ungodly men. The heavens and all elements thereof will be destroyed by fire and disappear with a roar. The earth and everything in it will be laid bear with a fire that will never be quenched.

This is what's in view here, and I hope it is taken very seriously because very soon nothing will be the same. The next global war that we all see in the horizon will kick everything into motion, bringing into the visible arena the end-times effects of the infinite decrees put in place by the Lord Jesus Christ during his 33-year earthly mission. The aftermath will be like nothing the world has ever seen since the beginning of time.

As for the apostle John being in the spirit on the Lord's Day, it simply signifies that his spirit was separated from his body and taken to a spiritual dimension as deemed appropriate to receive the prophetic word and to witness as he describes throughout the "Book of Revelation" the different events leading to the end of the world.

The possibility of such supernaturalism is found in *2 Corinthians 12:1-4* when the apostle Paul was caught up to the third heaven, where Paradise is located according to *verse 4,* and the apostle said he could not tell whether he was in the body or apart from the body. In other words, he doesn't know whether he was in the spirit or in the body.

So, as you can see, such phenomenon does exist, and when the Apostle John states that he was in the spirit on the Lord's Day he is neither referring to Saturday nor Sunday as generally believed, but certainly more is at issue as you now know.

From that perspective, the book of Revelation is simply about God judging the world and putting an end to this physical mess. Do you recall in *Genesis 1* when all the days were being created and God said, for each day before calling it a day, "there was the evening and there was the morning" and then called it a day? The evening, symbolizing darkness, came first, and then light came. A whole day was comprised of both darkness and light.

The same is true for the day of the Lord, which is symbolic of judgment day. The day of the Lord will begin counterintuitively with the appearance of the Antichrist and the false prophet as corollaries to *2 Peter 2:4,* which teaches that the angels who sinned were sent down to hell and kept in darkness until judgment day. Obviously, their incipience will only be short- lived as they will be thrown alive in the lake of fire by the Lord Jesus Christ himself after only a seven-year reign.

Nevertheless, the day of the Lord is truly symbolic of the thou- sand-year reign of Christ in the earth, but it certainly can mislead people, even well- intended people, because they have never experienced being in the spirit and be purposefully led through certain mysterious events.

People might confuse this with a vision or some sort of a dream, and if you only fit this category, you may have missed out on this supreme revelation of the power of God. This surpasses even the Apostle Paul's

The truth is, according to this statement and the one in chapter 4:1 the Apostle John was not only caught up to the throne of God in heaven, but he was also translated to the end of the world and lived through everything that is decreed to take place concerning the end times and judgment day as Jesus personally instructs him to write everything he sees.

Comparing Paul's statement of being caught up before the throne of God in the third heaven and John's testimony of being translated to the end of the world is similar to Jesus healing the paralytic in *Matthew 9:2* and asking the doubting scribes of his authority to forgive sins in the earth: "Which is easier to say? Your sins are forgiven or get up and walk." The event which followed precisely made the answer to the question very easy when Jesus most dumbfoundedly dropped the bomb and said to the paralytic, "Get up, pick up your bed and go home."

Now let me ask you! Between Paul's experience of being caught up to the third heaven and John's adventure of being translated to the end of the world, which is easier to believe? Well! it's impossible to acknowledge one and distrust the other. *Luke 1:37* simplifies it this way, "Nothing is impossible with God."

CHAPTER 4

At the beginning of *chapter 4,* Jesus in person takes John up into heaven and shows him the things that must take place hereafter. Contrary to the prophet Daniel in *Daniel 7:9,* who saw in a vision heaven and the ancient of days sitting on his throne, the Apostle John was translated at the throne of God and shown all that has taken place in eternity past and everything that will follow in times to come. In verse 4, surrounding the throne John sees twenty-four other thrones, on which twenty-four elders sit, all dressed up in white with golden crowns on their heads. In *verses 6-7* John talks about four living creatures that have six wings each and eyes all over their bodies. They incessantly say day and night, "Holy, Holy, Holy is the Lord God Almighty, who was, and is, and is to come."

Let's stop right here for a minute because John clearly refers to the God, whom he sees sitting on the throne in Heaven as a God who was, and is, and is to come. The Bible is clear that God is. From everlasting-to-everlasting God is. But the only time God ever was, was when Jesus was in the flesh for thirty-three years. So, the God Almighty described in *Daniel 7:9* as the ancient of days, whom John sees sitting on the throne in heaven and to whom it is referred to as a God who was, and is, and is to come is none other than Jesus Christ.

Furthermore, as Jesus is called King of Kings and Lord of Lords in *1 Timothy 6:15* we see a corroboration of this truth in *verse 11* when all twenty-four elders sitting on their thrones as kings throw their crown at Jesus feet and fall face down before Him and worship.

CHAPTER 5

In *chapter 5* John begins by describing a scroll sealed with seven seals being held in the right hand of him who sat on the throne. But no one in heaven, in the earth, or under the earth was found worthy to open and look inside it. John wept and wept. The word of God is so forever true that twice in Isaiah God says that He will not share His glory or give it to another *(Isaiah 42:8, 48:11)*. Here *chapter 5* confirms it to be true when no one in all of creation is found worthy to break the seals. Suddenly John was told to stop weeping, for the lion of the tribe of Judah, the root of David, has triumphed and is able to open the scroll and its seven seals. Then John saw Jesus **(The Lamb)** with seven horns and seven eyes, which are the seven spirits of God.

The definite article "the" before the word "seven" is an indication of the total number of divine spirits or the fullness of the Holy Spirit and then grappled with the number seven, which represents perfection and completeness, one cannot but conclude and agree with the teachings of Paul in *Colossians 2:9* about Christ representing the fullness of deity and in *Colossians 1:19* about God being pleased to have all his fullness dwell in Christ and through him to reconcile to himself all things whether on earth or in heaven, by making peace through his bloodshed on the cross, which gives inclusive evidence to what John is describing as taking place here in *chapter 5*.

Remember that God does not share his glory with no one *(Isaiah 48:11),* but here John is being a witness to Jesus receiving worship by all living creatures in heaven, on the earth, under the earth, on the ocean, and under the ocean. The four living creatures said "Amen" as the twenty-four kings fell down and worshipped him.

There is an important nuance that you should not let pass you by as the Bible only makes mention of things in heaven and on the earth being reconciled to God through the cross of Christ. But when it comes to Jesus being worshipped, all things are bowing to him as we see addendums of under the earth and under the ocean as places where living creatures also reside and from whom Jesus is also receiving adoration.

CHAPTER 6

The First Six Seals of a Total of Seven

The supernatural segment of the word of God is often rejected by people of all background, Christians and non-Christians alike, and this chapter, which represents the teaching of the Apostle Peter in *Acts 17:31*, states "that God has set a day when he will judge the world by the man he has appointed and that he has given proof of this to all men by raising him from the dead."

This is a very puzzling truth as we all have taken different attitudes toward life and death, and some of us don't even believe in life after death. Fortunately, our theological differences in that matter are at the verge of expiring.

Chapter 6 is the beginning of the end of all pluralistic theology, and the message is very clear from that point on with the opening of the first seal, the first of seven that Jesus will open, which consists of a series of unavoidable divine and invisible decrees about things that must take place in the universe both in the heavens, on the earth, and under the earth.

Each of the decrees, a few brief episodes apart, conveys a specific message with explicit actions to be carried out as in a symbiosis of good and evil. The first four decrees, as their respective seals are open, are read each by one of the four living creatures present at the throne with specific instructions and appropriate delegation of power to five horsemen symbolizing five powerful angels whose mission is the execution of the different plagues associated with each seal.

First Seal and the White Horse

The angel of the White horse, though his deeds are not specified, seems to have the upper hand because a crown was given to him, which puts him in a position of authority over the other four angels as their commander. And the fact that he is holding a bow and riding out as a conqueror sent on conquest tells us that he is a warrior engaged in warfare.

Second Seal and the Red Horse

The angel of the red horse receives a great sword and was told to specifically remove peace from the earth so that men slay each other. This angel symbolizes a military angel. This is a clear indication of the existence of a war between the nations of the earth, which experts might refer to as World War III (WW3). As the fourth seal will indicate, this will be the bloodiest of all preceding conflicts known to mankind. Anyone who has not read the scripture thoroughly will be at a loss concerning the significance of what is at issue here in connection with these end-times events that will take place.

God says in Zephaniah 1:2-3,

- "I will sweep away everything from the face of the earth.

- I will sweep away both men and animals.

- I will sweep away the birds of the air and the fish of the sea.

- When I remove all men from the face of the earth, the wicked will have only heaps of rubble, declares the Lord.

Peter says in *2 Peter 1:16,* "We did not follow cleverly invented stories when we talk about the power and the coming of the Lord Jesus Christ. We were eyewitness of his "Majesty". We ourselves heard the voice that came from heaven when we were with him on the sacred mountain.

He received "Honor and Glory" from God the Father when the voice came to him from the "Majestic Glory", saying, 'this is my Son' whom I love and with whom I am well pleased".

Again, this next war, "World War III" will be so devastating that only God could have prescribed it, leaving no possibility of any evasive endeavor. The world simply will have to resign to its fate as commanded.

Third Seal and the Black Horse

The angel of the black horse is holding a pair of scales in his hand, which is symbolic of a merchant whose apparent mission is to inject a severe depression on the earth, oppressing the economic system of the nations as a direct consequence of the war ensued at the opening of the second seal, affecting both national and international trades, and making it almost impossible to develop and store goods in sufficient quantities due to perhaps technological constraints.

In verse 6 we read, "a quart of wheat for a day's wages, and three quarts of barley for a day's wages," is a clear indication that the world will be faced with an acute shortage of food, where supply and demand will be in great disequilibrium forcing the market to be oligopolistic.

But praise be to God that his word and his promises abide forever. In verse 6, Jesus, after ordering that global economic scarcity, commands that no damage be done to the oil and the wine, which represent the community of believers.

As Jesus, in *Psalm 105* at the time of the great famine when all food supplies were destroyed, commanded that his anointed ones be protected against such plagues, here in *revelation 6* we see Jesus keeping his word and remembering his covenant when he commands that again his followers are not to be affected by these afflictions.

So, as you can see Jesus is simply reiterating what He commanded in *verse 15* of *Psalm 105:* "Do not touch my anointed ones and do my prophets no harm." He is also following through on what he said in *Isaiah 25:6* that He will prepare a banquet of aged and of the finest wines for his people.

"A thousand may fall at your side,
and ten thousand at your right hand; But it shall not come near you.
Only with your eyes shall you look and see the reward of the wicked."
"Because you have made the Lord, who is my refuge,
Even the "Most High", your dwelling place, no evil
shall befall you, nor shall any plague come near your dwelling; For He
shall give His angels charge over
you, to keep you in all your ways. In their hands they shall bear you up,
Lest you dash your foot against a stone. You shall tread upon the lion and
the cobra,
The young lion and the serpent you shall trample underfoot".

Obviously, this is the post-war era, and as you can see, the Church is still here in the earth but highly protected.

The Fourth Seal and the Two Horse Riders

When Jesus opened the fourth seal, one pale horse came forth but this time two angels, one identified as the angel of death and the other as the angel of hell conjointly rode on that horse so to speak, and to them was given power over one fourth of the earth to kill humankind by virtue of four dreadful judgments from God as mentioned in *Ezekiel 14:21*, sword, famine, plague, and wild beasts. Again, we see Jesus keeping his promise made in Ezekiel that not everybody will die during that dreadful period, which is behind the reason why He only gives those two angels permission over one fourth of the population of the earth representing in today's number, had the war been impending, about 2 billion people.

Latest official world population is estimated to be about 7.5 billion.

7,500,000,000 × ¼ = about 2 billion.

So, if the war broke out today, the world armies would be responsible for the killing of about 2 billion lives worldwide. Is this prophecy one to panic over? Not if you are a true follower of Christ. Jesus foretold that these things would take place. Nations would rise against nations, kingdoms against kingdoms. He further states that famines and earthquakes would also be part of our everyday life, but we are not to be alarmed because all these are only the beginning of sorrows, and he who stands firm to the end will be saved.

Jesus continues to say that wickedness will increase as the love of most will grow cold. But the good news is that the gospel of the kingdom will be preached in the entire world as a testimony to all nations and then the end will come *(Matthew 24:1-15)*.

Some people express doubt and question the reality of such calamity, especially in regard to the number of deaths that will result as a consequence of the war. If you think this contingency is a tale, I have news for you. By the time we reach the end of *chapter 19*, the truth is there won't be a single soul left alive anywhere in the entire world, as the prophet *Zephaniah* in *chapter 1:2* warned thousands of years ago, **"God will sweep away everything from the face of the earth. From men to animals, the birds of the air and the fish of the sea. All will be destroyed completely from the face of the earth".**

The last statement of this verse is very significant as it refers to the thousand-year reign of Christ and his followers. But this will be understood later. Again, the statement, "When I cut off man from the face of the earth, the wicked will have only heaps of rubble", simply signifies that when God totally remove mankind from the earth, **(complete destruction of mankind) the wicked (this word stands for the fallen angels)** will be left with a pile of trash. Like I said, this will be clarified later but simply have the guts to read on.

The Fifth Seal and the Post-War Era

When Jesus opened the fifth seal, John said he saw the souls of those who had been slain because of the word of God and the testimony that they held, crying with a loud voice, and saying to Jesus addressing him as the sovereign Lord, holy and true, "How long until you judge the inhabitants of the earth and avenge our blood?" They were given white robes and were told to wait a little longer until the number of their fellow servants and their brothers, who are supposed to be killed as they had been, was complete.

Some of the most significant works of God are being conveyed right here at the opening of the fifth seal, giving evidence to the identification of Jesus as the "Holy sovereign Lord and True God of the Heavens." And I pray that all disbelief that Jesus is at the same time, "the Father, the Son, and the Holy Spirit," satisfying the unification or the oneness of God that the Bible clearly teaches, from Genesis to Revelation, have been disposed of.

Here at the opening of the fifth seal, one cannot miss the presence of an altar symbolizing a platform where sacrifices are offered. We know the Old Testament prophets were very much accustomed to building altars and offering sacrifices. Moses himself was warned when he was about to build the tabernacle, which is a copy and a shadow of what is in Heaven, to see to it he made everything according to the pattern shown him on the mountain *(Hebrews 8:3-6)*.

Now we are in the presence of the true altar, the true sanctuary, one not made by human hands and not part of this creation. An altar that is in heaven *(Hebrews 9:24)* on which Christ offered his own blood and obtained an everlasting redemption for humanity *(Hebrews 9:11-14)*. For this reason, Christ is the mediator of a new covenant that those who are called may receive the promised eternal inheritance *(Hebrews 9:15)*.

In *Luke 11:50* Jesus promised to hold this generation accountable for the blood of all the prophets that has been shed. Consequently, it is made manifest here at the opening of the fifth seal as we see the souls of the Old Testament prophets being presented at the highest altar in heaven, though not worthy to be placed on the altar itself, but they were nevertheless under the altar partaking in the glory of Jesus.

This great phenomenon, which concerns the Old Testament prophets, that has taken place here at the opening of the fifth seal is the manifestation of the first phase of the Rapture relative to all true prophets whose deaths preceded the birth of Christ beginning with Adam's son Abel, the first prophet of God, and ending of course with John the Baptist, who bridged the Old and the New Testaments.

When I write first phase it is not a slip of the pen, but I do mean that the Rapture, though eventually synthesized, will be and has been dimensional and not subject to a single event as many are brought to believe. The Rapture has been interspersed throughout the history of the world, and will continue to be so during the tribulation period. In effect, first we will see the dead and the living sucked out of here simultaneously, and further in a second phase, the two witnesses of Christ who will be killed and left unburied for three and a half days will be revived physically by the Holy Spirit and then Raptured before all eyes.

Perhaps a little understanding of the following traits will be helpful.

- **The difference between soul and spirit.**

- **The difference between Jesus personal glory and the constituents of the glory around him.**

- **The solitariness of Jesus in the disposition and the dispensation relative to the opening of this fifth seal.**

SOUL vs. SPIRIT

Many have given their best at explaining the contrast between soul and spirit. However, I, being ignorant in the domain of the psyche, will stick to what the word of God has to say in that regard.

The Bible teaches two distinct souls being part of the human nature:

1- A physical soul

2- A spiritual soul

The Physical Soul

The physical soul is the emanation or the expression of all physical feelings and or physical emotions. Self-awareness of life in this side of the grave simply signifies that our physical soul is alive. A person as a whole, which wholeness is defined by Apostle Paul in *1 Thessalonians 5:23* as "Spirit-Soul-Body," is kept alive by the soul which is the blood in him. In *Ezekiel 18:4* God said: "Every living soul belongs to me. The soul who sins is the one who will die". This aspect of the soul is nothing more than the physical existence of man as being alive in the flesh.

The Spiritual Soul

However, when the Bible in *Genesis 4:10* talks about the soul of the prophet Abel crying to God after having been killed by his brother Cain, this is a whole other dimension of the soul. When Jesus said in *Mathew 10:28:* "Do not be afraid of those who can kill the body but cannot kill the soul," this is another range of teaching revealing that the **"spiritual soul"** does not perish at death and that it continues on living.

Understand that when the word of God uses the term "soul" to identify beings that are part of God's kingdom, it is referring to people who were once alive on the earth and who either physically knew death or were taken alive into heaven after a sudden physical transformation. As the Apostle Paul would tell you in *1 Corinthians 15:50*, flesh and blood stand for what is to perish. They represent corruption and the very sinful nature of our being. They cannot inherit the kingdom of God.

The Indivisible Glory of God

Preeminently one must consider the inherent Glory of God, which is an inseparable existential quality abiding permanently in his being. This ultimate Glory of God is not shared by or with any other being, whether in heaven or on the earth or under the earth *(Isaiah 42:8)*.

This fundamental truth is the reason behind the inspiration of the seemingly endless assertion throughout the Bible that "God is one." Though three different operations, one very distinct from the other in nature, were part of God's plan for humanity, thusly "Creation-Redemption-Salvation," God Himself has performed all three enactments, transforming Himself therefore pertinaciously into the three different and appropriate entities as it was deemed necessary.

We read the corroboration of this truth in *1 Corinthians 12:6*, where the Apostle Paul teaches that, indeed there are different kinds of working, but the same God works all of them in all men. This portion of the scripture in Paul's teaching *(1 Corinthians 12:4* and following) is a vivid illustration of the oneness of God in the diversity of his work through the manifestation of diverse gifts allotted to mankind by the Holy Spirit.

In summary I would say that God's intrinsic Glory is:

- His infinite wisdom

- His indefinite power

- His unapproachable light

If you have kept your eyes on Jesus, you would immediately identify our Lord Jesus Christ as the sole bearer of these three divine substances. *(Ephesians 1:17-23).*

The Constituents of God's Glory

What is man that you make so much of him?

What is man that you give him so much attention?

What is man that you examine him every morning? What is man that you never look away from him?

What is man that you never leave him alone even for an instant? (Job 7:17-19)

After reading these few statements of Job, the spirit immediately guided me to *Galatians 6:14,* where the Apostle Paul teaches that we ought to boast in the cross of our Lord Jesus Christ. And it was suddenly brought to my remembrance that "man" is the Glory of God *(1 Corinthians 11:7).* Yes, unbelievably true, we humans are the joy and the glory of God *(Proverbs 8:31).*

What's more striking as evidence of God's love for humanity is not so much his death on the cross as a human being even though in the physical sense this constitutes the ultimate sacrifice without which there would have been no salvation, but the fact that God in his foreknowledge, before the foundation of the earth, before the heavens were created, before the existence of any angels, slew himself as a forerunner and made himself sin for us in the mystery of Christ so that in him we might be redeemed and become the righteousness of God.

Proverbs 8:22-31 tells us exactly who we are in Christ and where we came from. Therefore, I will transcribe this passage of the scripture verbatim for your personal edification. It evidently talks about God the Father giving birth to Jesus in whom mankind exist before the foundation of the world, before the heavens and the earth were created, and before any angels came to existence. Yes, you read it right. The creation of mankind as living souls before sin (not human beings in the physical sense after sin) preceded the creation of angels. And I pray that this divine demarcation will compel you to come to know and love Jesus with all of your being.

Let's now contemplate the depth of the passage in *proverbs 8:22-31* as we meditate. "The Lord brought me forth as the first of his works. The earliest of his achievements of long ago. I was appointed from eternity, from the beginning before the world began. I was given birth before the heavens were created. Before there were springs abounding with water, before the mountains and the hills (meaning the angels) were settled in place, I was given birth as in labor pain. Before he made the earth or its fields or any of the dust of the world I was there. I was there when he set the heavens in place. I was there when he marked out the horizon on the face of the deep. I was there when he established the clouds above and fixed securely the fountains of the deep. I was there when he gave the sea its boundary so the waters would not over step his commands and when he marked out the foundations of the earth. I was the craftsman at his side through it all and I was filled with delight day after day rejoicing always in his presence, rejoicing in his whole world and delighting in mankind."

There you have it, "mankind," yes, you and me, we were the delight of Christ before the heavens and the earth and any angels were created. If this description is accurate, and it is, though what's going on here remains a mystery, it clearly answers a key question for humankind that has been of the greatest interest since our earliest days on the earth. The fact that it not only confirms the spiritual nature of man, but it also gives evidence of man's preeminence over the whole creation. No wonder the Apostle Paul calls this physical temple we now live in "the body of death," given where we came from. If only God would give us our memory back of the indescribable joy, of the milk and honey we enjoyed in the Garden as one people, the whole world would want to go back.

Unfortunately, this is not the case. God wants us to set our heart on going back because we love him, not because we remember our marvelous existence in the Garden of Eden. This is a minimal requirement and God, according to *Isaiah 65:17,* has purposefully erased our memory of heaven so that Jesus through his "Blood and the Cross" becomes our only key of humbleness, capable of inciting a spiritual contrition such as God esteems.

For Jesus' sake God made a spectacle of all demonic forces on the cross, making a way for our redemption and salvation, and that whosoever eats the flesh of Jesus and drinks his blood will be allowed to re-enter the kingdom of heaven, which cannot be compared to what we had in the Garden of Eden before we died and became the disgrace we are today in this decaying temple. At the conclusion of the millennium, when everything is said and done as we will later see, Jesus will re-enter the Father out of whom he was brought forth, to become one with him again so that the Father may be all in all as Jesus himself is all in all.

We know God speaks things into existence and could as well have spoken Jesus into life, had he willed to, as a different and separate entity, but that would have cheapened and supervened the sacrifice of the cross, costing God personally and absolutely nothing for our salvation. His Glory that he swore not to share with no one would have no meaning.

Consequently, and comparatively, the flagrancy of the analogy found in *2 Samuel 24:24* as we fathom King David's refusal to offer any sacrifices to God that do not cost him anything is such that it is with absolute obviousness that anyone other than God himself being slaughtered on the cross would have disowned his Glory and rendered God deficient and mendicant of a supplementary entity, which is the reason why the Bible insists on the absolute truth from beginning to end that God is one, God is one, and God is one, repeatedly.

God can very well manifest himself in any form or shape and still be fully God. Jesus on the cross is none other than God himself. Call him the "Father" call him the "Son," or call him the "Holy Spirit," but under no circumstances don't become obnoxious and forsake your blessings, by separating or dividing God into three different entities, which Jesus strongly forbids in *Mathew 19:6*.

Simply put, the Father is the Holy Spirit, or is it the other way around? *Matthew 1:20* indicates that the Holy Spirit is the Father of Jesus. But I thought God the Father was the Father of Jesus.

Obviously, as you can see, an abandonment of this linear thinking is greatly necessary in order to bring yourself closer to the ultimate truth that "God is Spirit" and therefore too complex to be understood by natural reasoning or human logic.

God is a SOLOIST

Far from my mind is the exertion of the musical ingenuity of God when the qualifying adjective "soloist" is being used here to describe the solitariness of God in his utmost work concerning humankind for whom God exhibits incomprehensible jealousy. The Bible is not weary of saying that God is a jealous God, He does not share his Glory with no one, and He is jealous for his Holy Name.

Implicatively, we see God by himself, all alone, with no help from any other being **(evidence of this pragmatism is throughout the scripture)** performing his three great works relatives to humanity.

- **Creation** - In six days Jesus did it all by himself.

- **Redemption** - Jesus was slaughtered in shame all by himself.

- **Salvation** - Jesus himself will come down from Heaven for his people. *(1 Thessalonians 4:16)*.

Let's make it very clear again in everyone's mind that the word "creation" as it relates to the physical world concerning humanity simply represents the transmigration of mankind from the living soul dimension to this humiliated, fleshly body as a result of sin *(Philippians 3:20)* on this cursed earth *(Genesis 3:17)* concurring with our new imposed limited lifespan as a second chance before entering "the second dimension of death forever," or return to heaven where we have our citizenship

Speaking of which, one of the promises of Jesus to his saints when he said, "Where I am you shall be also," certainly found the first stage of its fulfillment at the cross. In the book of Matthew, we read of a mysterious phenomenon that took place at the time of Jesus death and resurrection, which constitutes the first phase of mass resurrection of the dead and their Rapture to the very throne of God in heaven. This facet of the Rapture was seemingly limited to the Old Testament prophets, perhaps as described in *Luke 11:50,* beginning with Adam's son Abel the first prophet of God to Zechariah who was killed between the altar and the sanctuary.

Mathew gives us a vivid account of these mysterious episodes that immediately followed after Jesus cried in a loud voice and gave up the spirit. In *Mathew 27:50-53* we're told that the curtain of the temple was torn in two from top to bottom. The earth shook and the rocks split. The tombs broke open and the bodies of many saints who had died were raised to life. They came out of the tombs, and after the resurrection of Jesus, these resurrected saints went into the holy city and showed themselves to many.

When we couple the resurrection of these prophets, which coincided with that of our Lord Jesus Christ, and when we know that Jesus on that resurrection Sunday went up to heaven and presented himself as the eternal sacrifice on the holy everlasting altar that we read about in *Revelation 6:9,* and though only Jesus as the holy Son of God whose blood is worthy to be placed on that heavenly sanctuary, we see our Savior again keeping his word that where He is we shall be also, taking up into heaven with him the resurrected saints to partake in his glory, thus according to *Revelation 6:9* the resurrected saints were placed under the altar as it is written as follows.

Please recognize and understand this important spiritual principle. The Apostle John says that when Jesus opened the fifth seal, he (John) saw under the altar the souls of those who had been slain because of the word of God and the testimony they had maintained. Again, as mentioned earlier the resurrection and the Rapture is not a single one-time event as believed by the Christian community, but a divine multifaceted undertaking interspersed throughout the history of the world which will culminate in the book of Revelation as all its different phases are synthesized into a unified essence referred to in *Revelation 20:4-6* as the "First Resurrection."

The Sixth Seal and the Wrath of God

To understand what is going on here at the opening of the sixth seal one must consider the teachings of *Hebrews 12:26-29, Acts 26:12- 15,* and *Luke 17:24-36.* At the opening of the fifth seal, we saw the saints talking to Jesus and asking jointly in a loud voice, "How long Sovereign Lord, Holy and true before you judge the inhabitants of the earth and avenge our blood?

Well, the opening of the sixth seal has brought an answer to their request as we see a requital foretaste of the judge of the earth to the inhabitants of the world after having made his appearance in the sky during the opening of the fifth seal to Rapture his saints commonly referred to as the Church.

The Apostle John has described a number of incidents that are taking place at the opening of the sixth seal such as:

- **A great earthquake.**

- **The sun turning black.**

- **The moon turning red.**

- **The stars falling to the earth.**

- **The sky receding like a scroll.**

- **Mountains and islands being removed from their places.**

We know from the book of Psalms that the Lord does whatever He wants in the Heavens and on the earth, in the seas and all their depths *(Psalm 135:6)*. *Psalm 114* tells us that at the presence of God, the earth trembles, the sea looks and flees, and the mountains skip like rams and the hills like lambs. In *Psalm 96* we read that when the Lord comes to judge the earth, all the earth will tremble before him; all the nations will say, "The Lord reigns." In *Psalm 97* we read that when the Lord reigns, the multitude of islands will rejoice, his lightning will light up the world, the earth will see and tremble, mountains will melt like wax at the presence of the Lord of all the earth. The heavens will pro- claim his righteousness, and the people will see his glory. All who worship images and boast in idols will be put to shame.

After showing the connection between what the Psalmists and other prophets predicted and what is actually taking place with the opening of the sixth seal, we can say with confidence that the second phase of the resurrection and the ascension of both the living and the dead as promised in *1 Thessalonians 4:16* is at hand and is happening right before our eyes.

I am not really into numbers but there is a flagrant coincidence relative to the number six as seen during the crucifixion of Jesus correspondent to the sixth seal, not only in numbers but in similarity of deeds.

NUMBER 6

Matthew 27:45-54	Revelation 6:12-17
At the sixth hour on the cross	At the opening of the sixth seal
The earthquakes	The earthquakes
Rocks split	Mountains and islands removed from their places
Darkness covered all the earth	Sun turned black

When the Centurion and those with him saw the earthquake and all that happened, they were terrified and exclaimed, "Surely He was the Son of God"	Kings, generals, the rich, the mighty, slaves and free hide from the face of Him who sits on the throne, for the great day of his wrath has come and who can stand?

Contrary to the secrecy supposedly surrounding this great mysterious and wonderful event called the Rapture, the occurrence will be open and public as the Apostle John describes it as if he were reiterating the mysteries that took place at the cross when Jesus was glorified.

I hope you found this little contrast giving evidence of the second stage of the Rapture concerning this time both the living and the dead interesting. In *John 14:18* and *John 16:7* Jesus made a solemn promise to the Church concerning the Holy Spirit in the following manner. "I will not leave you as orphans, but I tell you the truth: it is for your good that I am going away. Unless I go away the Holy Spirit will not come to you; but if I go, I will send him to you".

The same way Jesus physical presence in the earth came to an end two thousand years ago on the cross, here at the opening of the sixth seal, the Holy Spirit, whose mission among others was to protect the Church against all evil in the earth, has reached his purpose and is now leaving the earth and all the saints are taken up with him.

Unsurprisingly we read in verse *1* of *chapter 7* about four angels standing at the four corners of the earth having power over the four winds of the earth. And another angel (a fifth one) having the seal of God calling out to them to delay all destructions to the land and the sea and the tree until a seal is put on the foreheads of the servants of our God, referring to the *144,000* Jews from the twelve tribes of Israel on the basis of *12,000* per tribe.

The *prophet Isaiah* in *chapter 65* beginning with verse 8 gives us an edifying insight concerning this portion of the scripture. The word "servants" used here is not to be confused with its regular meaning as it normally refers to "general believers." In this particular passage, the Old Testament connotation must be considered as when the servants of the Lord were commonly referred to as "prophets." Without going into too much detail, I will say this. In the Old Testament the Holy Spirit was not present in the world like when he personally took on flesh in the person of Christ. God used prophets as recipients of the Holy Spirit or vessels through which the Holy Spirit spoke to his people. Filled with the Spirit of Christ, their testimony was given in preparation for the birth of Jesus Christ as the "Messiah".

We read in *Hebrews 1:1* that in the past God spoke to our forefathers through prophets at many times and in various ways, but in these last days he has spoken to us by his son, whom he appointed heir of all things and through whom he made the universe. Interestingly enough the birth of the son resulted from the Holy Spirit overshadowing the Virgin Mary as spoken by the Angel Gabriel and through her was able to take on the appearance of a man with flesh and bones and blood as the soul.

Remember that God is *one*, and God is *holy*. For those who make more than one God out of the single holy God, I will say this: Nowhere in the Bible do we see the Holy Spirit and Jesus simultaneously present as two distinct entities and performing any work at the same time. Well, I take this back. It did happen once, and for your edification, witness for yourself what took place, and know the truth once and for all.

We know John the Baptist was the last prophet of the Old Testament, who bridged the old and the new. We also know, as the Bible teaches, that a prophet works under the direct instruction of the Holy Spirit and that John the Baptist was contemporaneous to Jesus.

Question! How is it possible that the Holy Spirit is operating as God through John the Baptist while Jesus is also physically present in the earth as God? Let's see what the text has to say.

When the Holy Spirit entered Mary to be born as Jesus to experience life as a true man, Jesus had to separate himself from the Holy Spirit as *Philippians 2:7* tells us: "Jesus stripped himself of his Glory, to take on the nature of a servant, and be made in human likeness and be found in appearance as a Man."

The Apostle Paul teaches in *2 Corinthians 3:7-18* that the Holy Spirit is the glory of God. But when did Jesus divest himself of the Holy Spirit? Angel Gabriel gave us an initial hint when he told Mary in *Luke 1:35* that "the Holy Spirit will come upon you and overshadow you": So, the "Holy one" to be born will be called the Son of God.

Mysteriously more is at issue than just the birth of a man. With the birth of Jesus Christ, a new covenant was introduced by God and now contrary to the Old Testament practices when the Holy Spirit would manifest himself through prophets, the Holy Spirit himself is now living among us as the Son of God.

But again, when did that self-deprivation of the Holy Spirit take place, and where was the Holy Spirit the first thirty years of Jesus life on the earth as a man.

Well, despite the meekness of Moses and the greatness of Enoch and Elijah, or any other Old Testament prophets, including Abraham, Isaac, and Jacob whose name symbolizes the name of the God Almighty, the Bible speaks of a man who is far greater than any of them.

Seven hundred years before the greatest man who ever walked the earth came to be, that is beside Jesus himself, his birth was prophesied in *Isaiah 40:3*, where the prophet referred to this great man, John the Baptist, as "a voice of one calling in the desert; preparing the way for the Lord; making straight in the wilderness a highway for our God, revealing the Glory of the Lord and all mankind together will see it". *(Isaiah 40:3 or John 1:23)*

The fact is, not a single physical miracle was ever performed by John the Baptist, yet Jesus in *Luke 7:28* said that among those born of women there is no one greater than John the Baptist.

Before the ministry of Christ was instituted, just to give you an idea how great and powerful this man John the Baptist was, his water baptismal had the same salvation power as the blood of Christ in the

New Testament. We read this in *Luke 7:30* as the Pharisees and the doctors of the law found that out bluntly, to their damnation.

Jesus, during a conversation between him and the Pharisees and other expert of the law, said to them, **"because you did not believe that John was from God and did not get baptized by John, you rejected God's purpose for yourselves, and Jesus referred to them in *Matthew 23:33* as snakes and children of snakes who will not escape going to hell.**

In other words, as Jesus said it with his own mouth, you can mock the son, ridicule everything concerning the son, or speak blasphemy against the son, and you will be forgiven. But anyone who speaks against the Holy Spirit is guilty of an eternal sin.

By their unrelenting hostility toward John the Baptist, his message, and his customary water baptismal, certain Pharisees and experts of the law have self-imposed an everlasting curse that even Jesus cannot forgive.

You see, John the Baptist was a special messenger from God. The man was so filled with the Holy Spirit from the womb that he lived a life that would be considered in today's culture as insane.

Unsurprisingly, this was exactly the opinion the Pharisees and other religious leaders had of John, saying that he was possessed by a demon, thus calling the Holy Spirit a "Devil". This blasphemy against the Holy Spirit, whom John the Baptist personified, cost them their eternal salvation, because like Jesus said in *Matthew 12:32,* blasphemy against the Holy Spirit is a sin that cannot be forgiven neither in this life nor in the one to come.

John the Baptist lived all his life in the desert, wearing clothes made of camel's skin and limiting his diet to locust and wild honey, but he was a true personification of the Holy Spirit. He was the temple that housed the Holy Spirit the first thirty years of Jesus in the earth until his mission ended at the baptismal of Christ when the Holy Spirit returned to his Holy Temple, the Lord Jesus Christ as described in *Matthew 3:13-17.*

The prominent and remarkable role of prophets, as they speak from God and for God under the inspiration of the Holy Spirit, earned them an unparalleled reverence from people of all religious backgrounds, but still our Lord Jesus Christ said in *Mathew 11:9* that John the Baptist was greater than a prophet. The man was so overshadowed by the Holy Spirit that he literally personified the spirit of God.

Luke 1:39 tells us that when the angel Gabriel left Mary, she immediately went to visit her cousin Elizabeth who was already six months pregnant with John the Baptist. As soon as she entered and greeted Elizabeth, the transfer of the Holy Spirit mysteriously took place from Mary to Elizabeth and consequently from Jesus to John the Baptist, enabling Jesus to be born and live as a true man while the Holy Spirit dwelled in John the Baptist as a temporary stowage. **Very mysterious!**

In the natural all this may not be too convincing, and most will unfortunately miss this great revelation, but as presented in the preceding paragraphs, the very concept is a matter of life and death which proclaims with certainty that rejecting John the Baptist was in fact a rejection of the Holy Spirit, and therefore deserving of eternal death.

According to the scripture, John the Baptist and Jesus were cousins, but they only met twice during their physical existence in the earth:

- Before they were born, when they were in their respective wombs *(Luke 1:40)*

- When Jesus was being baptized by John the Baptist at the river of Jordan *(Matthew 3:13-17)*.

John the Baptist attested in *John 3:29* and following that, "Jesus is from Heaven and is above all, and that Jesus must increase while he (John the Baptist) must decrease. In verse 29 he declares to be joyful, and his joy is now complete.

John the Baptist continues to say that Jesus, who is from Heaven, has the spirit without limit and the Father loves the son and has placed everything in his hands, and whoever believes in the son has eternal life, but whoever rejects the son will not see life, for God's wrath remains on him".

After the resurrection we read about Jesus in *John 20:22* physically appearing to his disciples and breathing on them saying, "Receive the Holy Spirit", but keeping each mission distinct, though related, as an integral part of his being, but only as a redeeming substance dwelling in them, giving them the new birth and keeping them" as promised.

The Spirit being One, one makeup or configuration has to leave and give place to the other as their functions differ. But it is the same God who performs each one. Like it was between Jesus and John the Baptist interchangeably using the Holy Spirit with full measure, we saw as Jesus increased in power, John decreased and was beheaded because his earthly mission had ended.

The same principle remains between the man Jesus and the Holy Spirit. So long Jesus could be seen as he was in the physical before his death, the Holy Spirit in conformity to the monotheistic nature of God as the central truth of the scripture, could not manifest himself as a separate entity except through other individuals; and even then, this could not be done while Jesus was physically present at the scene, because Jesus is the Holy Spirit.

This approach is a divine concept which ensures "Godly" unity and coherence. In *John 16:5-16*, Jesus told his disciples that it was for their own good that he goes away and that unless he goes away, the Holy Spirit cannot come, but if He goes, He will send Him to them.

Do you think it is a coincidence that nowhere in the scripture we ever read about the Apostles healing the sick or performing any other miracles on third parties while Jesus was physically present?

Jesus would simply empower them and send them away to work such wonders while he goes with them in the Spirit.

Given the seriousness of this portion of scripture in regards to the Oneness of the Holy Spirit and Christ, we should marvel at these patterns of behavior between Jesus and the Holy Spirit which confirms clearly their interchangeable faculties. The same way we saw the Holy Spirit throughout the Old Testament working through prophets until it was time for God to become "Immanuel" in the person of Jesus Christ and start a new covenant, Jesus earthly mission as a man also came to an end where he can no longer be seen physically, being now "The Spirit", and has been transposed since the resurrection as the invisible power of God, working and building the Church of God in readiness for this end times mystery that we see taking place here at the opening of the sixth seal.

Sounds exciting! Well, the Holy Spirit whose earthly mission to protect the saints now comes to an end and is leaving the earth with the people of God, both the living and the dead in order to make way for the second coming of Christ, which is to be preceded momentarily by the resurrection of the son of perdition, the Antichrist, the man doomed to destruction, who will oppose and will exalt himself over everything that is called God or is worshipped.

CHAPTER 7

The 144,000 Saints

Verses 1 and *9* of *chapter 7* both begin with the expressions "After this," giving a description of the effects brought about from the immediate courses of actions as a result of the Holy Spirit leaving the earth and making way for the apparition of the Lord Jesus Christ in the sky. A transition and a transformation which will occur in a twinkling of an eye, to receive to himself the saints, both the living and the dead.

To understand the depth of what is taking place here at the opening of the sixth seal, one must give special appreciation to the passage in *John 16:7* concerning Jesus and the Holy Spirit supplanting each other. Again, John teaches that one has to totally disappear for the other to appear and supersede.

This substitutional metamorphosis between Jesus and the Holy Spirit occurs when one has to step into the shoes of the other to perform specific works that must be done substantively from that necessary perspective for a particular purpose. But when neither is continuously present as in the Old Testament, God raises up prophets to represent Him in the earth, as we see taking place here at the opening of the sixth seal. In the Old Testament God raised up a multitude of prophets, each in his own time, during the first four thousand years until the Holy Spirit personally descended from heaven to become Jesus the redeemer, who has self-attributed a thirty-three-year mission on earth, which culminates on the cross with these words: "It is finished" *(John 19:30).*

In accordance with the truth, it is interesting to note that the Bible does not say that Jesus is a spirit but instead it says clearly that Jesus is the spirit as proclaimed in *2 Corinthians 3:17* by the Apostle Paul, reminding us of the existence of only one single, unique Holy Spirit.

It is crucial to understand that the three-phase earthly mission of Christ, namely, creation, redemption, and salvation, will come to an end according to *1 Corinthians 15:24* and *Revelation 20:7-10* when Jesus, having destroyed all dominion, authority, and power at the end of the millennium, hands over the kingdom of God to the Father so that the Father may be all in all as Christ himself is all in all *(Colossians 3:11)*.

Contrary to the Old Testament methodology, when prophets were chosen at various historical times, God at the opening of the sixth seal is now choosing *144,000* prophets simultaneously to represent Him in the world in these last very short days as the Holy Spirit and the Church have left the earth.

In *verse 9* of *chapter 7* we see a great multitude that no one could count from every nation, tribe, people, and language standing before the throne and in front of the Lamb, all wearing white robes, holding palm branches, and crying out in a loud voice: "Salvation belongs to our God who sits on the throne and to the Lamb." In other words, the totality of those innumerable people who were transited to heaven came together in one voice to give thanks to God and the Lamb for saving them and bringing them at the very throne of God in Heaven.

The most curious and satisfactory gratification is that the kingdom of heaven is made up of multiracial characters as confirmed by a conversation between John and one of the elders that these multitudes came from all the races of the earth out of the great tribulation. They have washed their robes and made them white in the blood of the Lamb. That is why they are before the throne of God and honored to serve him day and night in his temple.

Notice that these people are not referred to as "souls" like in the first stage of the resurrection and Rapture that occurred at the time of the resurrection of Christ in *Revelation 6:9*. But I wanted to bring to your attention the fact that in this context, when the Bible refers to people as "souls," allusion is made of individuals who were once alive in the earth but who experienced death. We know at death the soul is separated from the body and forever lives.

Jesus said in *Mathew 10:28:* "Do not be afraid of those who can kill the body but cannot kill the soul." Rather, be afraid of the one who can destroy both "soul and body" in hell. There are two fundamental aspects of this spiritual phenomenon that should interest us, and we will go to *John 11:25-26* and seek some enlightenment. As it is written, Jesus said in *John 11:25-26:* "I am the resurrection and the life. He who believes in me will live even though he dies; and whoever is alive and believes in me will never die."

The omission of the surname "soul," which appellation should have been common to all who have been raptured to heaven, is intentional to designate and differentiate those who did not experience death and the grave but went from this physical life directly to becoming spirit. A metamorphosis described in *1 Corinthians 15:52* that will occur in a twinkling of an eye, by which the living is clothed without going through death with immortality *(1 Corinthians 15:51-54)*.

As people often wonder, this is evidence that the Rapture precedes the physical appearance of the Antichrist and the false prophet. Keep in mind the great tribulation is a period during which the Antichrist and the false prophet as two powerful literal demons make their visible appearance and live in human bodies. Do not be deceived, the great tribulation is in no way the consequence of their physical manifestation, but rather, it is a direct repercussion of God recanting his personal presence from the earth, which takes momentum with the Rapture of his saints.

CHAPTER 8

The Seventh Seal

When Jesus opened the seventh seal, there was a silence in heaven for about a half hour *(Revelation 8:1)*. The word "about" inserted here in the phrase connotes something very significant, which stresses that it was not exactly thirty minutes. For understandable reasons and in this particular case, which concerns the physical existence of our Lord Jesus Christ in the earth as redeemer, it is equal to slightly over thirty minutes symbolizing the thirty plus three years spent as Immanuel.

In other words, this dramatic pause of all heavenly activities for about a half hour is a reminder of God's sacrifice, stripping himself of his glory, totally divesting himself of his worship, taking on a sinful appearance in the likeness of his people, to die in their place and to forgive their sins, and to destroy the works of the devil and finally to bring them back to heaven at the throne of God, where they belong.

Let this be conclusive evidence that Jesus is the Almighty God and Creator of all things, as taught in the Gospel of John. When God the Father through the Virgin Mary became Immanuel for thirty-three years, the "holy, holy, holy" songs and other heavenly worship practices came to a halt while Jesus was physically present in the earth. It was a very complicated situation even for the holy angels, who had to cease momentarily for "about" a half hour or thirty plus three years their ongoing adorations of God at the literal throne in heaven, not understanding the redeeming work being undertaken by their Creator, who was living in a mortal body, being mocked and ridiculed.

Undoubtedly, an immense complexity was inherent in the reality these holy angels faced for those thirty-three years having to bear helplessly the different circumstances concerning Christ, one less appealing than the other, despite their mightiness.

Hence, the half hour silence in heaven has at least two con- notations to it. It entails both a remembrance of the thirty-three years of physical sorrow of Jesus in the earth and the seemingly endless years of spiritual anxiousness of our Lord to see the manifestation of the new birth of his followers taking place, as promised, at his throne in heaven through the Rapture of his saints.

Jesus before his death told his disciples that in a little while they will see him no more and then after a little while they will see him again. Then their grief will turn to joy. We can see the end of the sorrow and the joy that follows as a consequence of the half hour silence in *John 16:21*, when Jesus uses the analogy of the pain a woman in labor endures and the sudden forsaking or disremembering of such anguish when the child is born.

The reality is that the half hour silence is putting an end to the agony of our Lord Jesus Christ, both physically and spiritually, and at the same time, giving place to an eternal joy seeing his saints having received the new birth and are now partaking in his kingdom.

Of course, unsurprisingly, to celebrate the arrival of the saints, Jesus, sitting on his throne and receiving adoration and worship by all creatures in heaven without distinction, suddenly stops everything and orders a complete silence in remembrance of the thirty-three years that all this cost him, which now finally culminates with the Rapture of his people to his eternal glory, as promised.

A look back at *chapter 5, verse 5* reminds us that the scroll has seven seals, and before the Lord Jesus could open any of the seals, John tells us that each of the four living creatures and the twenty-four kings had a harp and golden bowls full of incense, which are the prayers of the saints. They were all worshiping and singing in a loud voice, encircled by myriad of angels joining the worship ceremony, singing praise and honor and glory and power forever and ever.

One can certainly understand the silence, which was a necessary moment, following this humongous, loud and all-embracing worship, for the ceremonial presentation of the prayers of the saints offered as incense in a golden censer which smoke went up before God from a specially designated angel. We all remember the essence of their prayers from chapter 6, verse 10: "How long sovereign Lord, Holy and True until you judge the inhabitants of the earth and avenge our blood." And Jesus had told them to wait a little longer. But here at the opening of the last seal, the Lord Jesus Christ officially receives and is pleased with the prayers of the saints, and therefore responds by introducing the famous seven trumpets phenomenon which will be sounded by seven different angels present at the throne, causing a series of plagues on the earth. Then the angel with the prayers of the saints filled the censer with fire from the altar and hurled it on the earth, which caused great sounds of thunder, rumblings, flashes of lightning, and an earthquake.

The Seven Trumpets

Here in *verse 6,* John identifies seven angels who had each a trumpet and were ready to sound them. As each angel sounds his trumpet, a succession of plagues take effect in the earth, affecting every element that constitutes this physical universe, each one having an incidence on a specific target as one third of that subject is affected or destroyed. The plagues associated with the first four trumpets are destined to impact all created visible elements but with fewer repercussions on humankind, though we see a number of human deaths have resulted from these catastrophes.

However, the last three trumpets following the three woes in *verse 13* concern humankind more directly. As the first angel sounded his trumpet, we see a mixture of hail, fire, and blood being hurled down on the earth burning a third of the trees and a third of all green grass. When the second angel sounded his trumpet, we read that something like a huge mountain, all ablaze, was thrown into the sea, and a third of the sea turned into blood, killing a third of the living creatures in the sea and destroying a third of the ships. When the third angel sounded his trumpet, the Apostle John identified a star by the name of "Wormwood," blazing like a torch, which fell from the sky on a third of the rivers and on the springs of water. A third of the waters turned bitter and many people died from the bitter waters.

"When the fourth angel sounded his trumpet, a third of the sun, the moon, and the stars turned dark, which caused a third of the day and a third of the night to be without light ". *(Revelation 8:12)*. In *verse 13*, the Apostle John says that as he watched, he heard an eagle flying in midair and calling out in a loud voice, "Woe, woe, woe" to the inhabitants of the earth because of the last three trumpets the other three angels will sound. These three "Woes" in succession represent the greatness of the calamity that will befall in the earth affecting this time humankind.

CHAPTER 9

When the fifth angel sounded his trumpet, John said he saw a star that "had fallen" from the sky to the earth, but this star is not to be put in the same category with the one that fell when the third angel sounded his trumpet. The same verb, "to fall," is used by John, but the tense used when the third angel sounded his trumpet is simple past tense, which signifies that John was actually observing a star that is part of the cosmos as it fell from the sky on the rivers.

But notice the shift in the verb tense when the fifth angel sounded his trumpet, as John was describing what was taking place here. The star John saw here is one that had fallen from the sky to the earth. In other words, John is talking about a star that was already present in the earth when the angel sounded his trumpet and to whom was given the key to the shaft of the abyss, which is one dimension within the abyss itself. With this we know this particular star is an evil spirit or a fallen angel, and John further tells us in *Revelation 9:11* that this star is king of the abyss.

So, one can easily conclude that the star is Satan himself. Jesus in *Luke 10:18* said he saw Satan fall like lightning from heaven, and in *John 12:31* Jesus refers to Satan as the prince or the ruler of this world. The *Apostle Paul in 2 Corinthians 4:4* calls Satan the "god of this world." The plagues associated here with the fifth trumpet result directly from demon spirits who are released from the abyss to invade and inhabit the people of the world, spirit, soul, and body, to torment them for five months.

People will be in so much agony that they will seek death and long to die but to no avail, because the demon spirits were not given power to kill the people but only to torture them. The infliction was limited only to those who did not have the seal of God on their foreheads.

For some unexplainable reasons, demons, once out of the abyss, do not want to go back. And *Luke 8:26-39* gives us a vivid example of the affliction caused by demons when they dwell in an individual.

The story goes like this: Jesus after sailing to the region of the Gerasenes stepped ashore and was met by a demon-possessed man. For a long time, this man had not worn clothes or lived in a house but had lived in the tombs. When he saw Jesus, he cried out and fell at his feet, shouting at the top of his voice, "What do you want with me, Jesus, Son of the "Most High" God? I beg you, don't torture me!" For Jesus had commanded the evil spirit to come out of the man. Many times, it had seized him, and though under guard, he had broken his chains and had been driven by the demon into solitary places. Jesus asked him, "What is your name?" "Legion," he replied, because many demons had gone into him. **They begged Jesus repeatedly not to order them to go into the "abyss".** A large herd of pigs were feeding on the hillside. The demons begged Jesus who acquiescently let them go into the pigs. As ordered, the demons came out of the man and went into the pigs, and the herd was driven hastily down the steep bank into the lake and was killed by those invisible monsters.

Verse 13 – The Sixth Trumpet

The sixth trumpet is the second to last trumpet, which the sixth angel will sound, signaling the release of the four angels who were bound at the great river Euphrates, which goes from Turkey to the Persian Gulf passing through Syria and Iraq. Those angels were released to kill a third of humankind, which brings the number of men killed to date to about 60 percent of the world's population *(Revelation 6:8 and 9:18)*.

John says he saw horses and riders with breastplates that were fiery red, dark blue, and yellow as sulfur. Out of the mouths of the horses, whose heads resembled the heads of lions, came fire, smoke, and sulfur.

These three plagues are responsible for the deaths of another 2 billion people.

Again, those plagues, fire, smoke, and sulfur, are consequences of another great war that will break out in the earth as some sort of judgment to the inhabitants of the world having clearly become worshippers of demons. For in *verse 20* of *chapter 9* we read that the rest of humankind that were not killed by those plagues still did not repent of the work of their hands, they did not stop worshipping demons, nor did they repent of their murders, their magic arts, their sexual immorality, or their thefts.

CHAPTER 10

A Mighty Angel, A Little Scroll And The Two Witnesses

Here the Apostle John is describing a mighty angel who came down from heaven, robed in a cloud, and whose face was like the sun and whose legs like fiery pillars. He was holding a little scroll, which was open in his hand. He had his right foot on the sea and his left foot on the land. He shouted like a lion and spoke certain words. But John said he was told by a voice that came from heaven to keep those words secret.

The key word here is the word "secret," which confirms that more is at issue than the material being presented. But today we will marvel, for God has revealed the mystery John was told not to write.

By the way, it is essential to get some things squared away and establish the authority of certain principles. God made an irrefragable statement through the Apostle Paul in *Hebrews 1:1* that sets the dynamics of a new eschatological doctrine through a new covenant that started with the birth of Christ. The Apostle Paul tells us in *Hebrews 10:1* that the law and the prophets were only a shadow of the good things to come, not the realities. For this reason, God set aside the old and established the new to make us holy through the sacrifice of the body of Christ once and for all.

The most crucial detail to consider from this statement made by God in regards to the birth of Christ and the scheme surrounding his earthly mission, **(his baptism, his teachings, his death, his resurrection, and**

his ascension) is that no Old Testament prophets have any competence to be used by God as witnesses of Christ, because they simply do not satisfy the necessary prerequisites, as the New Testament entails new spiritual dynamics in Christ, whom God appointed heir of all things. The *Apostle Paul in Ephesians 3:4-5* conclusively states that the insight he and the other Apostles had of the mystery of Christ as a result of a revelation by the Holy Spirit was not made known to men in other generations before them.

In conjunction with that, Jesus, talking to his disciples in *Luke 10:24,* said that many prophets and kings (referring to the Old Testament era) wanted to see what you see but did not see it and wanted to hear what you hear but did not hear it. In *Hebrews 11,* the Bible goes as far as naming some of the most prominent names in the Old Testament, such as Abraham, Moses, David, Enoch, Samuel, Isaac, and Jacob, to name just a few that are mentioned, who died in their faith without receiving the things promised. Through the Spirit of Christ that was in them they welcomed them and prophesied about them. But they all died without seeing the promise. However, they were all commended by God for their outstanding faith.

Even Enoch who was removed from the earth without experiencing death is part of the list. Other prophets who are not mentioned by name are insinuated through their work as we read in *verse 30* of *Hebrews 11* about the prophet relative to the walls of Jericho tumbling down, alluding clearly to Joshua. In *verse 35* the Apostle also includes in the list a prophet whose reputation was to revive the dead in the Old Testament, and this undoubtedly refers to the prophet Elijah who also left the earth without dying, but without seeing the promise.

So, as you can see, *Hebrews 11* is all inclusive concerning the Old Testament prophets who were all commended for their faith, but left the earth without receiving what had been promised. These great Old Testament prophets only saw in their spirit the things concerning Christ and welcomed them from afar, and the reason being, *Hebrews 11:40* tells us that it's because God had planned something better for us in Christ so that only together with us would they be made perfect.

Of particular significance is the teaching of the book of Acts in its *chapter 1:4-8,* that moments before his ascension after having received all power in heaven, on the earth and under the earth, Jesus said to the eleven, "John the Baptist baptized with water, but in a few days you will be baptized with the Holy Spirit, and you will receive power when the Spirit comes on you, and you will be my witnesses in Jerusalem, and in all Judea and Samaria, and to the ends of the earth."

When you combine the teachings of *Hebrews 11* and this statement made by Jesus in *Acts 1:4-8,* you have a perfect divine prospectus accessibly ingrained in the prophetic arena of both the Old and the New Testaments, with their respective sense of proportion, or the lack thereof, clarifying these "centuries-old" misleading errancies concerning the identities of the two witnesses of Christ.

Straightaway, this statement made by Jesus and further corroborated by the Apostle Paul refutes the three most common names in the Old Testament as probable witnesses of Christ in the end time's events, namely Moses, Enoch, and Elijah. The Apostle John continues to say that the mighty angel raised his right hand to heaven and swore by Him who lives forever and ever, who created the heavens, the earth, and the sea, and all that is in them, and said time is no more, and when the seventh angel sounds his trumpet, the mystery of God will be accomplished, just as God announced to his servants the prophets.

Then John was told by the voice he had heard from heaven to go take the scroll from the angel. And the angel said to John, "Take it and eat it. It will be as sweet as honey in your mouth, but will turn your stomach sour."

Let's stop here for a moment and dig into the meaning of all this before we proceed. First of all, we know that John's life contrary to the other apostles was supernaturally preserved by God and subsequently became a very old man. In his latter years, the Apostle John was exiled on the island of Patmos to stop him from preaching the word of God. While a prisoner on the island as a very old man, John is being told to take the scroll from the mighty angel, to eat it and swallow it because he must prophesy again about many people, many nations, many languages, and many kings. This scroll, which contains the mysterious word of God, will be as "sweat as honey" in your mouth but "bitter" in your stomach, said the angel.

Scrolls in the Bible are like a parchment that incorporates the word of God in its twofold: "Blessing and judgment" that a prophet must preach to the people.

Sweet as honey   =   Blessing and life

Bitter   =   Judgment and death

King David told us in *Psalm 119* that the word of God is sweeter than honey to one's mouth when it is being preached. But *Proverbs 5:4- 5* tell us that bitterness leads to death and the grave.

Do you remember when the Apostle Paul was arrested in the book of Acts, and the Jews wanted him dead because of the word of God? Well, one-night Jesus appeared to Paul and said, "Take courage, as you have testified about me in Jerusalem, so you must also testify about me in Rome."

So, the plot to kill Paul **(a conspiracy involving the Jews, the commander, the governors, and even the kings)** failed. Moreover, even a deadly storm, which overtook them and dismayed all the crews, as death was sensed all around them when Paul was being transferred to Rome as a prisoner, could not prevail. It is written that the crew lost all interest so much as in food, for there was no more hope of surviving, but nothing could stop Paul from reaching Rome and prophesying again as decreed by the Lord Jesus Christ. The word of Jesus over-rules time, space, and death.

So, when Jesus appeared to the Apostle John, an old man at the eclipse of his life and a prisoner in the island of Patmos, and told him as we read in *Revelation 10:11* that he must prophesy again about many people, nations, languages, and kings, you had better believe it will come to pass as Jesus told him. This command of Jesus reveals one of the most important points in the Bible, as it undoubtedly reminds us of the appearance of the two witnesses that must precede the return of Christ with unassailable clarifications.

So, when John's mouth turns sweet from eating the scroll, it simply signifies that the Apostle John will in the future go around the world speaking and preaching the word of God to all people and all nations and tongues.

But the sad fact is that the bitterness in his stomach, as he swallows it, will result in the word of God costing him his life. Evidence of the witnesses being killed when they have finished their testimony is given in *Revelation 11:7* when the beast that comes from the abyss attacks them and puts them to death.

CHAPTER 11

I know the identity of the two witnesses is one of the most challenging questions in the scripture and based on what we have just read concerning the Apostle John, it should be unsurprisingly clear in your mind that John is one of the two witnesses.

Though the natural world argues against such supernaturalism, the truth is the truth. But of course, I can imagine the huffy reaction this will create. But again, the truth is the truth. The world and even Christians tend to underestimate the greatness of the mystery behind the power Jesus gave his twelve apostles and the Apostle Paul.

The Apostle Paul clearly teaches in *Acts 13:31* that the disciples who traveled with Jesus from Galilee to Jerusalem are his witnesses to the world. And as I said a few paragraphs earlier, in *Acts 1:8* Jesus told the eleven apostles after the resurrection that they will be baptized with the Holy Spirit, they will receive power, and they will be his witnesses in Jerusalem, in all Judea, and Samaria and to the ends of the earth, which basically confirms the apostles as the true witnesses of the Lord Jesus Christ. However, when Jesus says in *Revelation 11:3*, "I will give power to my two witnesses and they will prophesy for *1,260 days*," it is obvious that Jesus had chosen two of the eleven to particularly take part in the events preceding and leading to his return.

By common consent, three of the twelve apostles, Peter, James, and John, were the closest to Jesus, explicitly privileged as witnesses to certain mysteries of God that the other nine did not factor in.

But the death of only one of the three is mentioned in the Bible as predetermined supernaturally by God that the next event concerning him will be the first resurrection.

But as for Peter and John, the future remains open by necessity for any succession of events, because the word of God, which is final once proclaimed, has not yet declared them dead as in the case of James. **Do not underestimate the spiritual value of this.**

We propose to make the dissection of the two witnesses as much as possible less tedious, but the process needfully must include both for the analysis to be more convincing, as all the clues leading to their ordainments are congruent to both.

I know this may seem a bit surprising, but if you can believe there is a universe beyond this universe your spiritual imagination resulting from what the Spirit of God can pour into your spirit becomes limitless as God is infinite. All spiritual dementia simply vanished, leading to incredible enlightenment with confidence of the true nature of God.

Peter Identified as the Other Witness

The perspective of Peter as one of the two witnesses is ingrained in various parts of the New Testament. But the potential for misinterpretation of the facts is real because of the figurative way they are written.

One example before we move on. When Joseph in *Genesis 40:1-20* was interpreting the dreams of the butler and the baker, the two that were in charge of the beverages and the food service to the king of Egypt, no one could have imagined the infallible inferences concluded by Joseph from these two complete metaphorical representations, which, what's more, emanated from dreams.

Here is a summary of the story: They said to Joseph, "We have had dreams and there is no one to interpret them." And Joseph said to them, "Do not interpretations belong to God? Tell me your dreams."

So, the chief cup bearer said to Joseph, "In my dream I saw a vine in front me and on the vine were three branches. As soon as it budded, it blossomed and its clusters ripened into grapes. The king's cup was in my hand and I took the grapes squeezed them into the king's cup and put the cup in his hand."

Joseph answered and said, "The three branches are three days. Within three days the king will lift up your head and restore you to your position of cup bearer. When the chief baker heard how favor- able the interpretation was for the cup bearer, he said to Joseph, "I too had a dream, on my head were three baskets of bread, on the top basket were all sorts of baked goods for pharaoh, but the birds were eating them out of the basket on my head.

Sarcastically, Joseph said to the chief baker, "The three baskets are three days. In three days, king pharaoh will lift off your head and hang you on a tree. And the birds will eat away your flesh. Hence, three days later it came to pass just as Joseph had said to them in his interpretation.

Now, on a serious note, what does a bird pecking bread from a basket being carried by a man have to do with this man consequently being hanged/killed and left to be eaten by birds?

Do you see how the Bible is a hard nut to crack? Both Genesis and Revelation representing the beginning and the end of the world are so allegorically written with symbolisms pervading their entire contents that religious leaders digress left and right offering the world this distasteful multi-denominational mess the world has ever known.

The Bible is far from being epigrammatic; it is the living Word of God onto salvation. But to tell you the truth, none of the existing religions in the world today, Christian or non-Christian alike, has come to know and fully grasp the wonder experienced by the prophets and the apostles of the delectable divine heritage of the Creator of the universe and consequently cause the whole world to fall short of the total freedom that comes with the true revelation of the true God of heavens and earth. This religious imbroglio is a lack of knowledge of the truth. Jesus is the truth, and obedience to His teaching is the ear to which God whispers his deep secrets and reveals Himself without measure. Jesus said in *John 8:31*, "If you hold to my teaching you are really my disciples."

For this reason, the disciples of Jesus, having been exposed to the truth with intense interactions and reflections of great signs and wonders, have become confident witnesses of Christ. The Apostle Paul himself has come to regard James, Peter, and John as pillars or the foundation that supports the whole Church, so to speak. They, James, Peter, and John, had to validate—or maybe this is too strong of a word—nevertheless, James, Peter, and John had to give recognition that the grace Apostle Paul said he had was truly from God before he was allowed to fellowship with them *(Galatians 2:9)*.

When Peter got his name changed from Simon to Peter by the Lord because he had identified Jesus as the son of the Living God, Peter meaning "The Rock," Jesus made a promise to Peter that Peter will be the rock upon which He will build his Church.

In *Mark 6:7* we read that Jesus calling the twelve to Him **(including Judas Iscariot)**, sent them out two by two to preach the word of God and bring people to repentance. Jesus gave the twelve disciples **(including Judas Iscariot)** authority over evil spirits and power to heal every disease and sickness in all who believe, "but whoever does not believe will be condemned". *(Mark 16:16)*

In *Acts 1:1-10* we see the resurrected Christ commissioning the eleven apostles as His witnesses. But as a prerequisite they must be baptized with the Holy Spirit.

Corroboratively, Jesus seems to define in verse 8 a very simple but imperative process to be a witness:

- **The Holy Spirit must come upon you.**

- **Divine power must be received.**

- **Then you will be my witness throughout the earth.**

But on a deeper level these substantive passages are more and more convincing that the chosen apostles are the sole witnesses of the Lord Jesus Christ, considering the definition of Christ's endowment of a witness, established in the Bible.

According to the book of *Acts chapter 1 verse 22*, a witness is a disciple chosen by Jesus Himself to experience firsthand his life and ministry beginning with the baptism of John the Baptist in composition with his teachings, his miracles, his death, his resurrection, and finally his ascension back to heaven.

This criterion disqualifies any other character or prophet, or anybody else for that matter of both the Old and the New Testaments. This disqualification also applies to anybody whose birth was posterior to the ascension of Christ, including those who are alive today or will come into existence tomorrow.

Just food for thought, when Jesus raised Lazarus from the dead after being buried for four days, nobody would have known that Lazarus was from the dead unless they were familiar with the story. With God four days or 4 thousand years are totally congruent and make no difference whatsoever.

The *prophet Ezekiel* in *chapter 37* can tell you what God did with dead bodies whose scattered dry bones were their only remains; then sit down and pay your reverence.

Ridiculous theories about the identity of the two witnesses have brought much confusion that could not be further from the truth. In *Revelation 11:10* the Bible refers to the two witnesses as two prophets. Before that, Zechariah already in his time was told in a vision by the spirit of Jesus that these two witnesses, also known as the two olive trees, are two prophets who are anointed to serve the Lord of the earth.

Contrary to common belief, the two witnesses cannot be nonhuman because *Revelation 11:7-12* dissipates all possible ambiguity when Jesus says plainly that the two witnesses will be killed, and people will refuse them burial. In addition, the personification of the two witnesses by the

Apostle John is so prevalent that any omission of them being definite persons is levity to the power and the seriousness of the word of God.

Nonetheless, I will admit a measure of inconspicuousness in relation to the clarity of the scripture, unless it is revealed to someone with an obedient spirit. Even passages that are plain when taken in their immediate context have hidden profound spiritual meaning behind them, which is the mystery of the kingdom of God.

Indeed, *Matthew 13:34* tells us that Jesus spoke to the crowd in parables and He (Jesus) did not say anything without using a parable. *Mark 4:34,* however, gives us a word of comfort when he reassures us: "Though it is true that Jesus did not say anything without using a parable, but when Jesus was alone with the twelve, he explained everything."

According to *Mark 4:10* it is given to the believers, those chosen by God to know the sacred mystery of the kingdom of God, but to those outside **(non-believers)** all things are done in parables.

My next statement will probably come as a shock to some of you. But don't be fooled. You can be a pastor, a famous theologian, or a Bible scholar and still be a nonbeliever and be deprived of God's revelation.

I am sure not everyone would amenably accept the possibilities of John and Peter as the two witnesses. But let's go deeper. Let's look at some Bible verses that singled out Peter and John as the two chosen witnesses who will precede and represent Christ during the great tribulation period.

As Jesus was preparing to enter Jerusalem to be executed, *Luke 22:8* tells us, "Then came the day of unleavened bread on which the Passover lamb had to be sacrificed." And Jesus chose two of his disciples and sent them into the city to prepare the "Passover".

Conformably, the two chosen apostles preceded Jesus into the city and prepared the Passover just as Jesus had told them. Guess which two disciples Jesus chose and sent to prepare his coming to the Passover? You guessed it right, Peter and John. **What a coincidence! Or is it?**

Let's now consider the statement made by Jesus in *Matthew 16:8* after Simon identified him as God incarnate: "Simon you are a Rock and upon this rock I will build my church and the gates of hell will not prevail against it. I will give you the keys of the kingdom of heaven, whatever you bind on earth will be bound in heaven and whatever you loose on earth will be loosed in heaven."

The syntax used by Jesus in the construction of this statement is phenomenal. The definite future tense as a chosen morphology indicates clearly that reference is being made to the end of the world. We must not fail to understand that this particular conversation with Peter not only took place after the resurrection of Jesus, but what has irradiated the spiritual dimension of the whole incidence is that Jesus immediately afterward ascended to heaven. Yet Jesus still clearly used the future tense in decreeing the command, **"Upon this rock I will build my church and the gates of hell will not prevail against it"**. Jesus, in that same chapter just a few verses later corroborated his absolute allusion to the tribulation period and to the end of the world, explaining as he always does in great details to his disciples the significance of the parable told to Simon, now Peter, and describes its time frame.

"The Son of Man is going to come in the glory of his Father with his angels" *(verse 25)*. "Whoever wants to save his life will lose it, and whoever loses his life for my sake will find it" *(verse 28)*. "I tell you the truth, some who are alive today **(transporting the whole context of the proclamation to the end-times in relation to his second coming)** will not taste death before they see the Son of Man coming in his kingdom".

No one can deny that these propitious statements are referring to the Rapture and the second coming of Christ, which also undeniably corresponds to the period during which Peter will be given the keys of the kingdom of heaven and the gates of hell as mentioned in *verse 18* will have no power over him.

The reality of this episode is given to us in *Revelation 11:7*, when the two witnesses are killed and made a public disgrace as their corpses are left unburied for three days to overtly decay. And suddenly a great terror overcame the people who were contemplating the two cadavers as the spirit of life entered them and they stood on their feet, and a great voice from heaven is heard saying to them, "Come up here," and they went up to heaven in a cloud while their enemies looked on.

This is exactly what Jesus meant when he told Peter that the gates of hell, meaning death, will not prevail against him.

Another particularity worth noticing in the promise made by Jesus to Peter is the use of the expression "kingdom of heaven" instead of "kingdom of God."

The assertion of the phraseology "kingdom of heaven" in the sentence is by itself unequivocally denotative of the period surrounding the great tribulation and the second coming of Christ. An abusive interpretation of the expressions "kingdom of God" and "kingdom of heaven" interchangeably is gravely insidious when the Bible makes an unconcealed and formidable distinction both in terms of characteristics and superiority between the two utterances. It is vital to understand that the same eternal, sovereign God made himself lower than the angels, subsided his divine glory, thus his heavenly kingdom, transmuted it to our human dimension as a temporary allotment for the allocations of sin through and in Christ as king over the earthly transient kingdom referred to as the kingdom of God to subvert the kingdom of Satan which is earthly and hence physical and temporal.

Now when all is said and done, and the plan of salvation is complete and the spirit of sin and death and Satan himself are destroyed permanently, this provisional, conditional measure, namely the kingdom of God, will transmute back to its original state, its eternal nature with all redeemed souls transmigrating with Christ and entering the kingdom of heaven as Christ Himself becomes once again with the Father as it was before the beginning when Christ was hidden in or blended with the Father as *ONE*.

The Bible in *1 Corinthians 15:24-28* makes it quite clear that Jesus as the kingdom of God or king over the kingdom of God is temporal and will come to an end when all dominion and all authority and all power are brought to nothing. Christ must rule as king until all enemies are put under his feet. Then the end will come when Christ hands over the kingdom of God to the Father so that God the Father may be all in all as Christ is all in all.

Notice that every time the kingdom of God is mentioned, consideration of the here and now is appropriated. *Mathew 12:28* teaches that the physical presence of Jesus in the earth signifies that the kingdom of God is here among us. In *Luke 17:20-21* Jesus describes the kingdom of God as the power within us, such as when we are born again by the Holy Spirit, we become members of the kingdom of God here in the earth. The Apostle Paul in *Romans 14:17-18* teaches that anyone who serves Christ and his righteousness has peace and joy in the Holy Spirit and the kingdom of God is in him.

As a result, the kingdom of God, though spiritual in essence, is earthen and physical in nature. The physical and earthly agenda of the kingdom of God, with Christ as the head, consists primarily of building the Church of God and consolidate all believers as members in one body, hence members of his kingdom, the kingdom of God, which is to be handed over to God the Father as we just read in the preceding paragraph. Then the end will come as we all enter the kingdom of heaven in Christ as Christ himself is made subject to God the Father so that again God the Father may be all in all.

Conversely, the kingdom of heaven is never mentioned in terms of now or as a specimen of the present state of things. In *Mathew 3:2-12* the kingdom of heaven concerning the world is the ultimate supernatural power of God through his final wrath subduing all of the kingdoms of the world. When Jesus himself is referring to the kingdom in heaven, as in *Mathew 13:24* and *44-47,* he always uses a parable to describe what the kingdom of heaven is like.

John the Baptist, who is the forerunner of our Lord Jesus Christ, describes the kingdom of heaven as a future hope when he says in *verse 2 of Mathew 3* that the kingdom of heaven is near, and according to *verse 7,* it encompasses the wrath of God when Jesus baptizes with fire, which is at the end of the world, a winnowing fork in his hand, and clearing his threshing floor and gathering his wheat into the barn and burning up the shaft with unquenchable fire.

To close this segment, I will refer to *Matthew 7:21* concerning the kingdom of heaven alluded by Jesus when he returns as king of kings to judge the world. Jesus said, "Not everyone who says to me 'Lord, Lord' will enter the kingdom of heaven, but only he who does the will of my Father who is in heaven." There you have it. The judgment seat of Christ is the gateway to the kingdom of heaven and Jesus continues to say, "Many will say to me on that day 'Lord, Lord, did we not prophesy in your name and drive out demons and perform many miracles in your name?' Then I will tell them plainly, I never knew you. Depart from me you evil doers."

On the day of the Lord, which is the commencement toward the kingdom of heaven, the ultimate encroachment of Jesus on the whole world as he sits on his throne as judge is to set up the kingdom of heaven as a conclusive endowment for his followers putting an end in his kingdom, the kingdom of God as the kingdom of heaven subjoins to receive the souls of all those whose names were written in the Lamb's Book of Life.

Consequently, the enactment of the Apostle Peter having the keys of the kingdom of heaven is a great mystery, but it does have to do not only with him being one of the two witnesses of our Lord Jesus Christ during the tribulation period preceding the return of Christ to the earth, but it also has to do with attesting and giving solemn right to Jesus for the transmigration of our souls as the transmutation of the kingdom of God to the kingdom of heaven takes place.

The Bible is very clear that the establishment of every fact must be confirmed by the testimony of two or three witnesses *(2 Corinthians 13:1, Matthew 18:16, Deuteronomy 19:15)*.

The perspective of the presence of Peter and John as the two chosen witnesses of Jesus is perforce analogical to the appearance of Moses and Elijah on the mountain of transfiguration subjecting themselves to the holiness and the divinity of Christ, hence subjugating the "laws and the prophets."

The fundamental point is that just as Jesus needed two wit- nesses in the persons of Moses and Elijah as a representation of God-given laws and the prophets to establish his authority over sin, in the same vein, two witnesses of his redeeming mission are also needed to establish his authority over life, death, and the resurrection.

This being the case, and to say it amenably, the two witnesses can only be two of his contemporaries who have witnessed his life, his death, his resurrection, and his ascension to heaven, hence two of the chosen twelve apostles.

Let's look at a couple of other passages to further develop our understanding of the designation of Peter and John as the two chosen witnesses of Christ to be present during the tribulation period once the Holy Spirit exits the earth with the people of God, which is the focal and most significant segment of the Rapture.

In *John 3:34* we are told that Jesus has the Holy Spirit without measure and his words are Spirit and Life *(John 6:63)*. *Isaiah 55:11* is a reminder that the word spoken by God will not return to him empty, but will accomplish what God desires and achieve the purpose for which it was sent. If you take very seriously every word spoken by Jesus, the following commands or decrees made by Jesus concerning Peter and John should not be taken lightly unless you tend to attribute it to a slip of the tongue and thereby ridicule the entire Bible. But if your conviction of the deity of Christ, who is the truth, is strong, you know his every word will come to pass.

Peter, John, and other disciples were coming back from a vain fishing adventure when Jesus appeared to them on the shore and said to Peter:

Jesus said:	"Simon, son of Jonas, do you truly love me more than these?"
Peter said:	"Yes, Lord, you know that I love you."
Jesus said:	"Feed my lambs."

Jesus said again:	"Simon, son of Jonas, do you truly love me"?
Peter answered:	"Yes, Lord, you know that I love you."
Jesus said:	"Take care of my sleep."
Jesus said again (a third time):	"Simon, son of Jonas, do you love me?"
Peter said:	"Lord, you know all things; you know that I love you."
Jesus said:	"Feed my sleep"

It is very enlightening to consider the deliberate variations, each with its own distinct spiritual meaning, of the three commands given to Peter by Jesus subsequent to each of the three monotonous and tedious questions, "Do you love me?" And thereby giving him this exalted role of shepherding God's sheep.

The First Command: "Feed my Lambs"

Obviously here we see Jesus reminding Peter of Peter's peerless, superlative love for him, as many reasonable inferences concerning Peter suggest an unequal level of temerity and obstinacy and thus an uppermost devotion to our Lord Jesus Christ. Then Jesus concludes with his first command, "Feed my Lambs." With this first command of Jesus to Peter, Jesus has superposed Peter in relation to the other apostles. The word "lambs" means in this context the other apostles. Even Paul, who was gracefully chosen by the Lord Jesus Christ and who eventually became an apostle, had to receive recognition, like I said earlier, by Peter, James, and John before he was admitted in the "Apostolate".

In the book of Leviticus, we learn that lambs, goats, and bulls, when qualified, are animals that are slaughtered as sin offering. Jesus made it clear in *Mark 10* that the apostles will drink the cup he drinks and be baptized with the baptism he is baptized with. Simply put, the cup and the baptism indulged by Jesus, leading to his ineffable suffering and death, will also be the ultimate destiny of the apostles.

As it turns out, Jesus made this following statement to the eleven in *John 20:21,* "As the Father has sent me, I am sending you." With this decree Jesus has indeed commissioned the eleven apostles as his personal lambs in the world. Interestingly enough, Jesus during the relegation process, said to them in *Luke 10:3,* "I am sending you out like lambs among wolves."

The designation of the apostles as lambs is therefore evident, and so is the ordainment of Peter as the chief apostle when he received the "Feed my lambs" command from Jesus following the first of the three consecutive "Do you love me" questions.

I hope this little exercise has edified the meaning of the first command of Jesus to Peter, "Feed my Lambs."

The Second Command: "Take Care of my Sheep"

A notable variation involving both the verb and the object is being assured by Jesus in the second command.

At first glance or perhaps to a novice or an uninitiated mind, it may seem insignificant, but the linguistic nuance is very much intended by the Lord Jesus Christ to deliberately express the multilevel subscription of Peter's missions at different stages of his life. This makes a lot of intuitive sense for Jesus, who is only now present in the world as the Holy Spirit dwelling in us, to appoint his twelve lambs (first command) to carry out the gospel of salvation to the entire world, so that through the foolishness of preaching *(1 Corinthians 1:21)* the sheep will hear his voice and follow him. Understand that the word "sheep," is an appellation that designates royal priest and holy nations, a chosen people to become God's very own possession. *(1 Peter 2:9)*

Psalm 95:7 tells us that Jesus is our God, and we are the people of his pasture, the flock under his care. The second and the third commands are expressed in somewhat motley fashion. A comprehensive analysis of the apparent variation and the spiritual distinction beyond the natural linguistic dexterity of our Lord Jesus Christ in the use of two different action verbs to begin each of the imperative statements is fundamental in the designation of Peter as one of the two witnesses in the tribulation period.

There is no question of the mystery surrounding the privileged relationship enjoyed by Peter, James, and John, as if Jesus, after having chosen the twelve, created an inner circle as in a conclave for deeper secrets and revelations only for these three.

As it seemed, if one were to intensify the privileges of these three prime apostles, Peter would still be singled out as having the leadership to a number of events in the Bible. These three were so mysteriously privileged in the eyes of Jesus that only the history surrounding the death of James and the events leading to the death of Peter and John are recorded in the Bible.

But wait a minute! Neither the deaths of Peter nor John is recorded in the scriptures. As a matter of fact, the muteness of the Bible regarding the death of any other apostles beside James is very intriguing to me, when we know that Jesus himself confirmed the martyrdom of all the apostles in *Mark 10:39*. **Isn't this ironic?**

Or could it be that the omission of the deaths of Peter and John is not only deliberate but pregnant with high spiritual significance?

Given that non-biblical facts have no spiritual values, we will stick to the word of God, which, spoken or written, will come to pass as it is proclaimed.

According to the word of God, the written word is an absolute certainty and shall undergo no adverse modification. However, it also appears as true that when God says something and offsets it with an addendum, a reversal is possible.

This being said, if the Bible declares one dead with no offsetting addendum, his next interaction with God will be the first resurrection.

To illustrate, let's see a couple of examples. The first one concerns the twelve-year-old girl in *Luke 8:49*. When the girl was pronounced dead, Jesus said to the father, "Don't be afraid! Just believe and she will be healed." As the people were wailing and mourning for the girl's death, Jesus said, "Stop wailing! The girl is sleeping, she is not dead." And Jesus raised her from the dead.

The other story is the one concerning Lazarus. "When word got to Jesus that Lazarus was dead, Jesus said to his disciples, "Lazarus has fallen asleep and I am going to wake him up. You know the rest of the story *(John 11:11)*. So, Jesus went to where he was buried and raised him from the dead.

Of the twelve apostles, we know Judas went out and killed himself *(Matthew 27:5)*, and we are told that James, the brother of John, was put to death by King Herod *(Acts 12:2)*.

Considering these arguments as valid, if God had mentioned the deaths of the other eight apostles, bringing the number of declared deaths to ten, while simply omitting that of Peter and John, some of us would have picked up on it immediately. But that was not yet God's intention to make it known before its time.

Today, as promised, God is unraveling all mysteries. It's almost like the parable of the wheat and the tares. Because of the danger of uprooting the wheat while gathering the tares, God let both grow together until the harvest. Likewise, because of the identifying potential of Peter and John as the two witnesses had God mentioned the deaths of the other ten while only omitting theirs, God reasonably remains silent across the board.

Do you see why I said earlier that the muteness of the scripture regarding the deaths of the apostles is spiritually suspicious?

As it is expressed, it seems clear that if the word spoken by God does not suffer any offsetting addendum, it's a done deal. By the same token, if the word of God is mute on something, all events remain open, for nothing is impossible with God.

As a matter of biblical principle, the secret things belong to God, but the things revealed belong to us *(Deuteronomy 29:29)*. The teaching in *Isaiah 55:11* is clear that the word of God, once released, does not return to him void. But what's important to remember is that when God makes known certain details, it's always for the instruction and education of humankind and should be taken as a complement or an element of something bigger.

People seem to forget that Jesus is the incarnation of God, whose mission among other things is to initiate the new birth of humankind and to make decrees of things that must take place leading to the end of the world. To know the Father is to know Jesus. Who sees Jesus sees the Father. Whenever Jesus speaks, it is the Father who speaks, unless you want to join those who only believe the Bible to be a wonderful poetic literature.

Ezekiel 12:25-28 tells us, "The Lord will speak what he will, and it will be fulfilled". 'I will fulfill whatever I say, declares the Lord'. "The prophecy may be for a distant future and the visions, for many years from now. 'But whatever I say will be fulfilled,' declares the Lord."

It is so important to know that when Jesus speaks, he is not simply vaunting his linguistic skills, which he could rightfully brag about, but enactments are being put in place, and decrees are being established to warrant all of his manifestos according to their divine purposes. The same is also true of what we read anywhere in the Bible.

Let's say that Peter and John did die in the first century, perhaps John a little later at the beginning of the second centenary. Well! Guess what! Jesus will reiterate what he did for Lazarus by raising Peter and John from the dead. Lazarus was so much alive after he was brought back from the dead that he ate and drunk and went everywhere with Jesus as proof of the resurrection power of God, making the Jews so angry that they wanted to kill him again.

Now let's go back to Peter and his threefold command. The first had to do with the "lambs" of Jesus, which concerns the other apostles. The second and the third with the two consecutive "Feed my sheep" commands concerned obviously two categories of sheep that Jesus says in *John 10:16* that are from two different sheepfold which Peter is also given chargeability over.

One thing must immediately be squared away in order to have a correct understanding and fully grasp the appropriate intended purpose. There is evidently a correlation between the time of the junction and the context in which the encounter took place. Jesus was at his aftermost appearances to his disciples when he incidentally commissioned Peter with these three different assignments in propinquity to his ascension to heaven.

Another reminder is that Jesus between the time of his resurrection and his first appearance to his disciples on the evening of the first day of his resurrection ascended to the throne in heaven and took along with him the Old Testament saints who were resurrected when the earth shook, the rocks split, and the tombs broke open, subsequent to Jesus crying with a loud voice on the cross and giving up the ghost. The Old Testament saints who came back from the dead from under the earth were both physically and visibly so much alive that they went into Jerusalem and appeared unto many. *(Mathew 27:50-56)*

I said all this to say this: When Jesus referred to two separate sheep pen relative to the second and third command to Peter, it is not to be confused with bygone flock, which has already been taking care of at his death and resurrection but rather an impending prospectus of herd which will be comprised of two different categories of sheep at two different times in the future.

The second command concerns the first category of sheep, described in 1 Thessalonians, whose pedigree originated with the appearances of John the Baptist with extensiveness to the main Rapture which will occur prior to the arrival on the scene of the Antichrist and the false prophet. In other words, all believers in Christ, who constitute his body or his Church, are members of this present and foremost sheep fold, whose physical, psychological, and spiritual well-being are placed under the care of the apostles with Simon Peter assuming the leadership with continuous sacred transmissibility thereafter.

The apostle Paul in *Ephesians 4:11* clearly teaches that the apostles, the prophets, the evangelists, and the teachers of the law work as a chain of relief troops, until the Holy Spirit leaves the world and snatches away God's people, dead or alive, to be caught up together in the clouds to meet the Lord Jesus Christ and forever be with him. *(1 Thessalonians 4:16)*

About 2000 years ago when the New Testament was being written, the Apostle John wrote in *1 John 4* that the Antichrist was already in the world. However, we also know from *2 Thessalonians 2:3-12* that the presence of the Holy Spirit in the world is the power that keeps the Antichrist and the false prophet from appearing and being formally acknowledged.

This tells us how anxious the spirit of the Antichrist is to invade the earth and engross everyone and everything in this world. However, only when the Holy Spirit is taken away or leaves the earth with the people of God then the wicked one, the son of perdition, will be revealed, whom Jesus shall consume with the word of his mouth and shall destroy with his glory.

To put it in another way, the scope associated with the second "Feed my sheep" command extends from the time the Holy Spirit through John the Baptist began with the message of repentance until the departure of the Holy Spirit from the earth before the second coming of Christ. All those who believed the first message of John the Baptist and all others who have since joined the body of Christ through the years, together with those who will be alive and believe at the time of the Rapture, form the commonwealth of the sheepfold alluded in the second "Feed my sheep" command.

The Third Command: "Feed my Sheep"

The third "Feed my sheep" command immediately precedes the summons made by Jesus to Peter saying, "Follow me" as to adumbrate his presence for a particular unexpected purpose. The elicitation of the conversation between Jesus and Peter that immediately follows gives us the context in which all this enigma will take place. Impressively, after these three successive questions and commands, Jesus, still talking to Peter, added, "When you were young you dressed yourself and went where you wanted. But when you are old you will stretch your hands, and someone else will dress you and lead you where you do not want to go." We are told in verse 19 that Jesus said this to indicate to Peter the kind of death by which Peter would glorify God.

First and foremost, we see Jesus establishing a connection between Peter's third mission of feeding the sheep and his death, a kind of death by which God will be glorified *(John 21:19)*. Everyone would agree that the death of all the apostles must have equally given glory to God. But there is something very peculiar about the eventual death of Peter that prompts the Lord Jesus Christ to engross it with such prophetic scenery. The Bible, for reasons only known to God, is completely silent about the death of the apostles, except for James, the brother of the apostle John, which we read in *Acts 12:1-3*.

The third command, "Feed my sheep," seems to be definitely inherent in the process leading to Peter's death. Jesus immediately after the ordainment of Peter concludes with the circumstances surrounding his eventual death in a prophetic eloquence. Then Jesus says to Peter, "Follow me." Note at this point Jesus is about to ascend definitely back to heaven and still before he does, he is taking Peter aside to an undisclosed locale to, I imagine, further instruct him.

Interestingly enough, **and please do not think it's a coincidence,** *Revelation 11:1-6* tells us that the two witnesses have received clear and specific instructions from Jesus, as true prophets always receive from God, about their prophetic missions and the necessary power needed to fulfill them.

Strangely enough, after Jesus and Peter left for their secret con- clave, we read in *John 21:20* that Peter turns and sees the Apostle John following them. When Peter sees John, he asks Jesus, "Lord, what about John, how will he die?" In other words, how will John glorify God?

The first thing to discern here is that Jesus is taking these two apostles, Peter and John, on a special undisclosed venture. But fundamentally, what is striking is not so much Peter's intrigue about the Apostle John's ultimate fate, but the answer given by Jesus concerning that fate in a clear junction with his second coming. And Jesus in his omniscience, describing the setting and the atmosphere that Peter with this question evokes, reveals the period encircling the unfolding or the evolution of these events with this mind-boggling answer: "If I want John to remain alive until I return, what is that to you?"

Then he reiterates to Peter, "Follow me," which is the third time during Peter's acquaintanceship with Jesus that Jesus said this to him. The expression "until I return" in the answer Jesus gave to Peter concerning the circumstances leading to the fate of the Apostle John is a clear indication of the second coming when Jesus returns in his glory, at the end of the world.

When you cohere the different elements of this passage into a whole *(John 21:15-25)*, what do these different segments in a unified context convey?

All these concepts are manifestly inherently connected, and they converge to form a futuristic multitudinous episode involving the tribulation period, the reconquering of the souls of the remnants through the successful completion of the witnessing mission given to Peter and John as the two witnesses of Christ and also through the consolation that their deaths, by which God will be glorified, will bring to the world when they are raised from the dead and prove to the world that death will no longer triumph. At that very hour according to *verse 13 of Revelation 11,* there will be a severe earthquake and a tenth of the city will collapse. Seven thousand people will be killed, and the petrified survivors will give glory to the God of heaven.

So, you see the third command to Peter, "Feed my sheep," applies to a remnant that must be assimilated in fulfillment of what Jesus said in *John 10:16* concerning other inalienable sheep that are not part of the current sheep pen. Jesus said that these other sheep must be brought also. They will listen to his voice, and there shall be one flock and one shepherd.

Once the Rapture has taken place, and the most hideous treatment beyond imagination befalls humankind following the supernatural appearance of the two beasts, the two witnesses will be the glory of God in the earth.

To close this segment on Peter and John as the two chosen witnesses who will appear during the tribulation period, let's look at two other biblical facts and their misunderstood meaning and significance. The scriptures present ironically the deaths of both Lazarus and Jesus as glorifying to God and God's evocative response was such that God physically and publicly raised both of them from the dead. *(John 11:4 and John 12:23-34)*

Interestingly enough, both Peter and John had their eventual deaths associated with the glorification of God. Jesus said in *John 21:19* that God will be glorified in Peter's death. In *John 21:22,* based on Peter's inquiry to Jesus, the Apostle John's death will also glorify God.

No one will deny that the death of any child of God who die for the testimony of Jesus will glorify God, but strangely enough the only two glorifying proclamations openly spoken in the gospel are distinctively associated with the deaths of Peter and John.

One last "coincidence" that is too "coincidental" to omit is the fact that only Peter and John of all the apostles have verified the resurrection site and the very clothes Jesus was buried in and thereby can bear witness of the empty tomb. **Ponder on this!**

Before the next series of actions, we read in *Revelation 11:7* that when the two witnesses have finished their testimony, God will be glorified, and the beast that comes up from the abyss will kill them. People from all nations and languages will gloat over them, gaze on their bodies and refuse them burial. But after three days God will raise them from the dead and publicly snatch them up into heaven, while the whole world looks on.

The Seventh Trumpet—Chapter 11:15–19

Here in *verse 15* the utmost revelation of the true nature of the man named Jesus is given. In *Revelation 1:4,* the Apostle John referred to Jesus as the one who is and who was and who is to come.

At the sound of the seventh trumpet, we read that the kingdom of Satan is swallowed by the kingdom of our Lord and of his Christ. But more amazingly, we read that the angels and the twenty-four elders fall on their faces and worship the one seated on the throne who is the Creator, the Father, the God Almighty, calling him, the One who is and who was which is none other than Jesus Christ himself. This is irrefutable proof that this man called Jesus, who walked this earth, is truly the very God of the Bible, the Creator of all things, sitting on his throne in heaven being worshipped.

As mysterious as it seems that Moses, who wasn't born until Exodus, could have written the first three books of the Bible **(Genesis, Exodus, and Leviticus)** we are faced at the beginning of *chapter 12* with strange multiple non-contemporaneous events that transpired in the heavenly realm, in the spirit dimension primeval to the existence of any physical life whatsoever in the earth.

When these phenomena took place, the earth was still formless and void. These mysterious developments that evolved before men were put on the earth impel us to rightfully consider the book of Revelation as a mixture of past **(pre-humanity, nonphysical),** present **(from Genesis to Revelation),** and future **(life after death),** with Jesus Christ at the center of it all. In other words, the Bible, I must say, regardless of what page or section being read, will involve the past, the present, and the future. Past: the word of God will take you as far back to events that took place in the heavenly realm before humankind was ever put on the earth. Note that I did not say before humankind was created. There is a big difference and a big gap between the time men were created in the Garden and the time humankind was transferred or put on the earth. Present should be considered as everything from *Genesis 1 to Revelation 22* that humankind has experienced and will go through in this life. future is everything that is posterior to the kingdom of God in the earth **(the life-after-death dimension)** and relative to the world to come, even though things belonging to that category have been written as part of the salvation message from Genesis to Revelation.

However, the word of God, though spiritual in essence with contents not physically observable, was written by God for human consumption and therefore with an intrinsic language that identifies with our finite thinking and our limited indigenous earthly ways. Not only that, God somehow humbled himself and took on flesh to identify with our human general concept of existence and called himself the Son of God simply because it is presupposed by our understanding that all humans must have a genitor. Jesus, having been born of the Virgin Mary without the seed of any man, could only acceptably be at least considered to be the Son of God for earthly purposes.

Any transcendent domanial consideration relative to who Jesus was would have been of the highest blasphemy to the Jews at the time. Even some of the apostles were troubled by the idea of Jesus being God, because any modification of the oneness of God as prescribed in the scriptures would have been intolerable.

The idea of God being born of a woman was unthinkable. It is still not welcome today by many, which brings us to these mysterious passages in *Chapter 12* under the heading, "The woman and the Dragon."

CHAPTER 12

The Woman and the Dragon

For the sake of the seriousness of death, even physical death, let alone the second death, let's not treat the narrative of "the Woman and the Dragon" with flimsy nimbleness. Remember the whole story of the Bible from beginning to end is about Jesus and his work of creation, redemption, and salvation.

It's all about Jesus and none other. Jesus is the way, the truth and the life. No one comes to the Father but through Him. *(John 14:6)* No matter how it is proclaimed, what symbols are being used, Jesus is at the center of it all.

As the trial date draws near and the stage is being set here in *Revelation 12* with one of the most famous passages in the scripture, we cannot afford to miss the mark due to hunches or hypothesizes.

It is clear that the woman and the dragon could be justly renamed "the kingdom of God and the kingdom of Satan" or simply put "Jesus and the Devil", and you would have hit the nail right on the head. Moreover, the narrative should not be treated as if it were written in sequence relating to a specific order of succession of a series of related scenes.

The passage begins with four enigmatic elements:

- **A woman**

- **The sun**

– The moon

– A crown of twelve stars

The verse reads as follows:

"There appeared a great wonder in heaven: a woman clothed with the sun and the moon under her feet and upon her head a crown of twelve stars: she was pregnant and cried out in pain as she was about to give birth".

"And there appeared another wonder in heaven: and behold a great red dragon, having seven heads and ten horns, and seven crowns upon his heads. His tail drew the third part of the stars of heaven, and did cast them to the earth: and the dragon stood before the woman who was about to give birth, so that he might devour her child the moment it was born. She brought forth a son, a male child, who was to rule all nations with a rod of iron, and her child was caught up unto God and to his throne". "The woman fled into the wilderness to a place prepared for her by God, where she might be taken care of for *1,260 days*".

"And there was war in heaven: Michael and his angels fought against the dragon: and the dragon and his angels fought back and prevailed not: neither was their place found any more in heaven". "And the great dragon was hurled down, that old serpent, called the Devil, or Satan, who deceived the whole world: he was hurled to the earth and his angels with him". [This information about Satan and his angels being cast out of heaven together is phenomenally important. Please keep that in mind]. And John said he heard a loud voice in heaven saying, "Now have come the salvation, and the power, and the kingdom of our God, and the authority of his Christ: for the accuser of our brothers, who accused them before our God day and night is cast down. And they overcame him by the blood of the Lamb, and by the word of their testimony: and they loved not their lives unto the death".

"Therefore, rejoice you, heavens, and you who dwell in them. But woe to the inhabitants of the earth and of the sea, because the devil has gone down to you, having great wrath, because he knows that he has but a short time".

"And when the dragon saw that he was hurled down to the earth, he persecuted the woman who gave birth to the male child. And to the woman was given two wings of a great eagle, that she might fly into the wilderness, into her place, where she is nourished for a time, times and half a time, out of the serpent's reach. Then the serpent spewed water as a flood after the woman that he might cause her to be carried away by the flood. But the earth helped the woman, by opening its mouth and swallowed up the flood which the dragon had spewed out of his mouth. Then the dragon was enraged at the woman, and went to make war with the rest of her offspring, who keep the commandments of God, and have the testimony of Jesus Christ". *(Revelation 12:1-17)*

The issue here is very simple, and the first thing we need to draw attention to is in regard to our human culture of reproduction. Humanly speaking, only women can procreate. Therefore, any language associated with the birth of a child must be the result of a woman in travail at the origin.

Using biblical evidence, we will first identify who the male child is, and based on the facts in various meaningful aspects and their spiritual consequences, the designation of the mother who is called the "woman," will become obvious.

To my readers' disappointment, let me say firsthand: **The woman is not Mary, and the male child is not Jesus.**

This being said, let's make some biblical sense of the idioms and the imagery employed here in this portion of the scripture. The first information we are going to consider is verse 5, which tells us that the child will be snatched up to God and to his throne. The expression "to snatch up" is another way of talking about the Rapture. It means a quick, sudden removal almost invisible to the naked eye.

The Lord Jesus Christ was not snatched up to heaven. He ascended to heaven right before the very eyes of the apostles gazing the mysterious phenomena until a cloud hid Jesus from their sight. *(Acts 1: 9-11)*

In fact, the apostles were gazing for so long and so intently that God had to dispatch two angels to tell them not to worry and that the same Jesus, who had been taken from them into heaven, will come back in like manner. This alone proves that the child in question cannot be Jesus because the same Jesus who went up is coming back to destroy Satan and his demons with him. But the question we should really be asking ourselves is, what was born with a promise of being Raptured or snatched up to heaven and to the throne of God? I would imagine your guess to be "the Church," and this is correct. This is found in Mathew 16:18, where Jesus speaks of a Church that was being conceived, a Church under construction. This new doctrine, consequence of the new birth initiated by God through Christ is extended to all who believe and are baptized into the body of Christ with one spirit forming the Church of God as one people.

In *Ephesians 1:22-23,* the Church is also defined as the body of Christ, in which all believers become members of a single body. In *Galatians 3:26-29,* the Apostle Paul teaches that all believers in Christ are sons of God, and there is neither Jew nor Greek, slave nor free, male nor female, for we are all one (person) in union with Christ and we are all the seed (singular) of Abraham and heir according to the promise.

Moreover, In *Galatians 4:6-7,* the Apostle Paul talking to both men and women refers to them again as "sons," and because of the spirit of Christ, who is in all of us, Paul goes from plural to singular when he says in *verse 7* that we are no longer "a slave" but "a son," and as "a son" also an heir by the grace of God.

John 3:24 also teaches that all believers in Christ "live in him." John 1:12 emphasizes that all who believe in Jesus become children of God, not of natural descent but "born of God."

This is very impressive but far from being a mystery, for in *John 11:49-53* there was a "High Priest" contemporary to the ministry of Jesus, named Caiaphas who prophesied that if Jesus was killed, his death would gather together all the children of God scattered around the world as "ONE" in him. There you have the principle of the "oneness" of God's people who mysteriously have their being in Christ, and the bible in *John 11:51* is clear that the prophecy of the "High Priest" concerning the nations of the world becoming one in Christ was from the Holy Spirit himself.

You see, God is a God of absolute coherence. Do you recall in the book of Genesis when God created humans and made them male and female? Well in *Genesis 5:1-2* we read that God after creating them male and female referred to them both as "man" and thereby masculinizing their joint existence.

So, it is no surprise to see an emulation of that masculinity being ascribed here as well in conjunction with the book of Revelation and the Rapture. The Bible refers to all believers as "sons of God," masculinizing thereby the relationship of the Church with respect to God.

Insightfully the Lord Jesus Christ has two natures which are so tightly intertwined that any attempt of dissection is definitely impossible. He is fully man and full of deity, a very perplexing implication.

However, an introspection of the two representations of Christ may lead to a very profound conclusion with two specific themes in perspective by raising the following two questions when we know that Jesus is not only the Creator of the world but also the kingdom of God in the earth.

The two most vital questions are:

- **Who is Jesus Christ?**

- **What is Jesus Christ?**

I will not go to the particulars of who Jesus is because most people rightly believe that Jesus is God, and it's not very likely that we are going to learn anything beyond that.

However, the other noteworthy element at the center of the incumbency of Jesus impress the imponderable question, "What is Jesus?" But it is not always the case that people pose the problem particularly with that perspective in mind. The "Let there be light" decree in Genesis 1 instantaneously purports Jesus as the kingdom of God, though operating provisorily in parallel to the kingdom of darkness presided by Satan, respectively as day and night until the physical birth of Christ four thousand years later when Christ officially presents himself to the world as the foundation upon which the kingdom of God is built.

However, one must remember that the kingdom of God is still under construction today as we speak. It is a building process that started with the ministry of Christ, which was delegated to the twelve apostles with the erectness under perpetual construction until Christ returns to officially give birth to the Church which is the eternal establishment of God's people as sons of God in a single body, a single person, a male child, a son.

In other words, the kingdom of God is in continual gestation and will be composed of born-again believers throughout this generation from Pentecost to the return of Christ. Meanwhile and until the time set by the Father for the Rapture, this male child, the son, which is the Church, is subject to guardians and trustees under the Holy Spirit and his angels.

The fact that the passage in *Revelation 12* reads, "A woman clothed with the sun," makes everybody fall off the wagon. But it is not an exaggeration to say that the word "woman" in this particular context is purely metaphorical. This also can be considered as a form of condescension of God in a practical manner enabling us to fathom the woman as a prescriptive premise in respect to the natural implication of the message. It's just about meaning, it's just about language processing. Simply put, the idea of a woman is simply a representation prototype of the human culture because only women have the capability of giving birth in the natural realm. Another enigmatic emphasis is the expression "clothed with the sun." The word "sun" in the scripture has a multitude of meanings. It sometime means "light" as well as "life." But most significantly we have seen the word "sun" used in the Bible to also signify "glory."

Purposefully all three significations willfully converge into a single homogeneous play in cognizance of both who and what Jesus is.

- **Jesus is the "Light" of the world (*John 8:12*).**

- **Jesus is the "Life" of the world (*John 1:4*).**

- **Jesus is the "Glory" of God (*2 Corinthians 4:6*).**

Pragmatically and perhaps most importantly, we have to greatly consider *Psalm 84:11,* which teaches that "God the Father is a Sun," which thereby makes the "sun" a representation of the Father. So, when we read in *Psalm 84:11* that God the Father is a "sun," this is the nail that seals the coffin. Doesn't the Bible throughout its pages teach that Jesus is coming in the glory of his Father? One parallelism that can be exploited as a paradigm for this portion of the scripture is *Matthew 16:27,* which teaches that: "the Son of Man is going to come in the Glory of his Father with his Angels."

It should be noted that this is definitely a corollary to the "A woman clothed with the sun." Need I say anymore to establish the correlation between the two expressions? A woman clothed with the sun = Jesus in the glory of his Father. There you have it, the woman clothed with the sun is none other than Jesus coming in the glory of his Father to give birth to the Church as a separate entity **(no longer being in him as taught in the scripture)** and snatch them as God's people up into heaven. As for the moon under her feet, it represents darkness, evil, death, Satan, and all of his demons. In *Matthew 22:24* we read, "The Lord said to my Lord: 'Sit at my right hand until I make your enemies a footstool under your feet.'"

We know from the scriptures that sinners can be reconciled with God through the death of Jesus Christ *(Romans 5:10-11)*. But those who from the beginning polluted the creation through their deceitfulness, whom Jude 6 describes as the angels who did not keep their first estate but abandoned their own habitation, they are kept in darkness by the God Almighty, bound with everlasting chains for judgment on the great day.

The *Apostle Paul in Ephesians 6:12* is a little bit more specific in his description of these eternal enemies of God who will be put under Jesus' feet as footstools when he returns to judge the world. And they are as the Apostle Paul puts it, the rulers, the authorities and powers of the darkness. As if these personified evil entities were not enough, Paul seems to indicate a conspicuous convergence of these entities when he ends the list with what he titles as "the spiritual forces of evil in the invisible world."

Another element of great significance to consider is the dream of Joseph in *Genesis 37:9*, when he saw the sun, the moon, and eleven stars bow down to him. These exact terms are repeated here in *revelation 12* as part of the posture of the woman who is clothed with the sun, the moon under her feet, and a crown of twelve stars on her head.

Interestingly, *Psalm 147:19* tells us that God has revealed his word to Jacob. So, let's pay a visit to Israel, known as Jacob, and listen to what he says about the dream of his son Joseph.

In *Genesis 37:10*, Jacob, the father of Joseph, in his interpretation of the dream tells us that the sun represents the father, the moon represents his dead mother (which represents death) because Rachel, the mother of Joseph, had already passed away when Joseph had his dream, and the eleven stars are his brothers.

Therefore, as a corollary, the woman is figurative of Jesus, the sun represents God the Father, the moon under his feet represents Satan and his horde of demons, and the stars represent the holy angels. As we well know, angels are called in the scriptures "Sons of God," and Jesus himself being called the "Son of God" logically makes them, for the sole purpose of interpreting this passage of the scripture, brothers.

As cogent as these illustrations may seem to be, in the final analysis, you may still wonder how do we get the woman to be Christ.

If I said Christ gave birth to the **"church"**, that would be an easy pill to swallow. But If I said Christ gave birth to **"a son"**, that would be totally inconceivable.

You see, the relationship between God and his people has always been one of parenthood. Throughout the scriptures this relationship is clearly depicted as one of father and child. God the Creator is the Father of all. However, God's love and affection for his people is so tender and passionate that the Bible at times compares this incomparable intimacy to a motherly love. A love that is so strong that the scriptures commendably relate it to the most cherished love known to humankind that exist between a mother and her infant. So incredibly cozy, maternal affection is beyond all imagination.

It's no wonder that the feminization or the motherly imagery of God's affinity for his people is so prevalent throughout the scripture. God is indeed often pictured as a mother, and here are some of the maternal references.

- **In *Mathew 23:37*, God compares himself to a female chicken (a hen), which gathers her chicks under her wing.**

- **In *Deuteronomy 32:11-12*, God is described as a mother eagle that stirs up its nest and hovers over its young and spreads its wings to catch them and carries them on its pinions.**

- **In *Isaiah 49:15*, God presents himself as a mother who is nursing her baby.**

- **In *Isaiah 42:14*, God is as a woman in child birth crying and gasping and panting.**

- **In *Isaiah 66:13*, God is like a mother who comforts her child.**

- **In *Luke 15:8-10*, God is like a woman looking for her lost coin.**

- In *Numbers 11:11-12*, Moses gives us an irrefutable motherly imagery of God when he explicitly pictures God as being pregnant with his children, when he asked God: "Was it I who conceived all these people? Was it I who gave birth to them? Why do you tell me to carry them in my arms as a nurse carries an infant to the promised land?"

Perhaps these representations supporting the motherly picture of God are not so much inveterately introspective. To enhance our understanding, we will contemplate a passage written by the Apostle Peter presenting Christ as Zion and the entailment associated with it.

First and foremost, Zion is an eternal dwelling place for God, a spiritual holy house made of stones, "living stones," with Christ as the chosen and precious cornerstone as a supplement to God's people in a heap, being built into royalty to be a holy priesthood.

As we have just read, the *Apostle Peter in 1 Peter 2* describes Christ as the quintessential Zion for the people of God. The living stone was rejected by men. But to fully understand what the Apostle is driving at, one has to refer to the Old Testament to envision a few characteristics represented by this pregnant word, "Zion."

In the book of Psalms, God refers to "Zion" as:

- The City Of God
- The Holy Place Of The Most High
- The City Of Jerusalem
- The Temple Of God
- The City Of David
- The Holy Mountain
- The Land Of Judah
- The Joy Of The Earth

I could go on and on, but the most interesting particularity is what Jesus himself said about Zion or any other place of worship in a conversation with the Samaritan woman at the well of Jacob. The woman having perceived that Jesus was a "man of God" said to him, "Our fathers worshiped on this mountain, but the Jews claim that the place of worship is in Jerusalem."

Jesus answered by saying, "Believe me woman, there will come a time when people will worship the Father neither on this mountain nor in Jerusalem. Verily I say to you, the time has now come because I who speak to you am the Christ who was to come and I embody all these beautiful meanings ascribed to the holy mountain, the mountain Zion".

Now to get back to our point concerning the woman in Revelation 12, we have further chosen *Psalms 48* and *132* and *Isaiah 60* and *66* as convincing evidence that the woman is Christ.

Psalm 48 describes Mountain Zion as a beautiful, lofty place, which is the city of God, the city of the Great King, the joy of all the earth. But then in *verse 3*, Mount Zion is personified when God says, "I am her citadels and I am her fortress and I make her secure forever" (keep in mind *1 Peter 2-4*, which tells us that Christ is Zion). In Psalm *132:3*, we read that the Lord has chosen Zion and desired it for his dwelling, his resting place forever and ever. In *verse 25* God says, "I will bless her with abundant provisions and her poor will I satisfy with food. I will clothe her followers with salvation and her saints will ever sing for joy."

Let me stop here for just a minute. Those of you who studied grammar know that third person singular (personal pronouns) indicate gender, such as masculine (he, him) or feminine (she, her).

Paradoxically, here in *Psalm 132*, God uses Zion as if Zion were not only a female person but a woman with offspring. In *verse 17*, King David bridged Zion to Christ when God shifts from that beautiful feminine personification of Zion represented by the pronoun "her" to this loftier signification in the person of Christ, as the masculine pronoun "his" in a transitional move by God, is now being used in *verses 17 and 18* when God says, "I will set up a lamp for my anointed one and I will clothe his enemies with shame but the crown on his head will be resplendent."

The prophet Isaiah also had something to say about Zion. But still keep in mind that Christ is Zion according to the Apostle Peter. In *verse 12 of Isaiah 60*, God talking about Zion says, "The nation or kingdom that will not serve you will perish and will be utterly ruined." In *verse 14*, still referring to Zion, God says, "The sons of your oppressors will come bowing before you and all who despise you will bow down at your feet and will call you the city of the Lord and will call you 'Zion' of the Holy one of Israel. Although you have been forsaken and hated, I the Lord will make you the everlasting pride and the joy of all generations."

Now based on these irrefutable biblical references, can anyone not conclude that Zion and the Lord Jesus Christ are one and the same?

But that's not all. If you still have doubts that the woman giving birth to a male child is Christ giving birth to God's people or Zion giving birth to a son, let's read Isaiah 66 and watch your jaws drop. *Isaiah 66* is talking about the end of the world and the eternal chastisement that will befall those who rejected God at judgment day.

Starting at verse 6 we read:

"Hear that uproar from the city of God; Hear that noise from the Temple! It is the sound of the Lord repaying his enemies all they deserve.

Before Zion goes into labor she gives birth; Before the pains come upon her, she delivers 'a son'.

Yet no sooner is Zion in labor she gives birth to her children." **(Verse 8)**

You may have noticed, and I am hopeful you have, that the last two verses suggest the existence of a paradox. On the one hand, we read that Zion gives birth to "her children," which I am sure are many, yet on the other hand, the preceding verse tells us that Zion only delivers one child "a son." After scratching my head, I decided to consult the Apostle Paul, a steward of the mysteries of God, for some clarification. But first the following two questions had to be answered. They are found in *1 Corinthians 10:16-17.*

- **Is not the cup of blessing for which we give thanks a participation in the blood of Christ? (The answer is yes.)**

- **Is not the bread that we break a participation in the body of Christ? (The answer is yes.)**

Then the Apostle Paul explains in *verse 17,* "Because there is one Loaf, we who are many are one body, for we are all partakers of that one Loaf."

Going back to *Isaiah 66:20* once again which unambiguously refers to Zion as Jerusalem, the holy mountain of God, but this time we will look at another strange paradox the prophet brings to our attention when he indicates that the children of Zion are also her brothers whom will be brought out of all nations as a gift to Jehovah. **Bingo! Wouldn't you agree? The prophet says that the children of Zion are also her brothers. WOW!**

Now it is understood why the prophet says, starting with *verse 10,* "rejoice with Zion and be glad for her. We will nurse and be satisfied at her comforting breasts. We will drink deeply and delight in her overflowing abundance. We will nurse and be carried on her arm and dandle on her knees. As a mother comforts her child, God says, "I will comfort you and you will be comforted over Jerusalem".

To definitely close this segment, we will elaborate on Apostle Paul's teaching in *Acts 17* that all believers live in Christ. In *verse 29* the Apostle says we are God's offspring, which literally means that Christ gave birth to all of his followers.

The new birth, which is a requirement to enter the Kingdom of Heaven, is immediately received when one accepts the blood and the body of Christ as his or her new nutriment. However, the full effect of that birth will not take place until the Rapture, which will culminate with the millennium, when evidence of the "oneness" of the Church as "one body" becomes apparent, and those who have fallen asleep are brought back to life in an indistinguishable intimacy with the living to meet the Lord in the air.

You see, the birth of all believers will be simultaneous as the Apostle Paul describes it in *1 Thessalonians 4:16-17*. Like a pregnant mother whose infant is being nourished and kept alive in the womb, so it is with all believers, dead or alive, we live and move and have our being in Christ.

For the natural mother it is the prospective of a full term and the birth of a healthy child. For Christ, it is also the prospective of a full term, whose day and hour God has set from the foundation of the world to deliver and give birth to "the children of God," "the church," a "son," a "male child."

We read in *John 14* that Jesus is making all the preparations for the delivery, and when everything is complete, he will come back to receive us unto himself, and forever be with us and us with him. This will be the end of all fatuity regarding the "born again" notion when Christ returns and removes all accrued abstractness by following through with his greatest promise, the consummation of the Rapture, thus actualizing the new birth.

Let me conclude with this important recapitulation:

From Genesis 37:10   **The sun is indicative of the Father**

From Matthew 17:2   **The sun is suggestive of Glory**

From Psalm 84:11   **The Father is a Sun**

Did not Jesus himself say in *Matthew 16:27* that the Son of Man is going to come in the glory of his Father with his holy angels?

With all these revelations of the sun representing God the Father and his glory, we can therefore say with absolute certainty that the correlation between *Matthew 16:27*, which says that Jesus is coming in the Glory of the Father, and *Revelation 12,* which portrays a woman clothed with the sun, is undeniably conclusive.

To reiterate plainly, the woman clothed with the sun very well typifies the Lord Jesus Christ in the glory of the Father.

Next, we read that the woman has the moon under her feet. One scripture after another, we see how the word of God is coherent. The Bible teaches throughout its content that the moon is associated with darkness and, by extension, evil and death. The great patriarch Jacob, as we just saw, corroborates this truth when he tells us that the moon in Joseph's dream is symbolic of his mother Rachel who had already died.

Again, do you see the awesome constancy of the word of God? Way back in Genesis, Jacob was already telling us that the moon represents death and in so doing, darkness and evil.

Now things get really interesting, *Matthew 22:44, Psalm 110:1, Luke 20:43, Acts 2:35,* and more teach that God the Father said to the Lord Jesus Christ, "Sit at my right hand until I put all your enemies under your feet."

Jesus being the light, you don't have to be a deep-water diver to understand that darkness is the enemy of light.

As has been emphasized throughout the scripture, the first enemies of Christ are identified as Satan and his host of fallen angels about whom the prophet Jude *(verse 6)* said, "These angels who abandoned their estate were kept in darkness, bound with everlasting chains for judgment on the great day."

Therefore, when you read that the woman has the moon under her feet, it is simply a picture of the Lord Jesus Christ having the world of darkness as a footstool in cognizance to the promise of God the Father to put all his enemies under his feet.

Next, we read that the woman fled into the desert to a place prepared for her by God where she might be taken care of for *1,260 days.*

The word "desert" used in this passage is pregnant with spiritual signification. Sometimes the expressions "desert" and "wilderness" are interchangeably used depending on which version of the scripture you have in your hand. The Bible uses the word "desert" in a spiritual sense to signify a place full of green pastures where souls are restored. But Jesus also gave us a physical meaning of the word "desert" when he exhilarated the souls of the people by feeding the multitude.

We first saw the spiritual meaning of the word with king David in his famous *Psalm 23*, when David says that the Lord "makes me to lie down in green pastures leading me beside the still waters and to restore my soul and to lead me in the paths of righteousness." But closer to us, we read in Mark 1:4 that John the Baptist preached and baptized in the desert, where there is water in abundance. **Very paradoxical!**

Another wonderful paradox is the fact that the desert is also a place where there are a lot of green pastures. *Mark 6:39* tells us that Jesus in this desert place made the people sit in ranks by hundreds and by fifties on the green grass and with the five loaves and the two fishes fed the multitudes, and they did all eat and were filled.

When you read John's version of the same episodes in *John 6:10*, he reports that there was "plenty of grass" in the desert, with that much emphasis on the words "green grass"; it is obvious that the spiritual meaning is profound. King David was right in comparing the "Desert" with a place for restoration of souls.

With such undeniable evidence of the substantiative relationship that exists between the desert and soul restoration, it would be an insult to the Cross to think that anybody other than Christ would possess such authority, as the text is explicit that as soon as the woman gave birth to the child, she fled into the desert to a place prepared for her by God.

In essence, as the preceding passages clearly established, "Desert and Restoration of souls" are correlational. The works of Christ is to forgive and erase the sins of all his followers in readiness for the promised refreshing times which will come from the Father.

This mystery involved three episodic scenarios according to the apostle Peter in *Acts 3:18-21* which will conclude with the second coming of Christ.

- The proclamation of the eventual birth of Christ by the Old Testament prophets, his meekness and suffering.

- The actual birth of Christ, sent to engineer the Father's redemptive work which was ended on the cross.

- The fulfillment of the Father's promise in Acts 3:21 that the heaven will receive Christ **(the woman fleeing to the desert)** until the times of restitution of all things.

The connection is undeniable.

- **Christ gave birth to the "Church" and ascended to the highest heaven.**

- **The woman gave birth to the "Male child" and fled into the desert which the Father had prepared for her.**

Spectacularly, as foolish as it may sound, when Jesus gave the ghost on the cross, began the inception of his pregnancy with all God's people, chosen before the creation of the world, to be reconciled with God. Through Him came the "new birth" by virtue of repentance and forgiveness and God exalted him to his own right hand **(here is the desert again)** until labor and delivery time, which is another word for the "rapture", the last stage of this long pregnancy when the "child" or better yet the church as a "son" will see the "Light". **It's all about restoration of souls.**

In the final analysis, the woman in *Revelation 12* fleeing into the desert, as we now know to be representative of the Lord Jesus Christ, should remind us of that promise made by Jesus in *John 14:2-3,* "In my Father's house are many mansions".

This spiritual desert is the very place promised by Jesus that he was going to go and prepare for his own, and then come again and receive them unto himself, so that where he is, we may be also.

Now let's go back to *Revelation 12 verse 3*, which talks about another sign that appeared in the heavens referring to an enormous red dragon with seven heads and ten horns and seven crowns on his heads.

The first thing that strikes me is the number of heads, which is a clear indication that Satan is not "solo" in this adventure. It is obviously an "all for one and one for all" empire, as defined by Jesus in *Mathew 12:26* describing this evil quiddity as a unified, well-organized satanic kingdom, which is overseen, as we read here in *Revelation 12* by seventeen high-commanding (seven heads + ten horns) officers, whose powers converge to form this entity called "the Great Dragon."

Each officer may or may not be of a single essence depending on his nature and the attribution involved. The ten horns are also ten powerful nations or group of nations of the earth that are under the direct influence of the ten horns or ten evil spirits or fallen angels assigned for the purpose of fulfilling the interest of the seven heads of the beast.

Orders for example that will affect our way of life in this world will emanate from the seven heads concertedly, but those orders will be implemented by the ten horns through heads of states in concert with religious leaders. The seven heads represent seven especially exalted orders of angelic beings, including Lucifer himself, who is one of the seven but with the institutional role of a residing officer. These seven heads or seven powerful fallen angels are represented by four great beasts that came out of the sea, each different from the other according to *Daniel 7:3*.

Let's stay with Daniel a little bit because I think the book of Daniel is probably the best biblical reference to understand the meaning of the seven heads, the ten horns, and the seven crowns. In *Daniel 7:3*, we read that Daniel in his dream saw four great beasts that came out of the sea, and in *verse 17* he receives the interpretation of the dream by an angel. The angel confirms the origin of the four beasts when he uses the preposition "from" instead of "in" in the explication. According to the angel, the four beasts are four kingdoms that will rise "from the earth." Please note that the angel did not say "in" the earth, which is very significant. This clearly indicates they are coming up from under the earth.

The three areas of habitation revealed to mankind according to the Bible are:

1- **In heaven**

2- **On the earth**

3- **Under the earth or under the ocean**

The expression "out of the sea" or "from under the ocean" obviously indicates that the four beasts are from another sphere, another realm. Simply put, these four beasts are from the world under. They are the same ones used by God in *Revelation 6,* when the first four seals were opened. However, these four beasts among others which represent the power of darkness, are not to be confused with the four living creatures at the throne of God.

When each of the four living creatures speaks, it corresponds to a certain delegation of power to each of the four beasts, as each seal was being opened. But in reality, the four beasts correspond to five spirits because death and Hades, although traveling together as apparently one entity, are two distinct spirits.

Bear in mind that the four beasts in Daniel's dream very well denote the characteristics of the four horsemen found in *Revelation 6* according to their purpose. Together they are mysteriously the incorporation of the seven heads that constitute the Dragon.

Perhaps a little comparison of the two scriptures will help.

Daniel 7	Revelation 6	Revelation 12 The Seven Heads
Verse 4: The first beast was like a lion, which represents kingship	*Verse 2*: The first Horse rider (the white horse) was given a crown: This represents Kingship.	One Head
Verse 5: The second beast was like a bear, which receives the power to devour (kill) much flesh (people)	*Verse 3*: The second Horse rider (the red horse) was given a large sword and power to take peace from the earth and to make man kill each other	One Head
Verse 6: The third beast was like a leopard. This beast had four wings and four heads and dominion was given to it	*Verse 5*: The third Horse rider had a pair of scales which represents two sets of two-sided scales symbolizing each two spirits. So, the pair of the scales mentioned above represents four spirits and therefore four heads.	Four Heads

Verse 7: The fourth beast was very powerful, terrifying, and frightening and had ten horns, three of which were uprooted, and a little one came up along them	*Verse 7*: The fourth horse rider is identified as "Death" and "Hades." Two spirits acting in a concerted way as one.	One Head
four beasts	four horsemen	seven heads

We also read in *Revelation 12:3* that seven crowns are part of his countenance, each corresponding to one of his seven heads, but as a whole, suggesting ostensibly the oneness of the mind with which they operate in the pursuit of a concerted purpose as members of the Dragon compound.

The seven heads, like I said before, are seven very powerful fallen angels or evil spirits including Lucifer himself that make up the headquarters of the evil kingdom. The presence of the seven crowns, obviously one for each of the seven heads, is a definite indication that we are dealing with seven kings with again Lucifer as commanding officer or king of kings in the dark world.

In contrast, the ten horns that are on the seven heads of the dragon are lower-rank spirits in charge of the affairs of the world. These ten horns, like I said before, are also representative of their human counterparts. These human accomplices include powerful nations with very influential personalities. They will represent the Antichrist and the false prophet, both of whom had at one time in history normal lives in the earth as human beings, which goes back thousands of years. We will have the opportunity to study this in more detail in future paragraphs when it becomes more relevant.

Verse 4 of *Revelation 12* tells us that the tail of the dragon swept a third of the stars out of the sky and flung them to the earth.

The general understanding is that this refers to a third of the angels in heaven, who sinned against God. This cannot be further from the truth. This prevailing misinterpretation has not only gone unchallenged but has become widely accepted as truth, but it is indeed a false truth that disgracefully relegates the peremptory obsequiousness of the cross and thereby makes it negligible.

What better way to start the premise of the intended meaning of the symbol "stars" than to go pay another visit to Jacob to understand the explanation of Joseph's dream, when he saw the "sun," the "moon," and the "stars all bowing to him, provoking the jealousy of his brothers, filled with hatred toward him to the point of death, as a solid basis for the interpretation of *Revelation 12.*

<u>**Jacob stated very clearly that:**</u>

- **The sun represented the father**

- **The moon stood for his "dead" mother**

- **The stars were representative of his brothers**

Here is a straightforward and conspicuous evidence of stars representing people, and God, as a matter of interpretation, incidentally compares endlessly throughout the scripture the holiness of his people, the greatness of their character **"to stars"** such as told to our father Abraham by God in *Genesis 13:16.* God came to Abraham and said, "I will make your descendants like the dust of the earth". But later in *Genesis 15:5,* God took Abraham outside and said, "Look up at the sky and count the stars if you can; so, shall your descendants be." **No one can deny that God is giving prominence to Both the "quantity" and the "quality" of the children of Abraham when he compares them to the stars of heaven.**

Another element that I think will establish the link between stars and the people of God is the title "Bright Morning Star" Jesus self-ascribed to himself in *Revelation 22:16.* As this is true for Jesus, by tacit understanding, all of us being made in his image and likeness and having our being in Him as taught by the Apostle Paul in *Acts 17:28,* should also be considered as he is, having been transformed from dust to stars.

In brief, as these approaches suggest, it's amazing to see how the definition of stars parallels our earthly affiliation with God when he earnestly associates stars with godliness and by extension with "sonship," God being Father of all.

If we were to go beyond the obvious surface, we would realize that in essence, one is not a star simply because he or she is an angel. We are all stars because we are sons.

Since the first man Adam was created directly by God as a sinless spirit and placed in Paradise, the Garden of Eden (located in the third heaven, according to *2 Corinthians 12:2-4*), therefore Adam is a "son of God," which is taught by Luke 3:38 and obviously there shouldn't be any objections that Adam is a star from heaven.

Not so fast, you say. But certainly, the self-evidence of these facts immediately propounds a logical causal chain. All having died in Adam as stated in *1 Corinthians 15:22,* Adam being a star from heaven that has fallen from Paradise, from the Garden of Eden to the earth, as a matter of evidence, his progenies, being like him as living souls, are notably the stars that fell from heaven to the earth.

The word of God declares the soul that sins is the one that will die. By the same token, the scripture teaches clearly that we all came into this world as sinners. In order for this to be true, we must have had our prevenient existence somewhere prior to being formed in the womb. But because science can only trace us back to sperm and egg, our religious leaders for fear of seeming ridiculous have limited their focus on this earthly wisdom rather than on the Creator, whose power is unfathomable and limitless.

Well beyond any wisdom of this world or any understanding thereof, the Apostle Paul went to heaven and visited a place called Paradise and came back to earth. The Apostle John also went to heaven at the throne and came back to earth. Enoch and Elijah were both taken to heaven without seeing death.

In *Hebrews 11:5,* the Apostle Paul tells us that Enoch's ways pleased the Lord, and because of that, God took him to heaven so that he did not experience death, and he was no longer found.

These inexplicable phenomena are definite proofs that this physical world was truly made for sinners, and by way of illustration, God does justice to those who are totally devoted to Him by removing them from the earth and bringing them to one of heaven's dimensions away from this universe.

Again, it seems worth noting that Paradise or the Garden of Eden is not of this physical world. If God, who is the same yesterday, today, and forever, by doing justice to Enoch because Enoch was found righteous, took him to another dimension away from this filthy world, all the more reason not to think for one moment that Adam, who was created perfect like God and in the image of God, would have been left here to endure the horrible consequences of sin, he who knew no sin when he was created.

So, this great revelation of the outstanding power and character of God should heighten the sense of our awareness about what really took place immediately after Adam was created. The Rapture of Enoch and Elijah has dissipated the mystery of the buffer in regard to the spiritual phase of creation in Genesis, now that we know there is a place in heaven, call it what you will, "Garden or Paradise," reserved for sinless or for forgiven people.

As one might have expected, when God talks about a garden in *Genesis 2* where he put the first man Adam, where strangely the sun doesn't shine and we don't see the existence of the moon and the stars, I don't know how we could have missed that God is not talking about a physical place in the earth. It is evident that in the beginning passages of the Bible, we all had a sense of being lost but everyone kept it to themselves.

I will admit that the issue concerning the Garden and mankind is not only mysterious but beyond that which can be believed. Nevertheless, I will offer some generalizations then stop.

Perhaps the biggest mystery surrounding the Garden of Eden and humankind, which makes any possible conclusion very challenging, resides in the fact that after God retrieved Eve from Adam, he did exactly what Jesus repeated in the earth with the fish and the bread. The man and the woman responded to the command of God exactly as did the fish and the bread, multiplying into the existence of humanity as a whole.

Forgive me if I choked anyone. So, let's go another route and analyze different prospects.

Stars in the Bible have three dominant representations.

1- **They could mean literal stars in the sky.**

2- **They sometimes represent angels.**

3- **They sometimes symbolize people.**

The distinction is not a difficult one, and it's obviously not even necessary to do justice to all three possibilities. But any ambiguity will lead to horrible consequences and not bring out the essential message intended by God as the absolute foundation. Simply on the basis of redemptive perception, right off the bat, the third one should be the one understood to be correct.

However, in light of the challenges represented by this portion of the scripture and to ensure that the interpretation is as consentaneous as possible, we will consider a somewhat silly game called "Process of elimination," which will elucidate the true meaning that is in view, based on the three most dominant representations of the word "stars."

Let's begin by eliminating the choices that we know with certainty cannot possibly be right and explaining why.

According to the passage, these stars, at one time, had their existence in heaven and are now living in the earth. This is suggestive beyond any doubt that these stars cannot be literal stars.

No. 1 therefore is eliminated.

Next, we will examine why these stars that were flung to the earth by the tail of the dragon cannot be angels.

Do you remember we spoke in the preceding paragraphs about the three areas of habitation revealed to mankind according to the scripture?

1- **In heaven**

2- **On the earth**

3- **Under the earth or under the ocean**

In *Luke 10:18,* Jesus was careful not to specify the place Satan fell to when he said he saw Satan fall like lightning from heaven, and he stopped right at heaven. But we learned from other passages in the Bible that Satan and his demons fell to hell, which is another name for the abyss, located under the earth or under the ocean, bound with chains of darkness until the judgment day.

Revelation 12:7-9 tells us that there was a war in heaven, and Michael and his angels fought against the dragon and his angels. But because the dragon was not strong enough, he and his angels lost their place in heaven, and they were hurled to the earth. It's very significant for us to bear in mind that Satan and his angels were kicked out of heaven and fell to the earth together.

Now listen very carefully to yourself reading *verse 9 of Revelation 12* again. **"Satan was hurled to the earth and his angels with him."** This is the main factor that has to be acknowledged. Satan and all the fallen angels conjointly were and still are in this great conspiracy against God and his people.

Again, *verse 9* is clear that Satan and his angels were cast out of heaven together. Simply put, seeing that Satan and the whole squad have their residence or are confined under the earth jointly, the stars that followed had to have been distinct for the failed elusive goal of Satan of gaining the upper hand on humankind and becoming like God, to have made any sense.

What's even more interesting is that when you truly dive into the passage and set out to understand the proposed interactions, it becomes clear that the verse is self-evident.

Let's look at it together again. *Revelation 12:4,* **"The tail of the dragon drags one third of the stars of heaven and cast them to the earth, and the dragon stood before the woman who was about to give birth to devour the child as soon as he was born."**

The first element to consider is that Satan has gone from being a serpent to now a great dragon with expressible countenance such as "seven heads" and "ten horns" that are definitely phenotype of the entire evil spirit world, in much the same as expressions such like "All died in Adam" or "All will be made alive in Christ portentously, indicating that Adam represents all sinners, and Christ to symbolize all that will be saved." But what I find very strange in the subjacency of the verse is that there is a discernible depiction of antagonistic interests, Satan being the assailant and the stars are the innocent victims of Satan.

Subtly, what I find to be the major problem with this stereotype is that throughout the scripture, the interest of Satan and the interest of the rest of the fallen angels are never in conflict as the verse obviously depicts a furious dragon on the verge of falling, manifestly determined to bring down with him a number of stars from heaven with salient strenuousness as symbolized by the tail.

Therefore, when we consider that Satan and his angels are conjoint in this scheme against God and his Church and furthermore there would not be any self-gratification for Satan had those stars stricken by his tail simply been evil spirits, we can say with great confidence that the third of the stars that followed Satan into this universe cannot be angels.

Moreover, as we saw earlier, and this can be seen throughout the scripture, God used different appellations to identify or simply to designate what he has in mind. But they must be examined carefully in order to unveil their spiritual significance and attach any real understanding to the immediate context.

The most common epithets used by God in the scripture to describe angels and men interchangeably are:

– **Nations**

- **Stars**

- **Trees**

The book of *Ezekiel, chapter 31 verse 18,* describes a conversation between God and Lucifer in the Garden of Eden where Satan is represented by a cedar tree, **(The tallest and most fascinating)** and all the other angels under him, who were also present in the Garden, as simply trees of all other types.

But the buck does not stop here. In the preceding verse, God used the same appellation "trees" to describe humanity as a whole that was also present in the Garden.

In *verse 18,* God asks Lucifer, "Which of the trees of Eden can be compared to you in splendor and majesty? Yet you too will be brought down with the trees of Eden to the earth below and you will lie with the uncircumcised that will be killed by the sword."

There you have it as clear as crystal that the Garden of Eden is not of this physical dimension as God is specifically telling Lucifer that he and his angels with him will fall down from the Garden of Eden to the earth below *(Ezekiel 31:18).*

However, as Lucifer, the cedar tree, was handed over to the ruler of the nations to be dealt with according to his wickedness in the Garden of God, *Ezekiel 31:12* tells us that as the "Cedar Tree" was being cut down in the Garden, all the nations of the earth came out from under his shade and left him.

Consider what took place in *Genesis 3:8-10* after the fall of Adam and Eve and how it relates undeniably to what God is describing here in *Ezekiel 31.*

In *Genesis 3:8* the man and his wife hid themselves among the "Trees" because of their sins. From verses 9-15 God came into the Garden of Eden and called them out from amid the trees and separate them and interposed an enmity between them and the "Cedar Tree" before cursing the serpent **(Satan, Lucifer, The Cedar tree)**, call him what you want, and kicking him out of the Garden and vehemently casting him to the earth below.

Verse 16 of *Ezekiel 31* tells us that the nations **(his angels)** trembled at the sound of his fall, and because of him, all the trees of the field **(humanity as a whole)** withered away.

There is a logical continuity that is patent, and given the connection of these very coherent expressions and their relationships at different dimensions, one cannot but come to the only one possible conclusion that this divine doctrine ties in perfectly with the expressed philosophy of the scripture. What's even more astonishing is that verse 16 in its latter portion stipulates that, "Of all the trees in the Garden of Eden, **[this is the great mystery of predestination]** God chose the best of Lebanon to be well watered and consoled in the earth." **(This is talking about those chosen to be saved from before the foundation of the world).**

But those who remain in his shade, his allies among the nations, **(The fallen angels)** will also go to the grave with him, joining those that will be killed by the sword. **(Those to whom Jesus will say, "Depart from me I never knew you).**

As a final point, going back to our verse in question in *Revelation 12:4,* it should be noted that also inherent in the verse is the obvious relationship that is portrayed, relative to the woman and these stars that were just dragged to the earth.

The connection is manifest as the woman seems determined to come after these stars in total defiance against the daring of the devil threatening to kill her newborn child the moment he was born, referring to the newborn doctrine of the "Church" as one body for a spectacular rebound.

Most conspicuously, these stars, also known as the trees of the Garden of Eden according to *Ezekiel 31,* definitely don't belong to the devil, and given his knowledge of the facts and issues involved, he is ready to fight at all cost to avoid all possible reversions.

The devil is well aware of the consequences and certainly does not want to face the final destruction that awaits him and his angels without at least causing a measure of sorrow to the Holy Spirit, knowing the unfathomable love of God for his people, to the point of deserting his glory, taking on flesh and living as a sinful man who is ready to die in order to redeem his people from the power of darkness.

This is what it's all about, and though it may have seemed at first that this portion of scripture concerned the devil and his angels, the evidence proves this is not the case. These stars who followed Satan to this sinful world are not angels. This now brings us to the third and last possibility.

These stars that were swept out of the sky to the earth as you will see in the successive paragraphs, represent the *"People of God"*.

If you are surprised that the third of the stars that were dragged to the earth represents humanity in its entirety that followed Satan in this evil adventure, I suggest you go back and read *Ezekiel 31* and meditate on the relationship between humanity and the angels in the Garden of Eden on the one hand and on the other hand, the connection as all of this tie in with the redemptive plan of God for his people.

You might legitimately wonder, well, if the third of the stars that followed Satan to the earth are humans, where are the other two thirds? Because all men have sinned according to the scripture.

Great question! And you know what? God has given us the answer in the book of the prophet Isaiah. It's a privilege that French- speaking people enjoy perhaps without knowing it. This algebraic fraction (1/3) concerning mankind is mentioned in *Isaiah 40:12* in **"La Sainte Bible—Version Louis Second,"** but somehow, for some mysterious reason, it is not incorporated in none of the English versions. I invite everyone to Google *"Isaiah 40:12* from *La Sainte Bible"* in French and translate it in English and watch your jaw drop.

Impressively, the verse is very succinct but direct and clear as it supplies one of the most fundamental pieces of information in the

Bible concerning humankind. After reading the verse over and over, it's almost impossible to separate the information it conveys from its immediate surrounding relationship.

As it is, one cannot but come to the surprising conclusion that based on the information contained in this verse, humankind made up a third of heaven's total and diverse population.

So, when we read that the tail of the dragon swept a third of the stars out of the sky and flung them to the earth, God is simply telling us that the totality of the human race, which makes up a third of the heaven's population, fell into sin and was transmigrated to the earth.

Here is a proposed comparison for your appreciation:

"**Un tiers**" in French translates "**a third**" in English.

La Sainte	Any English Bible
Esaie 40:12	Isaiah 40:12
Qui a mesuré les eaux dans le creux de sa main, pris les dimensions des cieux et ramassé la poussière de la terre dans « <u>un tiers</u> » de mesure.	Who has measured the waters in the hollow of his hands, measured out the heavens with a span and included in the measure the dust of the earth.

You don't have to speak French to see "un tiers," which is a word fraction near the end of the French version. As you can see, the fraction, which is very significant, is not included in any of the English versions.

Thus, when I translate the French version of Isaiah 40:12 with the fraction "**Un Tiers**" which means "**A third**" in the passage, this is what I get:

Isaiah 40:12—French	Translation in English
Qui a mesuré les eaux dans le creux de sa main, pris les dimensions des cieux et ramassé la poussière de la terre dans « <u>un tiers</u> » de mesure.	Who has measured the waters in the hollow of his hands, measured out the heavens with a span and included the dust of the earth in "<u>a third</u>" measure.

Do you see the difference in meaning that the insertion of the fraction provokes? Unbelievable! This observation should help clarify the misconception surrounding the true itinerary of the people of God from creation and secure a more confident prosperity through a better foresight of the future events to come.

Even to people whose inclinations are contrary to what has been said; may the inclusion of this fraction (1/3) and its implication help attain new heights in our relations with God, with adequate potency for appropriate adjustments. There is no question that this in fact is a paradigm that involves the entire human race. The sad truth is, being the case; I don't think anyone can evaluate the centuries of damage this misjudgment has had on our willingness to repent, and how it most certainly continues to jeopardize our walk with God in these last days.

Now we're certainly beginning to understand why God used the expression "tail of the dragon" instead of simply "the dragon." Satan and his angels form an undivided kingdom *(Mathew 12:26)*, and as mentioned in *Revelation 12:9*, Satan and his angels were hurled down together, on the same flight, so to speak.

The tail as defined is what comes after. It is the hindmost part that follows the body. Deepening our thoughts, a bit, the tail gives allegiance to the body, which is exactly what Adam and Eve did in the Garden of Eden when they hearkened to the voice of the serpent. As a result of their disobedience to the word of God, they followed Satan into this sinful, dark world and all of us with them as members of the human race, thus members of the human kingdom, over which Adam, the first living soul, was created as king.

In *Ezekiel 18:20*, the sovereign God declares, "All living souls belong to Me, the Father as well as the Son, both belong to Me. The soul who sins is the one who will die." We also know from the Apostle Paul unambiguously that "all have sinned and lost the Glory of God" *(Romans 3:23)*.

Let me remind you that the single most important element that distinguishes between a living soul and a dead soul is the spirit of God.

Physically we are conceived in the womb as dead souls until the Holy Spirit on behalf of Christ abides in us and quickens us into a living spirit. However, this remedial principle obviously only applies to the dead as in physical birth. But Adam, when he was formed directly by the Living God, received the Holy Spirit as part of his nature, which made him a living soul, a sinless creature with automatic right and access to the Paradise of God, the Garden of Eden.

Recognizing the impossibility of self-attainment to such level of spiritual wonder, as it is a known biblical fact that we all came into this world as sinners and therefore lacking appropriate agentive capabilities, God through Christ, perforce a mysterious divine plan of redemption and salvation, made available the same Holy Spirit that quickened Adam into a living spirit to all who love him from before the foundation of the world, to bring us back to our former house in his "garden" as his chosen people.

In the spirit:

- **Spiritual birth parallels "living souls"**

- **Physical birth translates "death"**

- **Physical death is associated with somnolence**

Allow me to go off course momentarily. But this is for adult Christians only, those who can chew on spiritual chunks of meat without choking. In *John 5:19*, Jesus says, "I only do what I see my Father do." In *John 6:10*, Jesus multiplied five loaves and two fishes to feed the multitude, and Jesus, who cannot lie, said that he only replicates in the earth what the Father does in Heaven.

The implication of this statement is in essence very useful as it sheds the necessary light to the understanding of the multiplication phenomenon that was orchestrated by God in the Garden of Eden during the spiritual creation process when God made all kinds of trees grow out of the ground, which represent the entire human race **(Genesis 2:9)**.

Look very closely how Jesus distinctly proceeded with the multiplication process of the bread and the fish by recognizing their natural differences and dealing with them as separate elements. In *John 6:11,* we read that Jesus took the bread, gave thanks, and distributed to all as much as they wanted. The repletion was total, but bread exclusively multiplied into more bread.

Then, in the next sentence, we read that Jesus took the fish and did the same, multiplying them excessively to total satiety of the multitude present. In spite of the comprehensiveness of the redundancy, the multiplication process was performed by Jesus separately each according to its kind serving as an exegesis to the breeding of Adam and Eve in a sexless environment and the entire human race, which followed.

The Bible is clear that sex is a byproduct of sin, which logically explains why everyone is physically born dead as sinners. If already in the womb I am considered a dead sinner or a dead soul, my existence as a living soul or a sinless creature must have preceded the pregnancy of my mother and therefore anteceded my being born in this physical world.

Ooh this is scary!

Jesus said in *John 6:38* and *5:19,* "I came down from heaven to do the will of the Father and I only do what I see the Father doing. Whatever the Father does in heaven the Son also does in the "earth." In *1 Peter1:11* the bible reports that from Moses to Malachi, everything was written by the spirit of Christ that was in these prophets. All in all, the whole Bible from Genesis to Revelation was written by Jesus himself making therefore the entire scripture and the stories thereof an evidential replica of the works that took place or that the Father did in the invisible or spiritual world.

The scripture teaches that all came from Adam and were created in the image and likeness of God as sinless creatures and were made of one blood *(Genesis 1:26-27) (Acts 17:26).* The issue here is a little complex, given that we existed in the spirit before our physical birth, except that God initiated an interesting dynamic, masterful in nature, commanding a general engenderment of the human race from the first man Adam.

The process logically began with the extraction of the first woman "Eve" from Adam before the multiplication proceeding took place, whence Adam all males and hailing from Eve all females, each according to his or her kind.

Though all of this mystery is very necessary to understand, I think this is a bit too deep for some of you because faith is a God- given growing process. However, before we return to the surface, keep in mind that the Garden of Eden, like the invisible heaven, is not of this physical creation as clearly stated in *Ezekiel 31:18.*

In *Genesis 3:15,* God told the serpent after deceiving Adam and Eve that "I will put enmity between you and the woman and between your offspring and her offspring. Not that the woman in *Revelation 12* is symbolic of Eve, but the principle remains.

A summary of the account that followed is found here in *Revelation 12:7,* expressing how Satan and his angels were immediately kicked out of heaven and hurled down to the earth.

Ever since his fall to the earth, the dragon gave himself a single objective, which is to destroy the woman's child once born. The Old Testament entails many atrocities involving the killing of male children with Satan behind the scene as the provoker, forgetting that God's omniscience and omnipotence are impenetrable.

This war that took place in Heaven involved two groups of spirits. We know the principal objective of any war is to kill, destroy, and subdue the enemy. However, none of that was the consequence of the heavenly war, because spirits are eternal beings and cannot be killed nor destroyed while in their spiritual costumes. Keep this fact in mind— this is very fascinating.

Another intriguing aspect of this heavenly war is that it took place before physical time began in Genesis, as we know it. The earth was there but void and empty. The contrast with *Revelation 12:12,* which talks about the devil having come down to us, is totally another story. This is Satan with no more time on his watch, filled with fury coming down to the earth in the Antichrist, which cannot happen until the Church as the male child is Raptured to God and to his throne. In other words, Satan cannot manifest himself as the Antichrist until the Holy Spirit leaves the earth with the people of God, which is the male child, a son.

The Apostle Paul, in *2 Thessalonians 2:7*, teaches that the secret power of the man of lawlessness is already at work, but his physical appearance is being held back until the Holy Spirit, who is restraining him, is taken out of the way, and then the Antichrist will be revealed, whom the Lord Jesus Christ will overthrow with the breath of his mouth and the splendor of his coming.

In *Revelation 12:4,* we are told the dragon stood in front of the woman who was about to give birth so that he might devour the child the moment he was born. Inferentially, we are dealing here with a pregnant woman and her unborn child having to face the hostility of Satan standing impatiently in front of her to make sure the child is born dead. This obviously corresponds to the original casting out of Satan and his angels with him out of heaven immediately after he lost the war to Michael and his angels before physical time began in Genesis 1. This is a figurative reference to the enmity decreed by God in the Garden of Eden between Satan and the woman and the perpetual hostility between their respective progeny.

This is extraordinary evidence that these two events though seemingly related took place at very different times in history. When Jesus was physically alive in the earth he said, using the past tense, "I saw Satan fall like lightning from heaven," referring to Satan's defeat against Michael in the spirit realm and his eternal exclusion from heaven and his angels with him.

However, concerning the latter descent of Satan to the earth after the birth of the child, who was snatched up to God and to his throne, as described in *Revelation 12:13,* reference is being made to the new birth initiated by Jesus before his death with a purview, which culminates with the Rapture of his people before Satan comes down in and as the Antichrist for a final and an incontrovertible aggression against the rest of the body of Christ.

Obviously, Satan was powerless in the presence of the woman and could not carry out his initial well-thought-out objective, given the reality of the child that was to be born. The male child is a representation of the entire human race that belongs to God and to his Christ.

However, as *John 10:16* predicted, not all were of the sheepfold that is snatched up to heaven during the Rapture, and the rest must be brought in also so that there may be one flock and one shepherd. For we read in *Revelation 12:17* that the dragon, after the child is snatched up to the throne of God, was enraged at the woman and went off to make war against the rest of her offspring.

So, right away this tells us that the woman here in *Revelation 12,* who gave birth to the male child who was taken up into Heaven, had many other children. *Verse 17* describes the other children of the woman as those left behind after the rapture and who obey God's commandments and hold firm to the testimony of Jesus.

This gives me the opportunity to reiterate a very significant point. By now we all know that Jesus gave birth to the Church, which he refers to as the new birth, and all who receives this spiritual birth form one body and are members one of another representing the whole Church and the entire people of God. Furthermore, in *Ephesians 2:5,* the Apostle Paul teaches that when we receive the new birth, God raises us with Christ and seats us with him in the heavenly realms out of the reach of Satan.

I certainly hope you begin to see the parallelism. The woman having flown to the desert out of the reach of Satan *(Revelation 12:14)* can be rightly compared to Jesus ascension to the highest heaven out of the reach of all principalities and powers *(Ephesians 1:21)*. The Bible clearly indicates that neither the woman nor her child was at the reach of Satan, which infuriates the dragon and incites him to rage war against the other children of the woman.

This is sufficient proof that after the Rapture of the Church, a remnant will be spared by God in keeping with his promise made in *2 Kings 19:30-31*. "The zeal of the Lord will accomplish it, and the rest of the house of Judah will take root below and bear fruit above, and out of Jerusalem will come a remnant, out of mount Zion a band of survivors".

As these points have shown, those who will find themselves in the earth posterior to the Rapture and who do not take the mark of the beast in obedience to the antichrist will constitute a remnant, a band of survivors, the rest of the offspring of the woman described at the end of *Revelation 12*.

As we bridge *Revelation 12* and *13*, one cannot but notice a desperate hopeless dragon, mad as hell, standing on the shore of the sea and about to deploy and display all kind of counterfeit miracles, signs, and wonders that will deceive those who are perishing. The scripture says they will perish because they refused to love the truth and so be saved. For this reason, the Apostle Paul tells us that God sends them this powerful delusion so that they will believe the lie of the evil one and so that all will be condemned who have not believed the truth but have delighted in wickedness **(Thessalonians 2:9).**

CHAPTER 13

The Beast out of the Sea

Before we begin with the enlightenment of *chapter 13,* let me say that by the time *chapter 13* comes on the scene to initiate its episodes, the Church is no longer here. We have flown like eagles to meet the Lord in the air. Nonetheless the most intriguing aspect of this portion of the scripture is that Satan will devolve his authority and power to two individuals whom the Bible refers to as "two beasts," primarily because of their incarnation but coupled with that, their nondepletable strength and the supernatural powers they contemplate.

These two beasts **(the antichrist and the false prophet)** represent evil in its most loftiness. They cannot be destroyed physically even though their physical appearance will have the phenotype of a human being. *Revelation 19:20* tells us that at the onset of the return of Jesus for his thousand-year reign, he will capture the two beasts alive and they **(the two beasts)** will be thrown physically, undeceased, into Hell.

In this chapter we are also faced with a great mystery that no man has been able to decipher to date. This famous number 666 which represents the mark of the beast, the name of the beast or the number of its name, but which also in a better vernacular corresponds to the number of entities (the dragon, the antichrist and the false prophet) working as ONE in accordance with the works of Satan, displaying all sorts of power through lying signs and wonders to deceive those who are perishing.

We are also told in Revelation 13 that the number 666 is the number of a "Man". But "not just any "man" because Isaiah 14 gives us a lofty description of this angel called "Lucifer" who was violently kicked out of heaven after sin was found in him and fell to the earth where he has been reduced to a mere man, But still in possession of angelic powers. Don't be fooled! Both Apostles Paul and John referred to this fallen angel "Satan" as the "Prince" of this world, the "Ruler" of this world, and also the "god" of this world. (2 Corinthians 4:4, John 14:30).

In other words, subsequent to the appearance of sin in Heaven in Lucifer, Sin was given a "Kingdom" by God where Satan reigns as king of the "Abyss".

Beside Lucifer whom the Prophet Isaiah refers to as a "Man" to be regarded as the first six (6), the two other "Men" that will make up the other two (Sixes) 66 are the "Antichrist" and the "False Prophet" who will be raised from the dead and serve as the embodiment for the spirit of the antichrist.

Sadly, most people will shy away from these spiritual truths and ignore the eternal dimension of life or the spirit realm where such works are simply basic, but will unfortunately appear crazy to most carnal mind.

In the spirit, transcending the natural, we know that the physical universe is totally subjugated to the spiritual world and that "one spirit" can operate simultaneously in a multitude of people and that 666 is nothing more than an "evil spirit" operating in three different entities.

REMEMBER, "without me you can do nothing", said the Lord Jesus Christ in John 15:5… Unless it's given from above, no one "visible or invisible" for that matter can do anything. The truth is, these 3 men including Lucifer have had the word of God spoken over their lives that cannot be revoked.

The other fascinating truth is that even as "Men" these two emissaries of Satan can neither be conquered nor killed by any man. They will have at their disposal the very throne of Satan in the conquest of the entire world. They will have power to speak great phenomena into reality by spewing out of their mouths other evil spirits that will perform signs and wonders to deceive many.

The supernaturality of the word of God is the reason why unless a man is born of the Spirit, he cannot understand spiritual things. For they are foolishness to him because only in the Spirit they can be discerned. (1 Corinthians 2:14)

The number 666 undeniably refers to Lucifer as the first six (6) of this mysterious "puzzle". The other two sixes (66) are simply symbolic of the two superhumans of the end time prophecies, reckon up to the 3 major actors that will boggle the mind of the world:

1- **The Devil**

2- **The Antichrist**

3- **The False Prophet**

Beside Lucifer, these two evil spirits will incarnate in two different men and live like any natural human being until Jesus comes and personally puts an end to their existence and casts them directly into "Hell".

Given that dynamic, the casting of these two creatures alive into this place of ultimate torment, will not come as a result of their physical invincibility or corporal inviolability, but because they, the antichrist and the false prophet, had already experienced the first death physically, and as demons whose fate had already been pronounced by God from the beginning, they skip the last judgment and are sent straight to the lake of fire, which is the second death and eternal hell.

If you are surprised about the language and the tone being used here, let me assure you that this mysterious development is far from being metaphorical, and in fact will prove to be, as we get more understanding of the fundamentals of the spirit world, straightforwardly logical.

The personal names they will use have not been revealed, but one hint to look for that will bring them out into the open is their linguistic skills. They will master any and all languages like a native to better inspire the newly enervated world to quickly identify with them and their supposed ideologies. They won't have any legitimate past history that can be authenticated in regards to their line of descent, past youth surroundings, or their formative years.

Now let's try to decipher *Revelation 13* concerning the dragon and the two beasts herein described as the "Ocean Beast" and the "Earth Beast", better known as the Antichrist and the false prophet.

The Ocean Beast

We read that the dragon is standing on the shore of the sea, and from under the ocean came out the first beast, the ocean beast known as the Antichrist. This ocean beast has seven heads and a blasphemous name on each of the heads. He also has ten horns and ten crowns, one on each horn.

As if this fearful description of the ocean beast weren't enough, the Bible further tells us that the background of his compound is like a leopard with feet like those of a bear and a mouth like that of a lion. Moreover, the ocean beast, or the Antichrist, has the power, the authority, and the throne of the dragon at his disposition **(Revelation 13:2)**.

Based on this biblical text, the dragon is obviously a compounded creature convening seven powerful fallen angels or evil spirits in a concerted way, represented by the four great beasts described in Daniel 7:3 that came out of the sea.

The explanation the prophet Daniel received from the angel is that the four beasts are four kings or four kingdoms that will rise from the earth. Again, the preposition "from" used here by the Holy Spirit is an indication that their emanation is from the world under.

Retrospectively we read in *Matthew 4:8* that Satan took Jesus to an unusual **"High Mountain"** and showed him all the kingdoms (plural) of the world and their splendor and said to Jesus, "All this I will give you if you bow and worship me." We are all familiar with the answer Jesus gave him; "God alone is to be worshipped and served".

I hope you don't think that the word "mountain" here is typical of a physical, geographical landform that rises above the surrounding valleys. Mountains, as used in this context, signify extraterrestrial powers, and they should be understood as such when the Apostle Paul in *Philippians 2:10* defines kingdoms as having constituencies in heaven, in the earth, and under the earth.

We all know that kingdoms have kings over them, but when Satan showed Jesus the kingdoms of this world, he certainly was not unfurling the countries known today to be under a monarchy form of government, but rather spiritual forces at the command of the four corners of the earth. The expression "High Mountain" should be interpreted as a "spiritual kingdom" having a powerful fallen angel over it as king, which is a typical place of government where decrees emanate.

The concatenation of these seven kings or these seven powerful angels as the seven heads of the fourth beast also known as the ocean beast, that the prophet Daniel wondered so greatly about because of the enormous power and authority he has over the entire earth, is a clear evidence that the fourth beast herein described as the ocean beast greatly typifies what we now know from *Revelation 13* to be the "spirit of the Antichrist".

Revelation 13 gives us a description of the ocean beast as the embodiment of seven spirits in a concerted way personifying the first three beasts congruent to the ones the prophet Daniel saw in his vision, which were represented by a lion, a bear, and a leopard. The same icons are strangely reiterated here in *Revelation 13:2* to give us the profile of the Antichrist, who obviously looks like a leopard, has feet like those of a bear, and a mouth like that of a lion. **What a coincidence! Or is it?**

We read in verse 3 that one of the heads received a wound that would have been fatal to anybody else, but the Antichrist because of his indestructibleness was on his feet in no time, and the whole world was astonished and received him as their leader.

In *verse 4,* Satan's long treasured dream came true. Satan is worshipped because of the authority he gave to the beast. The beast is also worshipped because of his uniqueness and the fact that no one can make war against him and prevail.

Despite the greatness of the authority of the Antichrist over the whole earth, his days are numbered to only forty-two months or three and a half years according to *Revelation 13:5.* In *verse 7,* we are told the Antichrist made war against the saints and conquered them. Not to be confused with the Church because again the Church is no longer here but reference is being made to the 144,000 saints from the twelve tribes of Israel who had the seal of God on their foreheads as servants of the Most High in *Revelation 7.*

The Antichrist, or the ocean beast, will have authority over every tribe, every people, every language, and every nation. Verse 8 tells us that these are a compilation of the whole world and all its inhabitants, whose names have not been written in the Book of Life belonging to the Lamb that was slain from the Creation of the world. They all will worship the beast.

But there is still hope for those who will have missed the rapture, such as we read in *Revelation 14:12-13* which confirms that salvation is still open to those who will be left behind. However, those who find themselves in the earth beyond the Rapture and want to be saved will have to relinquish to captivity with faithfulness and endurance and be killed.

The Beast out of the Earth

The Apostle John tells us in *Revelation 13:11* that he saw another beast. But this second beast came out of the earth and has two horns like a lamb but speaks like a dragon. Tremendous attributions are associated with his prerogative as power is given to him to exercise the authority of the first beast on his behalf.

- The earth beast has power to make all the inhabitants of the earth to worship the first beast.

- He has power to cause fire to come down from heaven.

- He has power to give life to statutes.

- He has power to have all who refuse to worship the statute killed.

- He also has power to force everyone, small and great, rich and poor, free and slave, to receive a mark on his or her right hand or his or her forehead so that no one could buy or sell unless he has the mark, which is the name of the first beast or the number of his name.

I think enough is said here to incite all of us to step out of our comfort zone and take a moment to examine the universal trauma awaiting us that will decide the fate of the entire world.

This may sound like a joke, and I will admit it does sound like a joke when you consider all those industrialized and powerful nations and probably with the United States on top of the list, but I tell you the truth, as much as the prospect of having to face the end of times may seem an impossibility, we will witness science and technology and all that men have created become vanity right before our very eyes. This pulverization will create a worldwide panic starting with those very formidable nations, which will exacerbate the rest of the world purportedly until a global capitulation is reached.

Perhaps you ask, "How can these things be?" Well, since this man named Jesus came on the scene a little over two thousand years ago, died, and then rose from the dead, the world has openly become more supernatural than we dare contemplate. Both religion and politics at certain levels are very well aware of the invisible world and have become so scared of the spiritual reality that they have chosen to be confluent with evil spirits in exchange for wealth and human knowledge.

Most of the world have and must continue to conform to certain attitudes and influence as agreed with the forces of evil and must infringe the four corners of the earth, imposing a degrading spirit on all nations and, in the most hegemonic way, bring all people to a heinous conformation with an ineluctable outcome of total dejection.

What is going on in the world today has nothing to do with how rich or powerful a nation is. *Isaiah 40:17* puts it this way, "Before God all the nations are regarded as worthless and less than nothing." At best we are helping those fallen angels in the accomplishment of their evil deeds by creating and using our weaponry and other technologies to kill one another in absolute fulfillment of their wicked agenda.

The truth is our best armaments or artilleries are useless against the invisible mind-boggling forces of demons. The Apostle Paul made it clear in *Ephesians 6:12* that our battle is not against one another but against wicked spirits in the heavenly places. Therefore, it is critical that we understand the seriousness of the end times and the idiosyncrasy of the spiritual nature in which we live and consider with great curiosity how things are progressing in the world going from desperation to despicability, substantiating that evil wicked spirits are behind the scenes and avoid any mocking of the word of God, which is the only hope for humanity.

Philippians 2:10 teaches that at the name of Jesus, every knee of all that is in heaven, all that is on the earth, and all that is under the earth will bow. The latter, speaking of which (under the earth), is where the two beasts (the ocean beast and the earth beast), better known as the Antichrist and the false prophet, will emanate from.

One of the major objections of the Jews, who did not believe that Jesus was the Messiah or the Christ, despite his great wisdom and his miraculous signs and wonders, was the fact that people were cognizant of his parents and the place of his birth.

Because of their unbelief, *John 7:27* teaches that God made them prophesy that when the "Christ" comes (the false one) no one will know where he is from, not knowing they were prophesying about the appearance of the Antichrist, whom now we know is emerging from the world under. The place the bible refers to as the "Abyss", where Lucifer has his literal throne, and which is also the place where he and his angels precisely fell to following the war in heaven. As one can see this story accords with the deep doctrine of the scripture at the spiritual level as we are undeniably faced here with metaphysical elements that will play a major role in the end-time events when these two beasts incarnate.

The question is, if both beasts **(the Antichrist and the false prophet)** are coming up from the world under, why then the absolute distinction that one is specifically coming up from under the ocean whereas the other up from under the ground or out of the earth?

The answer I got from the spirit of Christ is that for the sake of revelation and knowledge, God in his eternal wisdom is making a distinction between two distinct eras:

1- **The ancient or the pre-deluge civilization from Adam to the flood of Noah.**

2- **The present or post-deluge world as we know it.**

In *Genesis 5:28,* at the time of Noah's birth, 600 years before the flood came, Lamech, the father of Noah, prophesied that God had judged and cursed the earth and that his newborn son Noah will be the one through whom God will bring comfort to the world. In view of the importance of that era in the end times and as strange as it may seem, *Revelation 20:13* reads that the sea will give up the dead that are in it. By the way, please do not think the Bible is referring to people who perished at seas and whose bodies were never found either when ships sink or airplanes crash into the ocean. I don't want to be rude, but it is absolute nonsense!

But bear with me. According to *Genesis 1:9,* (which is obviously before the flood), all the oceans were in one place, and there was a single landmass or the existence of only one continent. Then the flood came and covered the entire earth. The entire civilization was under water.

We are told in *Genesis 11:1* that the whole earth had one language and a common speech, which confirms intellectually the proximity, the cohesiveness of the pre-deluge population of the world and their co-extension.

However, according to Genesis 6, when the Lord saw how great man's wickedness on the earth had become and that every inclination of the thoughts of his heart was only evil all the time, he said to Noah in *verse 13,* "I am surely going to destroy and put an end to both all people and the earth."

So, you see, the passage clearly states that the earth was also destroyed in the process. While the flood covered the entire earth killing all men and all other living creatures, it is a known fact according to the scripture that the earth itself was destroyed.

Consequently, after the flood and for the very first time, starting with *Genesis 10:5,* the Bible begins to refer to different islands, different nations of the world which can only mean that when God put an end to the first civilization because of the wickedness of humankind, Noah and his family started out anew on fresh and provisorily sin-free land.

Multiple islands, big and small, that we today refer to as continents, emerged consequently according to the will of God.

The ancient world, or the pre-deluge civilization, is still under the cursed waters and will so remain until the return of Christ. The multitude that was judged by God and covered by the flood of Noah including those who had died going back to Adam, are considered the "dead of the sea." Today as I speak, the victims of the flood are still under the curse of that flood that came upon the earth. Thus under the "Sea".

Interestingly, death and Hades are not the localization of their souls, but the ocean, which came as a result of the judgment of God himself, is considered a separate entity that must give up the dead that are under its authority to be thrown into the lake of fire.

Contrariwise, on our side of the flood starting with Noah to the present, all who die whether on dry land or in waters are considered the "dead of the earth" and are placed under the authority of "death and Hades" with the exception of those who die in Christ, whose souls and spirits in total unison are immediately received and comforted by Christ himself in Heaven.

These two spirits, "death and Hades" that constitute with others the seven heads of the Antichrist, will take on human forms and subdue the whole world. Yes! Including all the great superpowers you can name. As a matter of fact, things will get so exceptionally supernatural that the powerful nations will capitulate first. I suppose they already have in many aspects, but that's another story.

In view of the importance of the spiritual juncture of the end times, let me say that these creatures, contrary to the general belief, will be nothing like we have seen or heard.

Demon possessions throughout history portend to what could be expected at any moment, but despite the prevalence of such supernaturalism, people have not seriously considered this phenomenon for what it's worth.

Not only do we know, as taught in the scripture, that people who are possessed by demons are subject to death, but it is also known that any malevolent preternatural being that takes control of an individual can be forced to exorcise and leave the victim.

But what is very intriguing concerning the two beasts is the fact that the Bible unequivocally teaches that mortality is ineffectual in regards to the Antichrist and the false prophet, thus making their bodies and spirits as if they were of the same essence or inseparable entities.

Throughout the New Testament, we have several instances where Jesus and his disciples drove out demons from their victims. But here in the book of Revelation, the Antichrist and the false prophet are presented as beyond physical destruction by nature, which obviously makes them nonhuman or of preternatural origin. This is foretold by God himself in *Genesis 3:14-15,* when God cursed the devil and declared a perennial enmity between the children of the devil and those of the woman.

In *Galatians 3:16-19,* the Apostle Paul tells us that Eve's offspring mentioned in *Genesis 3:14-15* is the Lord Jesus Christ himself against whom the children of Satan will collide.

With this sort of interpretation, who are the offspring of Satan? Most candid theologians, totally ignoring the entrapment, will probably concede to the theory of fallen angels, demons, or perhaps wicked individuals in connection with evil spirits. What we know for a fact is that throughout history, traditional or contemporaneous, atrocious individuals or wicked nations have always emerged, but none with suitability to be called "sons of the devil."

The biblical principle of "sonship" confirms that all who accept Christ as their savior are "sons of God", in contrast, all who reject Christ are referred to as "sons of the devil." But that's not what we're talking about here.

When you revert to the reality of biblical truth, like God who, despite the existence of a multitude of angels and humanity as a whole, considers himself having one single, unique child in the person of Jesus Christ, the devil also, despite all the obnoxious evil deeds the world has known since the beginning of time under successively wicked generations of leaders and all the demon possessions as his subordinates, has according to the scripture explicitly two sons.

These two sons are identified specifically as Cain, the son of Adam and Eve, and Judas Iscariot, which is found respectively in *1 John 3:12* and *John 17:12.* You might say, "Wait a minute, both Cain and Judas had natural parents physically." Well! So, did the Lord Jesus Christ physically from the Virgin Mary, so to speak.

In the spiritual sense however, both Cain and Judas are true personifications of the devil. They were not simply possessed by Satan as in demon possession, but they truly possessed the spirit of the devil as undivided breeder.

Concerning Judas Iscariot particularly, *Luke 22:3-6* tells us that on the night of the supper, Satan entered Judas, and Judas went away and conferred with the chief priests and other officers how he might betray Jesus to them in return for money. He is described by the Apostle John as an unrepentant thief *(John 12:6)*. But despite his lucre, Judas ironically had the same authority and power the other eleven apostles had (casting out demons, healing the sick, raising the dead, and so forth). We would not be wrong to think of Judas as a ticking time bomb that can't be defused, which was placed by Satan and approved by God, in the entourage of Jesus as the devil's artifice.

The word of God is clear that Judas had been walking in line with Satan all along and had reached the divine set time when Satan, as his commander, simply entered him and ordered that it is time to act.

Saint Jude is clear that evil spirits cannot be saved, whether you choose to call them "fallen angels" or "demons." In fact, Jesus tells us in *Matthew 25:41* that hell was created for them. And one would assume that Jesus, who created the angels that have become part of the demonic squadron, knows what he is talking about when he declares plainly in *John 6:70* that **Judas Iscariot is a "demon."**

Habitually, Jesus and his disciples would cast out demons and free their victims. But the emulsification of Judas by Satan was particularly intertwined with a specific mission of reassuring the emulation of Jesus by the evil one, and Judas, in total compliance, seemed to have had full knowledge of the facts and issues involved. This rendered all possibilities of exorcism null.

Anyone who has come to know Christ and the way of righteousness and turn back on the sacred command that was passed on to him is described in *2 Peter 22* as "a dog that returns to his vomit or a swine that is washed and then goes back to her wallowing in the mud". Such a person cannot be saved according to the scripture.

Besides, the insight concerning his death is proof that Judas was a "temple of the evil one." I think most people miss the spiritual significance of the passage in *Acts 1:18,* where Luke as a physician describes the gruesome physical damage sustained by Judas preceding his death as Satan forsook him before killing him.

I know it is very tempting to reverse the trend as it would make more sense to our natural mind that Judas first hung himself, and as he decayed, the integrity of his skin became compromised and because he was hung on a tree, most likely he fell off and burst out open spilling out his internal organs. **In the natural, this explanation certainly prevails.**

But this is pure verbiage, ignoring the real power of the supernatural surrounding us. It is true that any dead person left unburied will in no time become bloated to a degree as the first step in a series of events, and as a consequence, the body will most likely burst from the internal pressure.

But the explosion itself is not strong enough to exude violently the internal organs as described in Judas case by Doctor Luke, who is a physician. Besides, I don't think this detail of Judas organs oozing out was put in the Bible to uniquely make us want to puke.

A person's natural spirit is the breath of life from God which gives life to the physical body. Until this natural spirit exits the body, death is powerless. The body can sustain remarkable damage, physical and emotional, to the point where a coma may even result from such trauma, but the victim's coronary arteries will most certainly allow a pulse to be detected.

All esoterica aside, the snares of the devil and his power are not to be taken lightly, leaving yourself vulnerable to common satanic attacks. *Hebrews 1:7* teaches that angels are spirit beings, but because sin was found in the angelic community in heaven, God separated the angelic beings into two categories:

1- **The angels that remained faithful to God, are called "holy angels."**

2- **The angels that betrayed God, are called "devils."**

In the scripture, the angels who did not maintain their holiness are also designated as **"evil spirits or demons"**. *Ephesians 2:1-2* tells us that Satan is a spirit, and according to *Mathew 8:16,* all demons are spirits.

Of the appellative concordance there is no doubt that evil spirits, devils, and demons are one and the same.

Let us consider a few supporting texts in the Bible that confirm the coalescence of the most famous title given to the defected angels.

First, we will look at Satan himself, who is referred to in *Revelation 12:9* as the serpent, the dragon, the great dragon, and the devil. We already learned from *Ephesians 6:12* that Satan is an evil spirit, which makes him definitely an angel. It is also taught in both *Mathew 12:24* and *Ephesians 2:2* that Satan is the king of the kingdom of darkness and the ruler of all evil spirits.

Consider this! If Satan, who is the ruler of the fallen angels, can enter Judas Iscariot and demonize him not only to have Jesus killed but to proceed to take his own life, don't believe for one minute that demon possession is a remote undertaking reserved for a special category of spirits. In Mark 5:1-15, we read of a man with an evil spirit who lived in the tombs. When Jesus asked him what his name was, the evil spirit answered "legion" because the number of demons that had taken residence in this man were about two thousand. In verse 12, the Bible, now referring to them as "devils," teaches that they implored Jesus to send them into the swine. So here is proof that fallen angels are evil spirits, and evil spirits are demons.

Now let's look at another text. In Luke 4:33, we read, "In the synagogue there was a man possessed by a demon, an evil spirit." There you have it again, demons are evil spirits.

In *Mathew 12:22-36,* Jesus met a demon-possessed man who was blind and mute. After Jesus healed him, the man's speech and vision were restored. But what's impressive about the casting out of this demon is that in verse 26 Jesus refers to this demon as Satan himself. This is proof that the pervasive power of the spirit world to overtake humans should not be categorized or limited to a particular breed of demons, as if it were not an altruistic phenomenon.

The spiritual amenities associated with this preternatural malevolence are at the disposal of any and all evil spirits for their own well-being. But it is also true that, according to *Ephesians 6:12,* the spirit world is highly organized and divided into ranks, and it may be that certain attributions are assigned to different positions as orderly arranged. Those attributions remain spiritually universal when and as needed, as the evidence of the supporting texts above suggests.

When I hear people say in total ignorance and sometimes in pitiful disdain that Satan cannot do this, Satan cannot do that, I shake my head heartbreakingly, because *Matthew 24:24* is clear that Satan is capable of performing great miracles, signs, and wonders in so much as to mislead and deceive even the elect, **(God's chosen people)** if it were possible.

I am fully aware of the bitterness anent the reality of Satan and his angels. But the truth is the truth, and believe it or not, an insightful astuteness of his relentless malevolent activities can only benefit the true believer in Christ as a definite respite, and as Jesus says in *John 8:31-32,* "When you know the truth, the truth will set you free."

When an evil spirit enters a person there is no assuagement, the demon controls to the degree he wishes **(as allowed by God)** the whole person, "body, soul, and spirit". Unless the demon is cast out, he dwells permanently in the person until death do them part. If the evil spirit is a generational demon on a contract with his ancestors, as the possessed person's death is nearing, the demon gushes out and enters the next of kin prepared for that purpose, generation after generation, successively.

Demon possession affects people in different cultures in varied ways. The methods employed by those fallen angels in certain countries are perhaps more commonly accepted by the people of that particular culture. But don't be fooled! Their evil ways are extremely manifold, and the same destructive effect will result from a totally different spell tailor-made just for that particular belief system. One culture will mock the spiritual practice of another while the one they are accustomed to will lead to the same spiritual devastation.

I guess what I am trying to say is that Satanic methodology employed by evil spirits **(whether it be magic, hatred, lies, idolatry, racism, sex, drugs, guns, or wars)** should not be attributed or limited to any particular culture or better yet its power underestimated.

Let me stop right here with this demonology because the world of demons is neither the object nor the subject of this book, but I hope these few words are taken as an expository endowment to help you understand the mysterious nature and the seriousness of the time we live in as wicked spirits, and by that I mean satanic angels, embark on their ultimate mission to bring about a one world government under the sole leadership rule of the Antichrist as they are fervently working behind all the current policies being implemented in the world today.

It's all spiritual! In our everyday consciousness, spirituality as an innate subsidy influences us so deeply that the implication and the imponderability of life and death are always at the center of our struggle. Death is taught in *Hebrews 9:27* as an event that will occur once, and after that, we will face judgment. But strangely enough, both in the Old and the New Testaments we have had people raised from the dead to die again later. Elijah in *1 Kings 17:20-22* raised the son of Zarephath. In *2 Kings 4:32-36* he raised the son of Shunammite. Closer to us in the New Testament, raising the dead was a commonality for our Lord Jesus Christ and his disciples. All these folks that were raised from the dead died twice.

Is this a clear contradiction of the word of God? God forbids! In *Romans 3:4,* the Apostle Paul says, "Let God be True and every man a Liar." Like Pontius Pilate in *John 18:38,* you might wonder and ask: "What is truth?" Well, I tell you! Truth is a priori absolute and must prove beyond any shadow of a doubt to be universally valid.

As a matter of fact, the best analogy of the characteristic of truth is found in *James 2:10,* where the word of God teaches that even if one keeps the whole law yet fails in a tiny point, he is guilty of breaking the whole law.

So, you see, truth is either absolute or it is not truth at all. If what we hold as truth fails to maintain a limpid trueness at any point or at any time throughout the scripture from Genesis to Revelation, it is a false truth and therefore a deceiving lie. This false truth must be rejected and replaced by a valid truth, which sometimes cannot be discerned or perceived but can only be revealed.

Furthermore, all theologians will agree that truth is somewhat a mystery, which is the very essence of theology. But what they sometimes don't agree on is that the whole mystery of God is epitomized, as taught in *Colossians 1:26-27* and *Matthew 13:11,* in the Lord Jesus Christ.

Now, let's go a little deeper. The word of God clearly affirms that God will not contradict himself or violate his word. We have read just a few paragraphs earlier that according to the scripture, it is appointed unto men to die once and after that, the judgment. We have also read that people were raised from the dead and obviously died later a second time. These two statements are definitely irreconcilable and therefore irrespective to physical death as common to all.

In the spirit, however, one can effectively impugn the widely accepted definition of death with the appropriate connotation anent God's view of its true spiritual meaning.

As taught in the scripture, "physical birth" translates "death," and "physical death" is associated with somnolence."

In other words, God does not consider any person outside of Christ, from the womb to the last breath, to be alive. As a matter of truth, we are sent in the womb to be born as humans only after we died in the esoteric dimension of living souls. We were dead before conception in the womb and remain as such throughout our journey in the earth until and only if the Holy Spirit, be it the will of God, comes and quickens us. **(1 John 3:14)**

The meta-historicity of those who were raised from the dead and continued to live normal lives as human beings is a clear forewarning that the dead not only can be brought back from the dead, but most significantly, the spiritual factor to acknowledge is that the traditional understanding that man is appointed to die once then after that the judgment" is not at all referring to physical death as these evidences hold true. All things considered, the goal of these resurrections or revitalizations is to incite a deeper understanding beyond what a hasty skimming over the passages would simply allow, which can propitiously be a very impressionable foreshadowing of the supernatural events to come.

The temporary allotment by God of certain miracles, signs, and wonders that Satan will perform through the Antichrist and the false prophet to deceive those who reject Christ springs forth with Satan himself, as we read in *Revelation 13,* standing on the shore of the sea and raising from the dead both of them.

The Antichrist, known as the "ocean beast," will personify the angel of death, who rode the pale horse at the opening of the fourth seal. The scenery of the angel of Hades following closely behind the angel of death in *Revelation 6:7* is duplicated here in *Revelation 13* as the false prophet, known as the "earth beast," who will embody the angel of Hades that comes out of the earth immediately following the appearance of the Antichrist.

It is also very interesting to note that as soon as death and Hades incarnate and become human beings, this composite creature with seven heads called the Dragon will hand over his power and his throne to both beasts to use as they wish, to perform signs, wonders, and miracles.

A statue will be erected in honor of the Antichrist, whose head was fatally wounded but horrifically came back to life. The false prophet will be given power to breathe life into the statue, and the statue will become a living entity.

The first beast will make war against the saints and will conquer them. All people, all languages, all nations whose names have not been written in the Book of Life will worship the first beast. The scripture is clear that all who refuse to worship the statue will be killed.

Everyone is also forced to receive a mark on their right hand or on their forehead so that no one could buy or sell unless they had the mark, which is the name of the beast or the number of his name, which is 666.

I know this type of religious philosophy is unimaginable, and perhaps most people will shake their heads in total disbelief, and others in absolute complacency will disdainfully question the validity of these supernatural phenomena that can neither be stopped nor prevented.

The abnormal reluctances, especially in the Western world, concerning the supernatural can be regarded typically as the result of cultural brainwash, which by no means should be some sort of absolver to the truth of the global **(material and spiritual)** collapse to come as a consequence of the appearance of the two beasts.

The sad truth is that the subtle pervasion of Satan in world affairs from the Garden of Eden and throughout the history of the earth will now take a visible dimension with these two creatures, namely the Antichrist and the false prophet, who are nothing more and nothing less than two ghosts appearing real.

These two folks were at one time alive in the earth. They knew death and were buried as any normal human being. But power will be given to Satan by God to resurrect them from the dead to embody the spirit of death and the spirit of Hades, giving them a human appearance. These two are not just any ghost. They were forthrightly influenced by the power of Satan in the past when they were alive, and they abode delightfully and willfully in the spirit of Satan proving indisputably by their wicked actions to be extraordinarily treacherous to the God of Abraham, Isaac, and Jacob. It is very important to understand with a clear mind that the Antichrist and the false prophet, as taught in the scripture, will be raised from the dead. You may be surprised to see the reason for that is overly simple. A number of passages such as *Romans 14:9, Romans 15:4, 2 Timothy 3:16,* and others, will enhance certain distinctive characteristics in conjunction with these supernatural expectancies.

The Apostle Paul tells us in *Romans 14:9* that Jesus, the King of kings and Lord of lords, died and returned to life in order to be lord of both the dead and the living.

This affirmation from Paul suggests that at every dimension of existence, starting with the notion of pre-mortality in the Garden, where all men lived with God before their earthly transmutation as human beings, God has put on himself different garments suitable for each variance of existence to partake insightfully in their very nature in order to be God of all and maintain his sovereignty over the entire human protocol.

This principle set forth by the Apostle Paul is the bedrock doctrine that is fundamental in determining basic requirements of all dominations. Spiritually speaking, the general rule of thumb is that, in order to exercise power and authority over any social stratum, the ruling party must be of the same ingredient as the indigenes, evidently with unrivalled and superior insights.

One must be careful not to approach these mysteries with the natural mind as this guideline described by the Apostle Paul greatly minimizes the potential of misinterpretation concerning those metaphorical phenomena to come.

There are no alternatives. God in Jesus Christ:

- **Became man in order to have dominion and authority over all men.**

- **Became sin in order to have dominion over evil.**

- **Knew death in order to have dominion over the dead.**

- **Descended to hell in order to have dominion over hell and Hades.**

- **Returned to life in a special breed of spirits in order to have dominion over that dimension of spirits men will become.**

The Bible teaches that Jesus as a man had limited power and limited knowledge; in spite of this fact, he could heal the sick, cast out demons, raise the dead, and walk on water. However, the Bible also tells us that Jesus before he became man chose what power and knowledge he would have as a man, because no human being in his natural countenance has the capacity for containing the extraordinary power of spirits, good or evil, let alone the inexhaustible power and complexion of the God Almighty.

Only after his resurrection, when he became the spirit, did Jesus without a remainder have the potential to accommodate within his being the three essential divine qualities, omnipresence, omniscience, and omnipotence, which are solely the attainments of God the Creator, the supremeness of all spirit beings.

Until you grasp thoroughly the difference between the spiritual and the physical and the concept associated with each respectively, the irksome mystery of Revelation 13, where the dragon, a composite creature representing seven powerful wicked angles, gives his power, his authority, and even his throne to the Antichrist, will remain a great enigma that defies all rationalities.

My point is this! To think that a natural man, born of a woman, could supplant this angel of light called Satan, a cherub who was present when God created the physical universe, and exercise his power and authority, and sit on his throne in the earth, you have got another think coming. This general misinterpretation is very misleading and will restrain from attaining the truth that simply lies outside of the natural senses of the world.

These traits, when considered scrupulously, are but celestial, and the works associated with them can only be performed in the spirit and only by spirits. Even for a Christian to perform the miracles of Jesus, he must be in the spirit, meaning that the spirit must be "on him," not "in him," in order for the spirit to work through him. Though we have not seen such wonders since the apostles in the first century, as Apostles Peter, James, and John went from mere spectators to the vested position of privileged witnesses of all the works of Christ and were given to perform them as well, this esoteric miracle power is in the horizon and will soon manifest again in these last days.

According to John 5:19, Jesus, in all that he did, only replicates what was done in the spirit in heaven by the Father, making the invisible visible. He did nothing of his own will.

It became evident that Jesus chose Peter, James, and John and favored them to be constantly in his presence and instilled in them spiritual insights that others did not have.

As Peter, James, and John have witnessed firsthand all that pertain to the true nature of Christ and his power and were given supernatural propensity by the Creator to duplicate all the great miracles and wonders of Christ, all the more reason not to underestimate the power potential of Satan among other angels who witnessed firsthand the creation of the physical universe (Job 38:7-8). We know from Romans 11:9 that the calling and the gifts of God are without repentance. Therefore, it is conclusive to say that when Satan and his angels fell from heaven to the earth, they fell with deep heavenly secrets and supernatural powers that are only subject to spirits.

It naturally follows that in order for Satan to transfer his throne and everything associated with it to the Antichrist and the false prophet, one crucial requisite is for them to be brought back from the dead as coming out of the earth, and only as spirits will they be capacitated and duly empowered with the supernatural capabilities of the dragon.

The same expression, "Coming out of the earth," was used in the Old Testament involving a scenario where a deceased person was brought back from the dead after being buried *(1 Samuel 28:10-15)*. The Apostle Paul in *Romans 15:4* teaches that everything that was written in the past was written for our instruction, and in *2 Timothy 3:16*, we are told that all scripture is God's breathed and is profitable for teaching, rebuking, correcting, and doctrine.

The example from *1 Samuel 28* that is the equivalent of *Revelation 13* regarding the expression "Coming out of the earth" involved the Prophet Samuel, who had died and was buried; a woman who was only a medium brought him back from the dead. The fascinating thing is that even as a dead man, Samuel still possessed all his prophetic abilities.

According to *1 Samuel 28:11*, the woman seemed to have power over any dead. But the most profound issue is: If people who are simply human beings, by invoking Satan, can bring back from the dead a prophet of God, imagine what Satan himself can do.

Let's look at a little bit of the story together involving the woman and King Saul.

Woman "Woman shall I bring up for you?"

Saul "Bring up Samuel the prophet."

As the procedure is engaged, the woman cried out at the top of her voice and King Saul said to her, "What do you see? The woman answered, "I see a spirit coming out of the earth," which is the same exact expression used by John in *Revelation 13:11* when he says that he sees, "A beast coming out of the earth."

If in *1 Samuel 28* the expression "Coming out of the earth" denotes bringing the spirit of a dead man back into this physical realm, the same expression, "Coming out of the earth," used by John in *Revelation 13:11* certainly has the same connotation. The two expressions are not only verbatim, they are equivalent and dealing with the spirit and the soul of the dead.

Samuel, who was a prophet of the true God before he died, was able to maintain and exercise his prophetic aptitudes as a spirit even after he was brought back from the dead, so to speak. It is therefore clear that death does not relieve a prophet of his prophetic faculties. In addition, this also confirms Paul's teaching in *Romans 11:29* that the gifts of God and his calling are irrevocable.

Essentially, death in the physical sense is the end of all human wisdom. The cemetery is totally dead in every sense of the world, and nothing is necessary there. Dead is dead, physically speaking.

In the spirit, however, the truth is at death, depending on the ultimate fate of a person, the deceased is instantaneously and invisibly disintegrated into a combination of two natures, resulting from the three substances, spirit, soul, and body, which were the essential composition of our physical earthly existence as human beings.

The spirit, soul, and body in a combined alliance gave man his whole existence at conception, but at death a regressive process takes place, breaking up the original yoke of the three substances as their agreeable convenances become obsolete and revert each element back to its original place of inception.

Since the spirit and the soul are an impregnable coalescence that can only be divided by Jesus himself, at such time, as taught in *Hebrews 4:12,* the word of God which is the only power sharper than any double-edged sword that can divide the soul and the spirit intervenes during the entracte between the last breath and eternity to separate as necessary the body, the soul, and the spirit.

This spiritual disintegration always results in a combination of only two entities. The soul will either partner with the body or with the spirit, according to the will of God.

At death, all spirits, good and evil, return to God, who owns them. If a person is saved, at death his spirit and soul as one unit is instantaneously taken into the presence of God. His physical body returns to its original clay state, totally deprived of thoughts and knowledge and unconscious of any surroundings such as time and space.

Saved= body (versus) soul and spirit.

Unsaved = Body and soul (versus) spirit.

When the unsaved dies, a dividing of the soul and the spirit occurs. The spirit returns to God, who gave it (Ecclesiastes 12:7), and the soul and the body in a mysterious unison descends to this place of torment under the control of death and Hades.

This is another way of saying that the mysterious power of Satan is extremely complex, far more complex than we have yet imagined. The tentative nature of Satan's attack against Adam and Eve in the Garden can be confusing and the magnitude of what actually happened, underestimated. One way to evaluate the relative power of Satan is to consider the intriguing homology of the two Sons of God, the first Adam and the second Adam, in the person of the Lord Jesus Christ.

This crucial observation may share some evidence of the extent of the power acquired by the defrauder, Satan. For instance, the simple fact that the Lord Jesus Christ is referred to in *1 Corinthians 15:45* as the second Adam makes in inferential comparisons the configuration of the first Adam as significant with similar engrossment of powerful spiritual components equaled to those found in the humanity of Christ. Christ the second Adam being king, obviously makes the first Adam as described in Genesis having dominion over all that God created, also a king.

Though Satan has to some degree achieved his purpose, **having contemplated the monarchy symbolized by the first Adam and succeeded in overthrowing him and becoming his replacement as king over the most cherished kingdom that God the Creator had put in place, in so much that he has also become a source of wonderment for the angels under his command,** little did he know that his foolish undertaking would be a spiritual disaster that would bring death and give death a rich harvest even among the angels.

His multidimensional provisory kingdom, which is both physical and spiritual, includes on the one hand the visible world in all of its aspects: social, political, economic, and above all, religious, with all men from conception to the last breath totally subjugated to his clever ruse. And on the other hand, the extent of his kingdom includes a certain dimension of the invisible world, the world of dark and wicked spirits, where death reigns even decrepitly.

Before the death and resurrection of Jesus, all who died descended body and soul as taught in the scripture into one of the two sections of Hades. One section of Hades is a place of torment where the unsaved went and still go today, and the other section is referred to in the Bible as Abraham's bosom, where the saved used to go. This section of Hades involving the people of God has since the resurrection of Christ been transported to heaven.

Unfortunately, the contriver still remains in control of the souls that are in his prison. Like I said earlier, the incantation procedure of the medium woman proves a heart-stopping truth that Satan has extensive power over the dead, whose souls are within his jurisdiction. But let it be known also that the mind of a dead person is totally denatured and cannot be renewed. Nor is apprenticeship a commonality in Hades.

Therefore, it would be absolutely preposterous for Satan to bring a person back from the dead to be nothing more than a purposeless zombie in the world unless a word from God, which is eternal or multidimensional, was spoken over this person's life when he was alive. Every day, nevertheless, people on the breathing side of the grave are insidiously demonized by fallen angels left and right through some sort of bondage totally deluding as a self- aggrandizement. But that's totally another story.

Fortunately, Satan cannot freely take a stance to do as he wishes with the living outside of his reach. He must purportedly resolute his intention and solicit the necessary potentiality from God to carry out his deeds. As in the example of Job, he can only operate within the scope of the command given him as he receives the word of God. The word spoken by God is eternal and obviously encompasses the physical universe. The Apostle Paul tells us that neither principalities, nor powers, nor angels, nor demons, nor death can separate us from the love, the word, and the power of God.

When God releases a word over a prophet, every level of existential contingency is dealt with to perpetuate the life and the nature of the prophet, even at the metaphysical level, like we saw with Abel, the very first prophet of God, the second son of Adam. Though Abel was dead, killed by his brother Cain, he was able to communicate with God through his soul by crying out to God from the ground even as a dead man *(Genesis 4:10)*.

The extant characteristic of the gifts and calling of God results solely from God himself personally speaking or making a decree over someone's life without intermediary. Though sometimes we see the responsibility of the initiative given to his prophets, but at the appropriate time God will personally jump in with the necessary gifts and nudge his supernatural power over the recipient's life with an eternal seal.

As a supplementary remark, going back to the power of Satan over the dead in his kingdom, a distinction must be made between the prophets of God, who had the gifts and the calling of God over their lives but who are no longer within the reach of Satan for having been translated into heaven at the resurrection of Christ, and the others (only two are mentioned in the entire Bible) who had a physical encounter with God and were distrustfully but purposely empowered as prospective pioneers to coexist as future connivers of Satan in his ultimate abetment against Christ and his followers.

When Satan, a spirit being, had the green light from God concerning Job, he struck everything Job had. In fact, the Bible says that in just one day, or within a twenty-four-hour period, Job lost all his oxen, donkeys, sheep, and camels.

Paradoxically, in *verse 16 of Job 1,* we read that Satan called the fire of God down from heaven and killed the sheep and the servants of Job. In verse 18 we read that Satan commanded a strong whirlwind to strike the house where Job's sons and daughters were feasting and killed them all.

Despite the simultaneous deaths of Job's ten children, Satan, who was still not satisfied with the results, Job being the principal target of his focus, returned to God in great defiance for a second round of authorization but this time against Job's personal health, which he obtained favorably from God.

In *verse 7,* we read that Satan went out from the presence of God and afflicted Job with painful sores from the soles of his feet to the top of his head in combination with multifaceted symptoms such as nightmares, fever, bad breath, and pain day and night and also making sure that Job was totally neglected by his wife, family, and friends.

I hope you found this predicament very irrational, because it is. No matter what stance you take, the story of Job and the one earlier regarding the prophet Samuel should have in some way influenced your perception of Satan and compelled you to recognize his potency in both the physical and the spiritual worlds, over both the living and the dead.

The sad truth is that it seems that outside the power of creation, which is a glory God does not share with anyone, the omnifarious extent of the power of Satan goes beyond our imagination, given this evidence of an indisputable interaction between God and Satan.

The correlation is a mysterious one. As repugnant as this may sound, this does not absolve the fact that the first four seals that were opened in *Revelation 6* by the Lord Jesus Christ himself gave Satan precisely the necessary authority and power to perform supernatural signs and miracles as part of the deceptions of the last days.

The Apostle Paul tells us in *2 Thessalonians 2: 11-12* that in the last days, those who do not believe in the Lord Jesus Christ will be encrusted with a powerful delusion sent by God himself to believe the lying miracles, signs, and wonders of Satan that he will perform through the Antichrist and the false prophet.

One significant aspect of Satan's lies is that he will claim to be God. But for the world to buy into this utmost deception of Satan, he will have to prove himself wiser and more knowledgeable than Jesus by certainly surpassing the miracles, signs, and wonders that Jesus performed as a man.

These include, naming just a few:

1. **Feeding the multitudes miraculously.**

2. **Healing the sick.**

3. **Healing the limbs.**

4. **Casting out demons.**

5. **Commanding nature—rain, wind, lightning, the ocean, and so forth.**

6. **Raising the dead as in the example of Lazarus, who was dead and buried for four days.**

Simply on the basis of this relativity, discarding the fact that Satan has been or will be given the necessary power to resurrect the Antichrist and the false prophet, is not only uncongenial but lacking spiritual maturity.

Avowedly, in spite of all the literatures concerning the Antichrist and the false prophet, the essential that is generally considered mind- boggling is the identity of these two creatures.

Based on biblical evidences, as I already explained, the only two people that are respectively qualified to be the Antichrist and the false prophet are Cain, the son of Adam, and Judas Iscariot, one of the apostles of Christ.

The question is, why Judas of all men? The answer is simple, Judas is the only person in the entire scripture or outside of the scripture for that matter, since Adam, dead or alive, qualified to be the false prophet; which brings up the following questions that I will now proceed to consider.

What are the describing characteristics that depict the falsehood of a prophet?

In general, when people are asked about the nature of a true prophet, the first attribute that comes to mind is one of being able to foretell the future with specificity. Although this attributional image of the marksmanship of a true prophet is correct, the genuine recognition of this special man of God should not be based solely on these tangible ascriptions.

True prophetic workmanships go beyond the scrupulous outcome of his foreknowledge, to include God at the center of his clairvoyance, by preaching to the people repentance and obedience to Christ, and to forsake all evil ways, especially going after other gods to serve them.

A reasonable question at this point might be: Who would be qualified to be called a "true prophet"? If this is the case!

It appears there are at least three concepts regarding the divine will of God for humanity that must be relativized and distinguished in relation to the relinquishment of God's power and authority in the earth through Jesus Christ:

1. **The calling of God**

2. **The mark of God**

3. **The seal of God**

The manifestation of these divine exaltations requires a priori a degree of subversiveness to the monotonous teachings in place for two thousand years that keep Jesus detrimentally bound in the physical as the son of Mary or as the son of God if we are to be the recipients of deep revelations from the Lord Jesus Christ himself who is now the spirit.

In the Old Testament it is true that we are told in *Deuteronomy 18:22* that one of the ways to recognize a false prophet is when he prophesies something in the name of the Lord and it fails to come to pass. Paradoxically, *Deuteronomy 13:15* also strangely tells us that false prophets also have the ability to foretell the future accurately. However, when the miraculous signs and wonders they announce come to pass faithfully, some of the ways to recognize their falsehood, we are told in *Jeremiah 23:14,* is the adulterous life they are living, the lies they walk in, the wickedness that is common in their lives, and their pursuit of other gods.

In our days, it has become even more difficult to truthfully distinguish between true and false prophets. Jesus himself warns us in *Mathew 7:15,* "Beware of false prophets who come in sheep's clothing, but inwardly they are ferocious wolves." In *verse 21,* Jesus continues to say, "Not everyone who says to me 'Lord, Lord' will enter the Kingdom of Heaven but only he who does the will of my father.

On that day many will say to me, 'Lord, Lord, did we not prophesy in your name and in your name drove out demons and performed miracles?' And I will tell them plainly, 'I never knew you, away from me, you evildoers.'"

We also learned from *Mathew 24:11* that many false prophets will rise and will deceive many. In addition to all these epithets concerning the falsehood of prophets, *2 Peter 2:13* adjoins this contemporary reality that the love of money is also determinative of their falsehood whereby greed is their only compass.

As you can see, there are several key elements that understandably point out the falsehood of a prophet. But this last concern exclaimed by the apostle Peter is definitely part of our everyday lives, and who can deny it?

When you combine the Old and the New Testaments you have an exhaustive repertoire of both true and false prophets:

- **True prophets are intricate spawn of the Lord Jesus Christ as their pinnacle or their God.**

- **In contrast, Satan is worshiped as the headpiece of all false prophets.**

Despite such an extensive record of false prophets, past and present, and their variant degrees of despicability, no personal merit was ever awarded. It always was and still is a total delusion. What is scary in all of this amalgam of false prophets is the fact that many, according to the gospel, will believe in them and be deceived by their teaching.

What's even worse is that some of the false prophets themselves have been deceived and don't know it. They teach and they preach with great eloquence beating their chest in great arrest and deceiving many unknowingly. The blind leading the blind, so to speak.

Interestingly, in total defiance of all this evidence of false prophets, *Revelation 13* is clear that the one that will be found worthy to be validated by Satan for that ultimate evil position will be raised from the dead and empowered by Satan himself to become the true false prophet.

The key to understanding the uniqueness of Judas Iscariot and his Non Parallelism to any other prophet is that Judas has served both God and

Satan, which makes him unambiguously the only true false prophet that ever existed.

Judas was chosen by God personally to become a true prophet. Judas received both the calling and the mark of God. As an apostle of Christ, Judas received the appropriate power along with the other eleven to heal the sick, to cast out demons, and raise the dead, which he performed graciously according to *Acts 1:17*. No one can deny that Judas was one of the elect, but as we have come to find out, an elected devil, conformably to the Apostle John's view of him as described by the Lord Jesus Christ himself in this manner, "Have I not chosen you, the twelve? Yet, one of you is a devil".

One might totally ignore any rational grounds on which to base such an irony. But in order to understand the spiritual significance of the presence of Judas among the twelve apostles of Jesus, one must consider the basic spiritual principles concerning the origin of power which can be any creature's concoction, men or angels, as delegated by the Creator.

God is the source of all power. Neither man nor angel can do anything unless God has enabled him. Jesus says in *John 15:5,* "Without me you can do nothing." We have seen in the example of Job how Satan ineptly presented himself before God in the search of added power, not yet in his arsenal, which he obtained favorably, enabling him to strike Job to the nth degree, unreservedly.

In a similar vein, Christ, through whom God now speaks until the day of judgment, was only accessible to Satan and the demonic community while in the flesh between his birth and Calvary. For the Bible clearly teaches that when Christ resurrected, he ascended to the highest heaven and seated at the right hand of God where he dwells in an unapproachable light far above all principalities, powers, and dominions. **(Ephesians 1:21 and 1 Timothy 6:16).**

During the thirty-three years of Jesus humanity which culminated with his ascension back to heaven, Christ had to deal with all physical and spiritual contingencies on which all mandatory interactions conducive to the end of the world will rest. Certainly, this includes the empowerment of Satan through the person of Judas to perform the end-time miracles, signs, and wonders that Judas naturally harvested for having been one of the chosen twelve.

The supernatural inheritance bestowed on the twelve apostles by the Lord Jesus Christ is personal and can be transferred neither in this life nor in the next from one person to another. When Jesus said on the cross, "it was finished," everything that was, is, or yet to be was complete and there would be no future mandate.

Once again, the gifts and calling of God are not transferable at the will of the one who receives it. In *Romans 11:29,* we are taught that the gifts and calling of God are irrevocable and without repentance. Death itself has no strings, absolutely no consequence whatsoever on the authority of the calling of God.

It may not be a general sentiment, but the truth remains that nothing, good or evil, can be done in the world outside the divine will of God. And that does not absolve in any way the author of any evil, be it minor or major. When you consider God's power and his sovereignty over all things, good or evil, physical or spiritual, it would be a great delusion to think that any human initiative, as impressive as it may be, could amount to anything of spiritual significance.

Kings 19:25 gives us a little description of how God works. Everything that must be decided in days of old. Before the foundation of the world, God planned it, God ordained it, and when time is complete, God brings it to pass. The prophet Jeremiah is a vivid example of God's predestination power and of course his divine election, concerning this physical world. God says to *Jeremiah in chapter 1:45,* "Before I formed you in the womb I knew you, I set you apart and I appointed you as a prophet to the nations."

The commissioning of prophets is a divine election of God, who both equips and sustains those he ordains, giving them the manifest and the supernatural power necessary to carry out their mandate. On the surface, one would tend to categorize a false prophet as one who rejects

God and God's ways, but on a deeper level and most importantly, it is more subtly about someone whom God has chosen and brought near in his courts, accessing the good things of his Holy temple and then choosing to forsake the true God and to follow after other gods even while fundamentally and irrevocably invested with deep supernatural things of God.

A prophet must be considered in the highest biblical dimensions, having meaningful significance only in relation to God. In other words, the spiritual relativization of the word "prophet," whether true or false, must have antecessor with God as a conditional proposition in the determination of the condition of the prophet. A prophet cannot be labeled false had he not been at one time exposed to the truth, as a true prophet.

A prophet is therefore one who has been embedded in meta- physical or existential mysteries, fit to conformably represent the true God of the universe, who is spirit and who equips such like with extramundane tools to bring if necessary specific aspects of the physical world under subjection. When such a prophet erratically distorts his sacred God-given power, adopts spiritual loopholes, and engages in willful errancy by turning to crooked ways and honoring evil, he then becomes and can rightfully be labeled a "false prophet."

In other words, it is a resolute drifting away from the truth that makes one an apostate or a false prophet. Today, the word "prophet" is at its lowest demeanor and is being self-awarded left and right as if Bible schools or seminaries were true spiritual amenders capable of producing prophets, in the spiritual sense.

True prophetism is a divine concept that cannot be learned, taught, or developed by any human standards, or its application corrupted in any form by added theory with evidence of venality through recreant explanations. True prophetism is totally assumed by God the Creator himself, who anoints and appoints while we were yet in the pre-physical arena before the foundation of the world.

Once this core principle is understood, the potential for mis-interpretation greatly diminishes, and our intrinsic awareness of the roots of all prophetic abilities and power becomes clearer and clearer, God being the authority figure that defines all events and outcomes.

The very first false prophet in the history of mankind, who was also the very first liar ever and the very first murderer ever, was put under an everlasting curse by God, turning him into a restless wanderer on the earth, which brings us to a great wonderment I want to share with you, if only as food for thought.

I wonder if being the very first person to have told the very first lie in the history of the world does not make Cain "the father of all lies." **Jesus tells us in *John 8:44* that Satan is "the father of lies" and a murderer from the beginning.** Well, in *Genesis 4,* Cain, the very first son of Adam, committed the very first murder in the history of humankind, which amazingly took place at the very beginning, at the onset of time. You think about that!

That's not all. What is even more intriguing about the striking parallelism between Cain and Satan is that in *Genesis 4:10-16,* Cain is presented as a "restless wanderer on the earth" after being cursed by God, and this is clear enough in the book of Job when God asked Satan from whence he came, and Satan answered God in the most astonishing way: "From restlessly wandering on the earth," which are the exact consequences of the curse imposed by God to Cain in Genesis.

Despite the assassination of Abel by his brother Cain, God emphatically spoke the most auspicious word over Cain's life and put a mark on him, making him invincible to the point that he cannot be killed, and that no one would be able to kill him *(Genesis 4:13-15)*. Now tell me this is not amazing! The only other prophet in the entire scripture who had the unbreakable word of God spoken over his life directly by God himself and then mysteriously and impenitently turned away to evil is the famous Judas Iscariot. He was chosen by God to become one of the twelve apostles of Christ, weaving with the others and intimately partaking in deep mysteries of God as an emissary of Satan, incognizant the entire time to the other eleven, but fore- known from the beginning by the Lord Jesus himself. **Isn't this a strange mystery?**

Having said all this, I would like to conclude this segment on the identity of the Antichrist and the false prophet by simply adding this supplementary remark.

As we are cognizant of the implicitness of God in all spiritual and humanistic developments, we must also recognize that the strange interactions between God and Cain at the beginning of the Old Testament and between God and Judas Iscariot at the beginning of the New Testament are subjectively beyond all human understanding.

The intricacies relative to these two unique biblical experiences concerning the face-to-face interactions between God and Cain on the one hand and between God and Judas Iscariot on the other hand pertains to God's apparent transcendence of his natural exertion momentarily omitting his objurgatory judgment, when God evidently overlooks the dreadful vileness of these two wicked individuals and, furthermore, almost as an emolument, empowers them with metaphysical endowments.

Now if this does not send chills to your spiritual spine, I don't know what will.

Now that we have established the identity of the Antichrist and the false prophet respectively as Cain and Judas Iscariot, it is time to move on to the next series of actions.

From the beginning and throughout the Bible, it is taught that man is at the command of this world. *Psalm 115:16* reads that the highest heaven belongs to the Creator, but the earth he has given to man. Granting this position, the logical conclusion is that in this world everything naturally flows through man.

God, the Creator himself, had to become a man in order to have and exercise full corporal authority in the physical world. The same injunction applies to Satan, who is also a spirit and whose earthly dominion, likewise, yet even more so, must go through physical channels in order for him to exercise palpable authority in the earth.

Like fish out of water, the physical appearance of Satan or any of his squad as man can only be short-lived. There is a mysterious time frame within which this exhibition can take place, which will culminate with a sudden suspension of all activities, constraining them to immediately retract regardless of whether or not the task is complete. If for any reason the angelic/demonic spirit must depart leaving the "fake human body" that was used to appear humanlike, the fake body will look dead but will never decay because it was bloodless, thus soulless.

I just had to say this but the highly spiritual agenda of the end times, impressively involving the political and religious unification of the whole world and bringing it under the full authority of one entity, would be an elusive goal even for the great superpowers, but yet it is a possible achievement of two single individuals without any conventional weapons. These two single individuals will supernaturally conquer the whole world and set universal policies for both politics and religions for all nations to follow abiding under one single government presided by Lucifer himself.

The Bible is clear that we are not dealing with natural phenomena. But the sad fact is that people still naively think that the Antichrist and false prophet are going to be like our everyday normal people.

Let me reiterate once again that the expressions "out of the sea" and "out of the earth" signify being raised from the dead as spirits. The indwelling of humans by evil spirits is more common than people are truly cognizant, and it is taking place in all cultures, in all people, at all levels of society. But this is not what we're talking about here.

All in all, considering the infrangibility of using physical elements as an imperative mean for all effective and somatic control of the physical universe, man being the object central to the problem as principal overseer, could not be overshadowed even by the Creator himself, in violation of this core principle, who had to incarnate in the person of

Christ to subdue the whole world and legally exercise full authority in the earth.

As much as Satan would like to infringe on this ultimate spiritual principle that man alone is given dominion in the world, he is left with no choice but to use man to try to fully conquer the world as the end quickly approaches and totally bring it under direct evil submission before Christ returns.

These two invincible ghosts, who can no longer die or be killed physically, are kinsman of Satan, who will raise them from the dead as spirits but counterintuitively with normal manhood countenance, inasmuch as formerly they were human beings, to be his indestructible physical channels through which he will operate, giving them his throne and his power. Their physical countenance will be comparable to the appearance of Jesus, whom after he came back from the dead went about with his spirit nature concealed while appearing as an ordinary human being, physically palpable, able to cook and eat, and manage physical elements.

Retrospectively, it all started in the pre-physical dimension when Satan took control of Adam and Eve and through them the entire human race, created in the likeness of God, to satisfy his personal ambition to become like God.

Strangely enough the satanic possession of Adam and Eve only lead at the time to a somewhat tepid conversation between God and Satan. There was no sharp rebuke of Satan by God for what he did. Thus, a curse was spoken by God over his life. But the most intriguing aspect of the animadversions God imposed upon the serpent are the details of the "fatherhood" of Satan which will immediately ensue with God putting an eternal enmity between the son of Satan and the son of the woman as a precipice of war, which will culminate at the end of the millennium.

In *verse 20*, we read that Adam named his wife Eve, because Eve would be the mother of all the living, which manifestly tells us that Eve obviously would be the mother of the son God said that Satan would have.

This calls for great insight: the offspring of Satan mentioned in *Genesis 3:15*, who is the Antichrist personified by the first beast, is more of a warrior who will be invested with the throne and the power of Satan with unimaginable authority and who will prove himself to be superhuman by his immortality despite the mortal wound sustained in his head, which will marvel the whole world with its innocuousness and cause all inhabitants of the earth to worship him.

Please note that the first beast or the Antichrist is only presented of having a big mouth, uttering proud words and blasphemies but there are no mentions of miracles, signs, and wonders as part of his attributes. You see, one can only do what he is trained to do, as is given to do by the Creator.

It is important to remember that Jesus is the only God who has the power of creation. No other being has such privileges. Miracles, signs, and wonders are only his to do as he will, and only those, man or angel, to whom he has delegated such prerogative can likewise perform them.

Nowhere in the Old Testament it is recorded of Satan doing any miracles, signs, and wonders based on his own volition, because such qualities are not an innate faculty, even for angels. This privilege is only delegated by God to whomever he wants, man or angel, to do as he commands them.

This being said, Cain who is the offspring of Satan, thus the Antichrist, had neither seen nor taught the secret of performing miracles, signs, and wonders during his physical existence as a human being. The Bible is clear that once dead, the soul or the mind enters a state of invalidism, which dams all possibilities of intromission of new knowledge.

Therefore, Cain as the Antichrist, despite the throne and all the power conferred to him by Satan, still remains inane concerning the end time's miracles, signs, and wonders the Bible talks about simply for not having been accordingly endowed or exposed to such mysteries and consequently simply cannot perform them.

This is where the false prophet, the emissary of Satan in the person of Judas Iscariot, an once disciple of the Lord Jesus Christ who was embedded in deep inalienable supernatural secrets involving the mystery of mysteries, as comes into play the right hand of the Antichrist in complement to his in potential deficit the inspiration of humanity with delegated powers bestowed upon him to perform miracles, signs and wonders for having been one of the chosen twelve apostles.

The Bible portrays the Antichrist, or the ocean beast, as the one who supersedes the evil one in the earth with great authority and power and even the throne of the dragon. In fact, *Revelation 13* portrays the ocean beast, or the Antichrist, as a political figure with great military might who will conquer the whole world and totally subjugate all nations. No one will escape, he will even be given power to make war against the saints of God and kill them. He will be worshiped by all the inhabitants of the earth as he will be given authority over every tribe, people, language, and nation, all whose names have not been written in the book of life belonging to the Lamb that was slain from the creation of the world.

Despite all these apparent satanic forces conceived and displayed in ocean beast, his power is limited to the physical universe throughout cosmos. He can scare but not inspire. Satan simply does not have the characteristic of a lamb that can inspire humanity, and with just cosmic wonders, the grimness of the Antichrist would naturally be nothing short of a freakish and repugnant beast.

As the evidence proves, the necessity of a second beast is imperative to fill the potential void of the first beast inasmuch as certain miracles, signs, and wonders are definitely esoteric to the Lamb of God and to whomever he gives such delegation, in which Judas Iscariot was well versed as one of the chosen twelve.

Revelation 13:11 tells us that the false prophet, or the earth beast, has two horns like a lamb but spoke like a dragon. This reminds us of what Jesus says in *Mathew 7:15:* "Watch out for false prophets, they come in sheep's clothing, but inwardly they are ferocious wolves."

But there is more to it than just what we read in *Revelation 13:11*. The two horns represent two spirits: the gifts from the spirit of Christ, which are eternal, and the spirit of the evil one, who now takes residence in him.

God forbid that I would suggest any cohabitation of Christ and the devil in the same vessel. But the gifts from God are eternal, and they come solely as a result of one having received the spirit of Christ.

What I am trying to say is that Judas Iscariot, who once partook in the spirit of Christ as one of his prophets, was endowed with deep eternal supernatural traits that can never be taken away from him. The scripture says in *Luke 22:3* that at an appointed time, Satan entered Judas Iscariot and enticed him to betray Jesus, which inferentially means that the spirit of Christ had already departed from Judas. But the gift of miracles, signs, and wonders Judas had received as a conferment from Christ, being eternal and derivatively spiritual, coupled with the spirit of Satan, who is now dwelling in him, give evidence of the nature of the two horns or the two spirits sustained by Judas as the false prophet, conformably described as a lamb but who speaks like a dragon.

Revelation 13:12 teaches that all the authority of the ocean beast, who is subjected to the dragon, is delegated to the earth beast to implement through miracles, signs, and wonders, provoking the following universal denouements.

As I said earlier, one of the attributes of the earth beast **(the false prophet)** is to have all who refuse to worship the statue killed. This immane competence among others has great spiritual substance and is also revelator of a profound truth for those who are confused about the Rapture being "pre-tribulation" or "post-tribulation". The full significance of these variable aspects of this satanic picture of the conquest of the entire world is to exhaust all power and might known to man and to have the whole world demonized. If all who refuse the mark of the beast are killed, this means that the Rapture and already taken place because we know the followers of Jesus will be snatched up whole, body, soul, and spirit, without going through death *(1 Thessalonians 4:15-17)*.

Again, if **all** those who refuse the mark of the beast are killed, this further means that the world only has two categories of people at the time of the implementation of this life-and-death paradigmatic measure:

1. **Those who will be killed for refusing the mark.**

2. **Those whose lives are spared for taking the mark.**

Denying Jesus Christ at this point is the key for survival. The Bible says without ambiguity that **all** who do not adhere to the methods established by the two beasts will be killed.

Consequently, if you agree that all is totally inclusive and means undoubtedly **all,** by having all who refuse to worship the beast killed is clearly indicative that at that particular point in time, the Antichrist and the false prophet have the whole world to them- selves and their followers.

Correspondingly, *Revelation 13* marks the end of natural evangelistic sermons proclaiming the gospel of Jesus Christ by any human being. The next verse, which begins *chapter 14,* describes Jesus on Mount Zion ready to make his second physical appearance for the final victory of good over evil and putting definitely an end to this physical world as we know it.

CHAPTER 14

The Lamb and the Ransomed 144,00

The Apostle John tells us at the beginning of *chapter 14* that he looked and saw standing with the Lamb on Mount Zion the *144,000 Jews* who were killed by the Antichrist and the false prophet. These saints are described in *Revelation 7* as having been marked with the seal of God on their foreheads and were handpicked by God from the twelve tribes of Israel. Their souls were before the throne of God and were singing a song that only they know the lyrics. *Revelation 14:3* tells us that these *144,000* saints were redeemed from the earth pure and blameless. They were virgins for not having engaged in any sexual intercourse during their entire physical existence and in their mouths were found no lies.

Verses 6 through *13* of *Revelation 14* talk about three angels who will go throughout the earth with the eternal gospel to proclaim the judgment of God to every nation, tribe, language and people.

The first angel will declare the glory of the true God, who made the heavens and the earth, the sea and the rivers, saying, "Fear God and give him glory because the hour of his judgment has come."

The second angel will announce the fall of Babylon the great, who made all the nations drink of the madness of the wine of her fornication.

The third angel will herald in a loud voice that everyone who worships the beast and its image and receives his mark on the forehead or on the hand will drink of the wine of the anger of God and will be tormented with fire and sulphur forever and ever. In verse 13 of chapter 14, we have another confirmation that all who refuse to worship the beast and bear his mark will be killed. This is in reference to Christians who remain in the earth after the Rapture, and who will have to face death as their only escape. But the voice from heaven will proclaim concerning them, **"Blessed are the dead who die in the Lord from now on, they will rest from their labor for their deeds will follow them."**

This portion of scripture represents the parable of the weeds told by Jesus in *Mathew 13:24* concerning the harvest of the earth when it is ripe. Earlier we talked about the difference between the Kingdom of God and the Kingdom of heaven. The parable of the weeds refers to the kingdom of Heaven, which definitely indicates a transition from this life to the next.

Jesus told it this way in *Mathew 13:24,* "The kingdom of Heaven is like a man who sowed good seed in his field. But while everyone was sleeping, his enemy came and sowed weeds among the wheat and went away. When the wheat sprouted and formed heads, then the weeds also appeared". The owner's servants came to him and said, "Sir, didn't you sow good seed in your field? Where then did the weeds come from?" "An enemy did this," he replied. The servants asked him, "Do you want us to go and pull them up?" "No," he answered, "because while you are pulling the weeds, you may root up the wheat with them. Let both grow together until the time of the harvest. At that time, I will tell the harvesters: 'First collect the weeds and tie them in bundles to be burned; then gather the wheat and bring it into my barn.'"

When Jesus was alone with his disciples, he explained the parable to them in this manner:

– **The Son of Man is the sower of good seed.**

– **The world is the field.**

– **The children of God are the good seed.**

– **The children of the devil are the weeds.**

– **Satan is the enemy who sows them.**

– **The harvest is the end of the world.**

– **The harvesters are the angels of God.**

– **The barn is the kingdom of Heaven.**

Verse 40 continues to say, "As the weeds are pulled up and burned in the fire, so it will be at the end of the world." The Son of Man will send out his angels, and they will weed out of his kingdom everything that causes sin and all who do evil. They will throw them into the fiery furnace, where there will be weeping and gnashing of teeth. This is the end of the Antichrist and the false prophet. Then the righteous will shine like the sun in the Kingdom of the Father, which represents the millennium and beyond.

Before we move on, let's make sure you understand the significance of this parable and the content of *Revelation 14,* which are parallels.

I strongly recommend you read *verse 40* of *Mathew 13* again and compare it with *Revelation 14 verses 6-11* to realize that none of it concerns the living but the dead at the resurrection.

- **We have angels flying in midair (verse 6).**

- **The glory and judgment of God at hand (verse 7).**

- **The destruction of Satan (verse 8).**

- **The wrath of God being poured out (verse 10).**

- **The dead, which worshiped the beast, and his image being tormented with burning sulphur forever and ever (verses 10-11).**

- **The dead in Christ being blessed as they rest from their labor, for their deeds followed them (verse 13).**

Verses 14-20 describe the context in which all this take place. We see Jesus, still on Mount Zion sitting on a cloud with a golden crown on his head and a sharp sickle in his hand. Another angel came out of the temple and called in a loud voice for Jesus to swing the sickle over the earth and harvest the earth because the time to reap has come, for the harvest of the earth is ripe. Verse 17 tells us yet of another angel who also had a sharp sickle in his hand, and of course in verse 18 there is still another angel, but this one is in charge of the fire, calling in a loud voice to the angel in verse 17, who had the sharp sickle, to gather the clusters of grapes from the earth's vine, because its grapes are ripe. And the angel (verse 19) swung his sickle on the earth and gathered its grapes and threw them into the great wine press of God's wrath.

Here in Chapter 14 we have three elements that are most certainly indicative of the end-time judgment:

- **The wrath of God (verse 19), which is figurative of the judgment of God.**

- **The fire (verse 18), which is also symbolic of the judgment of God.**

- **The Harvest of the earth, which certainly represents the end of the world as well as the judgment of God.**

Revelation 14 pictures a general context with an overall impression surrounding these specific events of the end times, but as we begin reading *Revelation 15,* particularities of each characteristic are developed as part of the overall situation dealing and leading to the second coming of Christ for his thousand-year reign, at the end of which the power of Satan and all his angels with him will be destroyed forever.

CHAPTER 15

The Seven Angels

Revelation 15 offers a series of wonders that will happen in the spirit realm, the kind of events one cannot expect to see with the naked eye. We read about seven angels that are holding the seven last plagues, which will bring to completion the wrath of God concerning the earth.

The Apostle John describes the setting as a sea of glass mixed with fire, and all those who were killed by the Antichrist and the false prophet, perhaps a human paradox, are considered by their deaths victorious over the beast and his image and over the number of his name. They are all standing next to the sea of glass in heaven, in the presence of God, holding harps given them by God and singing the song of Moses and the song of the Lamb.

When the worship ceremony is over, John makes mention of the tabernacle of the testimony being opened and out of which came out the seven angels with the seven plagues that will complete the wrath of God. One of the four holy angels who stand in the center and around the throne of God gives to the seven angels seven golden bowls filled with the wrath of God, who lives forever and ever. The Holy Temple was filled with the glory of God as smoke spreads so much throughout the celestial tabernacle that no one could enter in until the seven plagues of the seven angels were complete.

CHAPTER 16

Then a voice addressing the seven angels from within the temple says, "Go and pour out the seven bowls of God's wrath on the earth." It is no surprise that the bowl of each of the seven angels will affect elements of different dimensions, both in the physical and in the spiritual.

- **The first bowl affects the health of the people.**

- **The second bowl applies to the sea.**

- **The third bowl relates to all rivers and streams.**

- **The fourth bowl impacts on the sun.**

- **The fifth bowl concerns the throne of the beast.**

- **The sixth bowl acts specifically on the Euphrates in readiness of the great day of God Almighty.**

- **The seventh bowl pertains to the earth's general atmospheric pressure.**

The First Angel (verse 2)

When the bowl of the first angel enters the earth's atmosphere, it produces some severe health disturbances resulting in the breakout of ugly and painful sores on all who have the mark of the beast and worship his image.

The Second Angel (verse 4)

The second angel pours out his bowl on the ocean and it turns into blood like that of a dead man, and all living things in the sea die.

The Third Angel (verse 3)

The third angel pours out his bowl on the rivers and springs of water, and they too became blood.

Referring to Jesus, the angel in charge of the waters says, "You are just in these judgments, you who are and who were, the Holy One, because you have so judged. For they have shed the blood of your saints and prophets and now you have given them blood to drink as they deserve." The altar responds, "Yes, Lord God Almighty, true and just are your judgments."

The Fourth Angel (verse 8)

The fourth angel pours out his bowl on the sun, and the sun was given power to scorch people with fire, searing them intensely. They curse the name of God who has control over these plagues, but they refuse to repent and glorify him.

The Fifth Angel (verse 10)

The fifth angel pours out his bowl on the throne of the beast, and his kingdom became like hell on earth as his followers gnaw their tongues in agony and keep on cursing the God of heaven because of their pains and their sores. But they still refuse to repent of their disobedience.

The Sixth Angel (verse 12)

The sixth angel pours out his bowl on the great river of Euphrates, and its water dries up to prepare the way for the kings (plural) from the east. You and I both know that rivers have never dissuaded military invasions or keep enemies away from a hostile territory. The term "kings" used here in this specific context represents powerful nations or countries, and by using the Euphrates as a symbol, a precise geographical region is definitely being designated. The geostrategic significance of the Euphrates in connection with the nations as far north as in the continent of Asia flowing through the Arab nations of the Middle East before ending its course in the Persian Gulf will play a central role in end-time prophecy before the return of Christ and his dreadful day.

The Euphrates River goes back before time began, thus having deep spiritual significance, as we read the account of the heavens and the earth when they were created, making mention of it for the very first time in the *Genesis 2:4* before sin entered the world and kicked off the physical time clock of the natural world as we know it. Though the physical geographical location of the Euphrates involves both Asian and Middle East nations, a careful consideration of its geopolitical significance could stretch its territorial importance as far as to include Eastern Europe.

The spiritual dimension concerning the effacement of the Euphrates or simply its physical inconspicuousness simply means that all the social unrest and the terrible political and religious divisions inherent to that particular region of the world will be forced to a halt in an unprecedented political, social, and religious symbiosis in perspective of an unparalleled world war that will authoritatively lead to the one-world government of the "Antichrist". Surprisingly, the drying up of these rivers will be very unconventional, and because of what it will symbolize, it will be very difficult for the rest of the world to come to terms with the new political restructuring of that particular region. This revolutionary geographical innovation will exert unity, encroaching all territorial borders in a single geopolitical unison in preparation of a concerted impulsion for the upcoming world war and eventually against the return of Jesus Christ.

This concatenation will eventually include all the nations of the earth for having been deceived through miraculous signs and wonders from these evil spirits sent forth by Satan, the Antichrist, and the false prophet. We read in *verse 16*, "Then these evil spirits will gather the Kings together at the place that in Hebrew is called 'Armageddon.'" But in *verse 15*, Jesus says, "Behold I come like a thief. Blessed is he who stays awake and keeps his clothes with him, so that he may not go naked and be shamefully exposed."

The Seventh Angel (verse 17)

The seventh angel pours out his bowl into the air, and out of the temple came a loud voice from the throne saying, "It is done."

John 2:19 tells us that Jesus is the Temple of God; therefore, it is tremendously comforting to all Christians to know that the same mystery of the last word of Jesus on the cross, "It is finished," paying in full the debt of humankind to his Father and putting an end to the redemption era, is reiterated here in *Revelation 16:17* by Jesus himself from the throne in heaven uttering and proclaiming, "It is done," and therewith kicking off the process of the end of the world and the end of the kingdom of darkness.

"It is finished" on the cross was the end of the power of sin on those who eat the flesh and drink the blood of Christ, thus the beginning of the redemption process.

"It is done" in the book of Revelation is the maturity date to put an end of the "one" who has the power of sin and death (Satan) and the consummation of salvation for the church.

With this loud voice uttered by Jesus from the throne saying, "It is done" in reverberation of his last word on the cross, "It is finished," Jesus made complete both the Old and the New Testament prophecies, combining them into one and destroying all kingdoms, powers, rulers, and every authority under heaven.

The Apostle Paul teaches in *1 Corinthians 15:24* that the end will come when Jesus, after having destroyed all dominion, authority, and power which oppose God, hands over the kingdom to God the Father so that God may be all in all.

Immediately following the loud voice, came flashes of lightning, rumbling, peals of thunder, and a tremendous unprecedented earthquake. Jerusalem will split into three parts, and the cities of other nations will collapse.

Revelation 11:8 tells us that "the Great city" is the city where Jesus Christ was crucified. Though the expression "the Great city" is undoubtedly a substitution for Jerusalem, *verse 8* tells us that in the spirit it represents Sodom and Egypt, giving exertion to the wicked agenda of the seven heads of the beast as an integral movement going back to the beginning of the world.

As the earthquake is taking place, we read in *verse 19* that God is also dealing with Babylon the great as God gives her the cup filled with the wine of the fury of God's wrath. Babylon the great being referred to here is symbolic of Lucifer himself. By no means does it point to a geographical location in the earth like most people tend to believe. In fact, the next verse tells us that when the islands and the mountains (principalities and powers) realize the manifestation of God's ferocity upon Babylon, they fled away.

Chapter 16 ends with hailstones weighing about a hundred pounds each falling upon men from the sky and as a result they curse God because of this horrific plague of hail.

CHAPTER 17

The Prostitute

One of the seven angels who had the seven bowls carried John away in the spirit and showed him the punishment of the great prostitute who sits on many waters.

In *verse 2,* the Apostle John tells us that the kings of the earth and the inhabitants of the earth committed adultery with the prostitute, so much as to become intoxicated with the wine of her fornication. The kings of the earth in this particular context are not only symbolic of all political and religious leaders throughout the world who have certain sovereignty over a geographical territory or a multitude of people, but most importantly it's referring to fallen angels who are in charge of the four corners of the earth.

In *verse 3* we read that John saw the woman sitting on a scarlet beast covered with blasphemous names. The beast had seven heads and ten horns, which are not only indicative of his demonic character but also descriptive of both his invisible and indivisible countenance as the embodiment of the four great beasts in the Prophet Daniel's vision, whose coalescence adds up coincidentally to these exact seven heads and ten horns.

I am far from being exegetical, but when it comes to the identity of meaning even from multiple nomenclatures, synonymizing different entities, the similarity of their nature should become so evident that even to a mind without wisdom the possibility of dissection is patent. We know Satan is not the beast but the power behind the beast. In other words, Satan is the creature controlling the beast as the *rider* of the beast, representing both Babylon the Great and the woman who sits on many waters.

The word of God is full with interspersions to diversify the scope of an object while using different aggregation for the same entity. In *Revelation 12,* we read about the woman and the dragon, the woman being Christ and the dragon symbolizing Satan. But here in *chapter 17,* the same appellation, "the woman" used just a couple of chapters ago to describe the Lord Jesus Christ is now being employed as a substitute for Satan, exerting ancestor-progeny as well as mentor-apprentice relationship in a perfect twine similar to the integration of a mother and her fetus.

We know the beast is the Antichrist, and his unique mentor is his master Satan. Therefore, I could rightfully rephrase the title "the woman on the beast," as the beast and its rider in a clear depiction of Satan as the mastermind, the mentor, and the rider.

At the beginning of the chapter, we saw the woman sitting on many waters, and now she is also being referred to as the great prostitute.

Now, because there are so many ways to interpret the use of water in the Bible, I will simply summarize its significance in an effort to exert the perspective of this context. Water, whether its usage is being considered in the Old or New Testament, has always been brought into play in connection with people. So, when we read that Satan sits on many waters, it simply signifies that Satan has power over a multitude of people by keeping them in bondage both physically and spiritually.

In the physical sense, the Lord Jesus Christ refers to Satan in *John 14:30* as "Prince of this world," but in the book of Revelation, Satan is presented as "King of the Abyss" with both dimensions spiritually intertwining to form "the Kingdom of darkness."

Verse 4 gives a description of the outward countenance of Satan being dressed up in purple and scarlet and glittered with gold, precious stones, and pearls. In order to grasp this entire figurative vernacular, it is necessary to have recourse to the Old Testament prophets whose prophecies of the end times can stand as reminders and symbols of current events.

Here in *Revelation 17*, Satan is painted as "the woman on the beast," but thousands of years earlier, the Prophet Ezekiel in *chapter 28:13* gave us the outward appearance of Satan and what he once represented in the following manner:

"You were the model of perfection, full of wisdom and perfect in beauty. You were in Eden, the garden of God. Every precious stone was your covering. Your settings and mountings were made of Gold. They were prepared for you on the day you were created. You were anointed as a guardian Cherub, for so I ordained you. You were on the holy mountain of God. You walked back and forth in the midst of fiery stones. You were perfect in your ways from the day you were created, until iniquity was found in you. By the abundance of your trading, you became filled with violence within, and you sinned".

"Therefore, I cast you as a profane thing out of the mountain of God, and I destroyed you, O covering cherub. I expelled you from the midst of the fiery stones. Your heart became proud because of your beauty and you corrupted your wisdom because of your splendor. So, I threw you to the earth and made a spectacle of you before kings. By your many sins and dishonest trade, you defiled your sanctuaries. Therefore, I made a fire come out from you and it consumed you, reducing you to ashes on the ground in the sight of all who were watching. All the nations who knew you are astonished at you. You have come to a horrible end and shall be no more forever".

With a title written on the woman's forehead, we are told in verse 5 that:

- **Satan is a mystery.**

- **Satan is Babylon the Great.**

- **Satan is the mother of prostitutes.**

- **Satan is the mother of the abominations of the earth.**

- **We already know from John 8:44 that Satan is the father of all non-believers.**

- **Satan is a murderer from the beginning.**

- **Satan is the father of lies.**

In *verse 6* of *Revelation 17,* the Apostle John says that he was greatly astonished at the sight of the woman **(Satan)** being drunk with the blood of the saints, the blood of those who bore testimony of Jesus. But the angel said to John in *verse 7,"* Let me explain to you the mystery of the woman and of the beast she rides, which has the seven heads and ten horns". In verse 8, the angel explains, "The beast that you see was once alive in the earth, now he is not, and will come up out of the Abyss and go to his destruction."

It is essential we understand that we're not dealing here with milk and bottles. This is not even "Life and Death" as usual, as we know it in the natural. This is spirituality at its best. The eschatology is so serious that it transcends anything humankind has ever dealt with.

This is very interesting! The Antichrist and Jesus seem to have similar factual background. Except, as we write this book, Jesus still "is" versus the person of the Antichrist who once was but now is not. But will come again.

- **Jesus "was", "is" and is coming again *(Revelation 1:8)***

- **The Antichrist "was", now "is not" (because he is still dead) but is coming again *(Revelation 17:8)."***

The angel is unequivocally telling us that the beast out of the ocean (the Antichrist) is a man who was once alive in the earth and who died and will be resurrected in the future.

We were told in *Revelation 13* that the first beast (the Antichrist) will be coming out of the sea. But again, to make sure there is no misinterpretation of this mystery, the angel is clearly corroborative by repeating this great mystery in *chapter 17:7* and repeating it again one more time in *verse 8* that the Antichrist will come out of the abyss, meaning from the deepest part of the ocean, a zone typically in perpetual darkness, impenetrable by direct sunlight.

Reasonably of course, *verse 9* says, "This calls for a mind with wisdom." And just prior to that, in *verse 8,* we read that people whose names have not been written in the Book of Life from the creation of the world will be astonished when they see the beast, because he once was, now is not, and yet will come.

Still in *verse 9,* the angel says, "The seven heads are seven hills on which the woman sits. They are also seven kings".

Again, let's pause here for a minute. And I beg you, readers, not to confuse the seven kings mentioned here with "kingdoms and monarchs of this visible world," who are but nothing in the sight of God.

Given this mysterious atmosphere and so much emphasis on the recondite origin of the two beasts, I suppose we ought to put all expressions in their appropriate contexts for the edification of the readers. With all due respect, humanity, whatever its stature, is simply dust and a breath away, and God would not waste his time referring to men as kings in the end-time conflict against God's Kingdom.

The prophet Isaiah says it this way, referring to the nations of this world. *(Isaiah 40:15-17)*:

- **The nations of this world are like a drop in the bucket.**

- **The nations of this world are regarded as dust on the scales.**

- **The nations of this world are as nothing before God.**

- **The nations of this world are regarded by God as worthless.**

- **The nations of this world are less than nothing.**

This being clarified, let's now continue paying attention to what the angel is saying. The woman, whom we now know to be symbolic of

Satan and who is also the rider of the beast, is actually sitting on seven hills representing the seven heads of the four great beasts seen by the prophet Daniel.

Verse 10 tells us that the seven heads are seven kings, but the angel refers to them as "hills" rather than "mountains" (though some translations define them as mountains). In the scripture, "mountains" denote a high order of angelic beings such as the four living creatures that incorporate each the power of both a seraph and a cherub combined.

Certain categories of angels at the top ranks are described as **"mountain"**, **"high mountain"** or **"great high mountain."**

As we saw earlier, a brief description of the hierarchy of the angels as given in *Ezekiel 6:3* is as follows:

1. **Mountains**

2. **Hills**

3. **Ravines**

4. **Valleys**

This ranking order may seem simple and straightforward at first site, but it certainly reflects a superior, a transcendent disposition to which one does not dare to do justice.

In the New Testament the Apostle Paul defines the angelic ranks somewhat as follows:

1. **Principalities**

2. **Powers**

3. **Rulers**

4. **Spiritual forces of evil**

However, being referred to as "hills" or "mountains" here in *Revelation 17* is indicative that Satan and these six other powerful spirits forming the seven heads of the Antichrist were high-ranking celestial beings, who concerted their forces in a powerful concatenation as a last resort against Christ and his saints.

The First Five Heads Of The Dragon

We are told by John that FIVE of the SEVEN heads of the dragon have fallen and that "**one**" as we speak "**is**", which equals to six, and the last one has not yet come, making up the seven heads. But when the "seventh one" (Lucifer Himself) comes, **he will only be for a little while.** Please keep that in mind.

Again, the one that now is, which is the number six, is the spirit of the antichrist who will be represented by the two superhumans, **(the antichrist and the false prophet),** who will sit on the throne of Satan with power and great authority.

It's very important to keep in mind that the name "Satan" is defined or represented by all evil spirits. However, we do know the personal name of the "Prince of this world" is "Lucifer." But these six other angels, beside Lucifer, forming the seven heads of the beast as the most "wicked" evil spirits are somewhat anonymous to us as to their personal identity, except that the Apostle Paul tells us in *1 Corinthians 15:26* that the last enemy or spirit that will be destroyed is "death."

In principle, it should not be too simplistic to say that "death" here represents Lucifer. To get down to practical matters all demons typify "death", and don't be too surprised if I told you that the epithet "Satan" epitomizes all "fallen angels".

This is to show you how figurative language can be interestingly precise but also pregnant with diversified spiritual meaning.

This portion of scripture is very intriguing and it brings to mind different pictures that each one of us, based on his or her experience, gets from these various metaphors.

But I don't think we have a figure of speech when the bible talks about Satan, the angel of death, the antichrist or the false prophet. They may be a bit elusive in character but very well denote symbols that are very conventional, because they are going to hell as physical beings.

In fact, *Revelation 20* gives us the epithets of five evil spirits that will be put in the lake of fire by Christ when he returns to judge the world.

These five spirits are:

1. The Antichrist (*Revelation 19:20*).

2. The false prophet (*Revelation 19:20*).

3. Death (*Revelation 20:14*).

4. Hades (*Revelation 20:14*).

5. Lucifer (*Revelation 20:10*).

A few paragraphs earlier we read that five of the seven heads have fallen, suggesting that each of the five was responsible at one time in history for a certain evil mission against God and his people, but in every one of those satanic assignments, the evil spirit behind the undertaking was defeated and put out of service by God personally.

Although the identities of those five heads remain a mystery, the territoriality of their evil missions is revealed accordingly:

1- Garden of Eden.

2- Noah's flood.

3- Sodom and Gomorrah.

4- Moses and the Red Sea.

5- On the Cross at Calvary

Garden of Eden

Defeat of the First Head

In *Genesis 3* we are told that the serpent, who was more cunning than any beast the Lord God had made, deceived Eve—and through her,

Adam—into sinning against God. In *verse 14* (the first vanquish of Jesus over the first head) the Lord God said to the serpent, "Because you have done this, cursed are you above all the livestock and all the wild animals. You will crawl on your belly and you will eat dust all the days of your life."

Noah's Flood

Defeat of the Second Head

In *Genesis 6:4* we read that in the days of Noah, angels came in onto the daughters of men and they bore them children. The Lord God said, "I will destroy mankind from the face of the earth, both men and animals, for I repent for having created them." This word "repent" is used by God and for God when our disobedience has crossed over the boundaries of his patience, his grace and compassion, forcing Him to intervene and exercise judgment.

The nature of the problem is clear and it is safe to say that the word "animals" in this statement made by God does not refer to alligators, horses, or donkeys, but it is epithetic to angels or demons as defined in context. Even though literal animals were also killed in the process.

Do you recall *Genesis 3:1?* The serpent, who is Lucifer, was craftier than any of the other animals the Lord had made. So as God judged the earth by sending the flood to wipe out all flesh that moved upon the earth, *2 Peter 2:4-5* corroboratively established an unambiguous link between the judgment of God through the flood and fallen angels, in that, because of what they did, God bound them with everlasting chains until judgment day.

Sodom and Gomorrah

Defeat of the Third Head

The Lord said to Abraham, "The outcry against Sodom and Gomorrah is so great and their sin so grievous that I will go down and see if what they have done is as bad as the outcry." The wickedness of the people was so great that the angels sent by God destroyed both cities with burning sulfur out of the heavens killing all and laying waste the vegetation in the land.

We learn from Saint Jude *verses 6* and *7* that the angels who left their estate and abandoned their assignments were behind the sexual immorality and perversion in Sodom and Gomorrah. Jude refers to these angels as dreamers who pollute their own bodies, reject authorities, and slander celestial beings.

Moses and the Red Sea

Defeat of the Fourth Head

When the time came for God to intervene and free his people of Israel from spiritual and physical bondage in Egypt, he sent Moses to king Pharaoh saying, "Let my people go." After Pharaoh was impelled to let the people go, the Lord told Moses to turn back and encamp near Pi Hahiroth between Migdol and the sea. "I will harden Pharaoh's heart," said the Lord, to pursue them. "But I will gain glory for myself through Pharaoh and all his Army, and the Egyptians will know that I am the Lord."

As Pharaoh and his Army approached, Moses said to the people, "Do not be afraid, stand firm and you will see the deliverance the Lord will bring you today. The Egyptians you see today you will never see them again." *Exodus 8* gives us an exhaustive account on how the Lord dealt with the gods of Egypt to free his people. God also dealt with the Egyptians and all Pharaoh's horses, chariots, and horseman, which followed his loved ones into the sea. After parting the sea for his people to go through on dry land, God made the water flow back and covered the entire army, and not one of them survived.

But that's not all, Saint Jude again tells us in Jude 5 that after the Lord delivered his people out of Egypt, he later destroyed those who did not believe, and the angels who were involved, having abandoned their own home, were kept in darkness by God, bound with everlasting chains for judgment day.

Defeat of the Fifth Head

In *Colossians 2:13* we read the following: "When we were dead in our sins and in the uncircumcision of our sinful nature, God made us alive with Christ on the cross. God forgave us of all our sins and cancelled the written code with its regulation that was against us and stood opposed to us. God took it away and nailed it to the cross, for on the cross, God triumphed over all evil, disarming the powers and authorities and making a public spectacle of them.

HEAD # 6

The Antichrist

These five vanquishments of Jesus over these evil spirits constitute the five defeats sustained by five of the seven heads comprising the total countenance of the beast. However, of the two that remain of the total seven heads, one now is, conveying that as I write this opuscule, head #6 is currently in the world roaming and ruling. He is the mastermind behind the new-world order, influencing all aspects of humanity from its basic sociological level to the most sophisticated scientific principles, encompassing and polarizing both religion and politics, to subtly slip the entire world into a global chaos and confusion in readiness for his physical apparition in the very near future.

The Apostle Paul in *2 Thessalonians 2:7* had this to say about the spirit of the Antichrist two thousand years ago: "The secret power of lawlessness" or "the spirit of the Antichrist" is already at work; but the one who now holds him back, the Holy Spirit, will continue to do so until he and his subsidiaries are taken away, and then the Antichrist will be revealed, and the Lord Jesus Christ will overthrow him with the breath of his mouth and destroy him by the splendor of his coming.

Paul continues to say that "the apparition of the Antichrist will be in accordance with the work of Satan, displayed in all kinds of power, signs and lying wonders and in every sort of evil that deceives those who are perishing." They will perish because they have refused the love of Jesus that they might be saved. For this reason, God will send them a powerful delusion so that they believe the lie, and so that all will be condemned who did not believe the truth but have had pleasure in wickedness. The latter part of *verse 10 in chapter 17* talks about the seventh head, who has not yet come but will only remain for a little while when he does come. The seventh head is Lucifer himself, who will appear only after the millennium for a short time, according to *Revelation 20.*

This we read: "An angel came down from heaven with a great chain, seized the dragon, that ancient serpent, which is the devil or Satan, and bound him for a thousand years. The angel threw him into the Abyss and locked and sealed it over him. After the thousand years are over, Satan will be set free for a short time to make his apparition in the four corners of the earth to deceive the nations. But fire came down from heaven and devoured them. And Lucifer was thrown into the lake of burning sulfur where the beast and the false prophet had been thrown. They will be tormented day and night forever and ever."

Now let's go back to our head #6, which is the spirit of the Antichrist, and let me bring to your remembrance *Revelation 6,* when Jesus opened the fourth seal and a pale horse came forth, which seemed to have had two riders, death and Hades. *Revelation 6* is clear that although death and Hades are associated with the same pale horse, they are two distinct entities but of the same spirit.

Passages such as these, talking about death riding on horses or a beast with multiple heads can be very confusing, but when you consider certain spiritual assumptions and believe the truth being exhibited, you may find that these allegories are simply a reflection of biblical-historical phenomena, proposed long ago by God, that can be unraveled through correlative bygones as efficient formula for today's enigma.

In *Numbers 11:16-30* for instance, when the burden was too heavy for Moses to carry by himself, he prayed to God, and God through an apportionment took of the spirit that was on Moses and put the same spirit on seventy elders. Now you have seventy-one people functioning under the same spirit.

Hence, to understand the mystery of the sixth head, which is the spirit of the Antichrist and who is currently in the world, and why he is going to use two distinct quiddities for his evil deeds, one must be aware of the complexity of the two great world systems, religion and politics, polarized to such a degree and full of hatred that men no longer think they have a common destiny. The first beast will prove to be extremely crafty through his course of action in global political matters, while the second beast will handle religious issues worldwide with sublime shrewdness.

Back in *Revelation 13* we saw Lucifer standing on the shore of the sea bringing out from under the ocean the first beast, which is the Antichrist, and a few verses later he also brought out from under the earth a second beast to personify the false prophet. These remarks are meant to express the conception of a new era with a supernatural objective. The purpose of all this mysticism will probably be apparent to some as it sheds lights on the origin of the two beasts, which actually are congenerous, comparable to Siamese twins but separated at birth.

I want to make it very clear for the readers to understand that by raising from the dead these two creatures, namely the Antichrist and the false prophet, Lucifer is simply availing the spirit of the Antichrist in such a manner to imitate the multidimensionality of the Spirit of Christ that was on Moses and of which a parting was made by God to the seventy elders. In other words, these two beasts will be of the same spirit, like we have seen with Moses and the seventy elders.

What's even more intriguing is the fact that when the beasts are raised from the dead to reign as kings in the physical world, they will rule conjointly, giving evidence of their royalties as "King # 8, because their dominions will have come from the seven heads or the seven kings of the kingdom of darkness.

When you read *Revelation 17:11,* the inference is beyond any doubt, clearly and congruously injected on the "Two Beasts" which represent the "Eleventh" horn.

Now again the two beasts that will be raised from the dead as the Antichrist and the false prophet are in reality "One Beast" with two heads, so to speak, because, like I said earlier, they are of the same "spirit".

We saw a few paragraphs earlier that the seven heads are seven kings. Let me reiterate that in the kingdom of darkness the spirit of the Antichrist is one of the seven heads, thus one of the seven kings.

So, when the spirit of the Antichrist, who is one of the seven kings, is personified by the two beasts, (the Antichrist and the false prophet) they will receive authority as kings in the earth which will make them the "Eight King". As you can see, being the bearers of the same spirit, they are not considered to be two separate kings. Though they will be two distinct personalities, the two conjointly represent the "Eleventh" horn spoken by the angel in *Daniel 7:24-25* that we also read here in *Revelation 17:11-13*.

The two, having been sprung from the seven kings or the seven heads of the beast, are themselves kings, but of a single essence, and are therefore considered as the "Eight King" which will rule the entire earth, but he belongs to the seven as stated in *verse 11,* and he is going to his destruction, referring to the spirit of the Antichrist as one and a single entity but which controls both beasts.

As any blind can see, more is at issue here than meets the eye. We saw together earlier that the Antichrist and the false prophet are two individuals who will be raised from the dead, which to some degree explains their invincibility. But this is not enough to take away the intricacies associated with their character.

Jesus himself, who was God incarnate, died. Why then these two men not only cannot be put to death physically by any man, but Jesus himself, as strangely as it may sound, when he comes, though he will kill everyone associated with them, will only capture them and throw them alive with their physical bodies into the fiery lake of burning sulfur? Now tell me this is not a true paradox!

This is beyond the finest human philosophy with its narrow- mindedness and limitations, bearing merely upon ordered concepts in the natural realm. The metaphysical phenomenon taking place here in *Revelation 19:20-21*, as silly as it may seem, transcends the apex of all human knowledge, when the Bible clearly substantiates the end of physical death concerning humankind throughout the world as all human life mysteriously come to an end by the sword that came out of the mouth of Jesus.

This implies that all interactions from here on out, starting with *chapter 20* and leading to the final destruction of the devil after the end of the millennium, will no longer involve any human being in the physical sense, because humankind will no longer be physically in the earth at the end of *chapter 19*.

In *verse 12*, John says that the ten horns of the beast are ten kings who have not yet received a kingdom. But these kings who do not yet have kingdoms will receive authority as kings alongside the beast for one hour. This is another mind-boggling statement, a twofold mystery. Whether we realize it or not, this varied appreciation of the characteristics of the beast is to help to deepen our understanding and carry us to that dimension of the spirit and to realize we are like a pile of ants in front of a bunch of elephants.

Like I said earlier, the ten horns represent both the spirits behind the scene and their human counterparts or the governments they control. The angel, in his explanation to Daniel, utterly said that the fourth beast is a fourth kingdom that will appear on earth. This kingdom will be different from all the other kingdoms and will devour the whole earth, trampling it down and crushing it *(Daniel 7:23)*. This is the spirit of the Antichrist, which is not to be confused with the person of the Antichrist.

This kingdom, according to *Daniel 7:24*, will include ten horns as earthly kings, not necessarily individuals but powerful political and religious groups or nations in a heap with extensive territorial authority. Let me reiterate clearly that the spirit of the Antichrist is exactly what it is, a spirit, and he is one of the seven heads of the beast, thus one of the seven invisible kings.

Now the person of the Antichrist, as a visible earthly king, is an eleventh horn that the angel said will come up among the ten horns, and he will incorporate three of the horns within himself as a sign of great power, namely the spirit of the Antichrist, the spirit of Death, and the spirit of Hades, of which the false prophet will also be a partaker.

In the natural realm however, the ten horns also represent ten of the most powerful nations or alliances that will come alongside the beast, for having been under the direct influence of these ten evil spirits, but ironically three of the horns or three of these countries will be totally destroyed by the beast in the substantiation of his predominance.

This eleventh horn looked more imposing than the others; he had the eyes of a man and a mouth that spoke boastfully *(Daniel 7:20)*. He will speak against the Most High and oppress his saints and try to change the set time and the laws. The saints will be handed over to him for a time, times, and half a time. But the court will sit, and his power will be taken away and completely destroyed forever. Then the sovereignty and the power and the greatness of the kingdoms under the whole heaven will be handed to the saints as an everlasting kingdom, and all rulers will worship and obey the Most High. The angel added, "This is the end of the matter."

In *verse 15 of chapter 17,* we read that "the waters on which the prostitute sits are peoples, multitudes, nations, and languages", which enlighten the spiritual dimension of the word "prostitute" in depiction of the dragon. But beginning with *verse 16,* an earthly parallel is being contemplated as the representation of the word "prostitute" is now downgraded to designate human wickedness at its utmost degree, taking into consideration the most wicked nation on earth, perhaps one of the most powerful, to be eliminated as an obliterative example to the rest of the world, bringing the whole earth to its knees.

Strangely enough, despite its abominating ways and its impious outlawries, perhaps in conjunction with its outstanding opulency, this particular nation in its boastfulness as a "lone ranger" will not be one of the ten horns of the beast, causing a general loathsomeness against it. In *Revelation 17:16,* we read that "the beast and the ten horns in a unified rapport will hate the "prostitute" (this nation) and will concert a deadly strike against it, bringing her to ruin, and she will be totally consumed with fire". "For God has put into the hearts of the ten horns to give their power to the eleventh horn which is the Antichrist to rule until God's words are fulfilled and because the 'woman' (who is the dragon controlling the beast) is the great city that rules over the kings of the earth. "*(Revelation 17:15-18).*

CHAPTER 18

Before we continue with these marvelous wonderments, let's recapitulate a little bit concerning the "woman," covered with blasphemous names, who is sitting on the beast that had seven heads and ten horns.

Being the subject of this whole current chapter, the woman's lavishness on sin is graphically exposed in a rather symbiotic narrative involving both the spiritual and the natural, but with two specific targets in God's mind.

In the spirit dimension, Lucifer is depicted as the master profaner, whereas in the natural, the emphasis is strangely on this great nation, singled out as a comparable earthly entity, on which God has deliberately poured his judgment.

I suggest you get rid of all hastiness in any conclusion concerning the identity of this nation, because physical and spiritual are two extremes, and their parallelism may suggest great variance and may simply turn out to be totally disproving.

For example, we know according to *John 19:20* that Jesus was crucified and buried outside of Jerusalem in Israel, but in the spirit, the Bible refers to the place of crucifixion of Jesus as "Sodom and Egypt." You see how easy it is to fall off the wagon. The same spiritual principle applies here for this evil nation that's going to be judged by God in these end times, but just because at the end of the chapter we read that the nation in question is where the prophets and the saints were killed, reference is not necessarily being made to Jerusalem (Israel) or Rome (Italy).

This mysterious "prostitute woman" according to Revelation 17:5 is also:

- Babylon the Great.

- The mother of prostitutes.

- The mother of the abominations of the earth.

The entire chapter is an illustration of God's judgment against Lucifer and this wicked nation that will be destroyed by the eleven horns concertedly. The whole section is reproduced for you here with no further comments:

"After this I saw another angel coming down from heaven. He had great authority, and the earth was illuminated by his splendor. With a mighty voice he shouted: Fallen! Fallen is Babylon the Great! She has become a home for demons and a haunt for every evil spirit, a haunt for every unclean and detestable bird, for all the nations have drunk the maddening wine of her adulteries."

"The kings of the earth committed adultery with her, and the merchants of the earth grew rich from her excessive luxuries." "Then I heard another voice from heaven say: Come out of her, my people, so that you will not share in her sins, and receive any of her plagues. Her sins are piled up to heaven, and God has remembered her crimes. Give back to her as she has given. Pay her back double for what she has done. Mix her a double portion from her own cup. Give her as much torture and grief as the glory and luxury she gave herself.

In her heart she boasts, I sit as queen. I am not a widow, and I will never mourn. Therefore, in one day her plagues will overtake her: death, mourning and famine. She will be consumed by fire, for Mighty is the Lord God who judges her.

When the kings of the earth who committed adultery with her and shared her luxury see the smoke of her burning, they will weep and mourn over her. Terrified at her torment, they will stand far off and cry: Woe! Woe, O great city, O Babylon, city of power! In one hour, your doom has come!"

"The merchants of the earth will weep and mourn over her because no one buys their cargoes any more, cargoes of gold, silver, precious stones, pearls, fine linen, purple, silk and scarlet cloth. Every sort of citron wood, and articles of every kind made of ivory, costly wood, bronze, iron and marble; cargoes of cinnamon and spice, of incense, myrrh and frank-incense, of wine and olive oil, of fine flour and wheat; cattle and sheep; horses and carriages; and bodies and souls of men." They will say, "The fruit you longed for is gone from you. All your riches and splendor have vanished, never to be recovered." The merchants who sold these things and gained their wealth from her will stand far off, terrified at her torment. They will weep and mourn and cry out:"

"Woe! Woe, O great city, dressed in fine linen, purple and scarlet, and glittering with gold, precious stones and pearls! In one hour, such great wealth has been brought to ruin! Every sea captain, and all who travel by ship, the sailors, and all who earn their living from the sea, will stand far off. When they see the smoke of her burning, they will exclaim:" "Was there ever a city like this great city? They will throw dust on their heads, and with weeping and mourning cry out: Woe! Woe, O great city, where all who had ships on the sea became rich through her wealth!"

In one hour, she has been brought to ruin! Rejoice over her, O heaven! Rejoice, saints and apostles and prophets! God has judged her for the way she treated you.

Then a mighty angel picked up a boulder the size of a large millstone and threw it into the sea, and said: "With such violence the great city of Babylon will be thrown down, and never to be found again". The music of harpists and musicians, flute players and trumpeters, will never be heard in you again. No workman of any trade will ever be found in you again. The sound of a millstone will never be heard in you again. The light of a lamp will never shine in you again. The voice of bridegroom and bride will never be heard in you again. Your merchants were the world's great men. By your magic spell all the nations were led astray. In her was found the blood of prophets and of the saints, and of all who have been killed on the earth."

CHAPTER 19

The Return of Christ

At this point all hopes are forever lost for those who were consentient in their adverse inclination to the "Gospel of Christ" and its detrimental implications.

This conclusion may seem a bit surprising, but as we examine the text in its ultimacy, the Bible clearly teaches that everything is complete, and there is nothing more expected to be overcome by humankind as natural beings in this world at this point.

Fundamentally, the Antichrist and the false prophet are in hell, Lucifer is in a penitentiary for a thousand years, and death is no more.

After the judgment of the "prostitute," the Apostle John said he heard a loud noise in heaven and a great multitude was shouting, "Hallelujah, salvation and glory and honor and power unto our God, for God has condemned the great prostitute who corrupted the earth by her adulteries and made her pay by avenging the blood of his servants at her hand."

The twenty-four elders·and the four living creatures fell down and worshiped God, who was seated on the throne, crying:

Amen, Hallelujah!

Then the great multitude said, "Let us rejoice and be glad and give him glory, for the wedding of the Lamb has come, and his bride has made herself ready with fine linen, bright and clean representing the righteousness of the saints." Then the angel asked John to write the following: "Blessed are those who are invited to the marriage supper of the Lamb." And he added, "These are the true words of God."

At this point John wanted to worship the angel, but the angel said, "Don't do that" I am a fellow servant with you and with your brothers who hold the testimony of Jesus. Worship God! For the testimony of Jesus is the spirit of prophecy.

Then John said he saw heaven opened and a white horse appeared whose rider is called "Faithful and True." He had many crowns on his head, and his eyes were like blazing fire. He was dressed in a robe full of blood, and his name was, "the Word of God." The armies of Heaven, all dressed up in fine linen, white and clean, were following him riding on white horses. Out of his mouth came a sharp sword with which to strike the nations. He treads the wine-press of the fury of the wrath of God Almighty, and he will rule them with a rod of iron. On his robe and on his thigh, it is written the name, "King of kings and Lord of lords."

Beginning with *verse 17* is a graphic and gruesome picture of what is taking place in the earth as the Lord Jesus Christ makes his apparition on the scene. The Apostle tells us that all the inhabitants of the earth are killed. All people, free and slave, small and great, kings, generals, and all the mighty men, horses and their riders, all are killed by the sword that came out of the mouth of Jesus. Then all the birds that the angel had commanded to gather together for the "all you can eat" supper of God in *verses 17-18* gorged themselves on their flesh.

The two beasts (the Antichrist and the false prophet) are captured alive and thrown undeceased into the fiery lake of burning sulfur. You don't have to be a biblical expert to convince yourself of this irrefutable evidence that the earth now stands without any human life, physically speaking.

A brief recapitulation is by all means necessary for the establishment of this sad and joyful truth.

During the episode of the Antichrist and the false prophet back in Revelation 13, the Bible is definite that all who did not take the mark and worship the beast were killed, leaving the entire earth exclusively to the beasts and their worshipers. Conversely, now we are in Revelation 19, and as Jesus returns to the earth to reign, he captures both the Antichrist and the false prophet and puts them in hell. We are told that he also killed all who had received the mark of the beast and worshiped his image.

Bluntly put, this portion of scripture corroborates the Apostle Paul's teaching in *2 Timothy 4:1* that the Lord Jesus Christ will come again to judge the living and the dead.

The expression "to judge the living" does not mean, as you might at first sight be inclined to believe, that if Jesus came today, he would have a throne set up in a country somewhere and men and women would be called before his court to defend their evil misconduct. This is nonsense!

Naturally, this kind of thinking is a grave misconception of the power of God and who God is, totally ignoring the prominence of the spiritual characteristics of his ways established throughout the scripture. Acknowledge that when God judges, he destroys and kills, angels or men. I know it may be very hard to wrap our mind around such a concept, but the implication is obvious, and it certainly does not involve any argumentum for adjustments as allowed in human courts. God's judgment is always past tense. When you reject Christ, you have already been judged.

Given the evidence of that crossed line by the people of the tribulation period, deliberately rejecting the loving God as they meld their vows with a proud and candid mark in favor of the devil, is of course another way of saying, "God, we don't need you."

With such a definite stance it is fair to say that this is sin at its utmost. This is a violation of the first commandment, "Thou shall have no other gods before me," and is certainly deserving of death. Shall I say without equivocation that this is exactly what Jesus did, or will do, putting an end to all physical life in the earth in the establishment of his millennium.

CHAPTER 20

Lucifer in Prison

The Millennium

Up to the end of *chapter 19,* things were going so favorably for Satan and his squadrons that all nations regardless of their power and might were destroyed, giving place literally only to his kingdom. But at the end of *chapter 19,* as Christ made his appearance and exhausted the power of the two beasts, the conditions were such that death had reaped the richest of his harvest leaving no human survivors behind.

This is where the prophecy of the Apostle Paul concerning angels being judged by men is taking form as things finish just as the Bible predicted throughout its pages.

The Apostle Paul in his description of the role of the people of God through his foresight of the future said in *1 Corinthians 6:3* that, among other things, at an appointed time, we will judge the angels. And like I said earlier, from here on out, the battle is spiritual involving exclusively spirits on both sides: Jesus and his followers as spirit beings on the one hand, and certainly Satan and all his demons on the other.

Chapter 20 begins this way. "An angel having the key of the Abyss and a great chain seized Lucifer and bound him for a thousand years, locking and sealing the abyss over him and keeping him from deceiving the "nations" anymore."

Nations at this present moment exclusively refer to all the evil spirits, commonly called devils-fallen angels or demons, but after that, he (Satan) will be set free for a short time.

Again, this is proof that Lucifer is the last head, or the seventh head of the beast to be destroyed. The statement "After that, he will be set free for a short time" is paralleled to the one found in *Revelation 17:10*, which reads, "The seven heads are seven kings, five have fallen, one is, the other has not yet come, but when he does come, **he will only remain for a little while**". The Bible says that **at the end of the millennium, Satan will be set free, but it will only be short lived.**

There is one very important factor that needs to be acknowledged. Otherwise, t he potential for misinterpretation will overtake you. Like I said at the beginning of the book, evil spirits, fallen angels, or demons, call them what you want, are here and everywhere like natural human beings, driving on our highways and engaging in ordinary conversations with the general public with total unawareness while they still have the power to transmute between both worlds.

But all this will come to an end soon with the destruction of the Antichrist and the false prophet and the binding of Satan. *Daniel 7:11* tells us that when the Antichrist and the false prophet are captured and thrown into the lake of fire, the rest of the beasts, corresponding to the rest of the evil spirits, will be stripped of their power, but their lives will be purportedly prolonged for a time to endure the adjudication of the millennium in fulfillment of what Jude 6 foretold of the angels who became evil spirits, whom God had kept bound with everlasting chains of darkness for judgment on the great day. The great day is beyond a shadow of a doubt the thousand-year reign of Christ and his followers.

It sure is interesting to see the onset of the millennium begins with thrones being put in place and the spirits of those who came back to life during the first resurrection sitting on them as kings. Very impressive! Anyway, by now you shouldn't be surprised to see the Bible come alive as the connection between Paul's teaching in *1 Corinthians 6:3-4* assuring us of eventually judging the angels and the reality of the message gloriously coming to pass right here in *Revelation 20*.

We are told that in addition to those who were privileged by the Rapture, these kings also include those who were beheaded because of the word of God and the testimony of Jesus, along with those who during the tribulation period honored death over the receipt of the mark of the beast on their foreheads or on their hands. In a perfect congruence, they conjoined and reigned with Christ for the thousand years.

These resurrected souls are the Jews spoken by the prophet Ezekiel that God had taken out of the nations where they had gone and brought them on the Mountain of Israel as one nation. They are no longer two nations divided into two kingdoms. There will be one king over them, referring to the kingdom of heaven which obviously begins with the thousand-year reign of Christ. They will no longer defile themselves with idols and vile images, for "I the Lord will cleanse them and save them from all their sinful backsliding." They will be my people and I will be their God" *(Ezekiel 37:23)*.

"On this mountain, they and their children and their children's children will live forever. I will make an everlasting covenant of peace with them, and I will put my sanctuary among them forever. My dwelling place will be with them. I will be their God and they will be my people. Then the nations will know that I the Lord make Israel holy, when my sanctuary is among them forever" *(Ezekiel 37:20-28)*.

The focal point of the majority of the messages of the Old Testament is the Rapture of God's people from a sinful and wicked world to reign with Christ over the nations.

Now it's time for the submarines to surface, the nations that had been living or confined under the earth dimension, the evil spirits that had been residing in the abyss, they will surface to live as mere men on the earth for the millennium with no more transitional power back and forth between the two dimensions, because the submarine's chief officer, the source of their power, Lucifer, is bound during the thousand-year reign of Christ and his followers, awaiting his final destruction.

I know this sounds incredible. But the Apostle Paul foretold of this mysterious phenomenon in *1 Corinthians 6:3* when he clearly states that we humans (the saints) will one day judge the angels, and it is happening right here in *chapter 20* as we are given dominion and authority in the earth with Christ over the whole community of fallen angels for a thousand years.

Whether we want to believe it or not, during the entire millennium, God's people at the side of Christ will judge and rule over the totality of fallen angels throughout the earth, while these evil spirits wander in total darkness as physical beings during which time the sun and the moon will be no more, and the oceans and all the streams will have fled away.

Yet these fallen angels or demons despite their dereliction are nevertheless able to survive the entire thousand years. They can't die the kind of death known to humankind because not only death in the physical sense is no more, but they themselves personify the spirit of death.

As we saw in Genesis the hazing that followed the transformation and the transmutation of both the man and the woman from **"living souls to humankind"** in this physical painful body as a result of sin, here in *Revelation 20,* the angels, in a similar fashion, because of the violation of their spiritual mandate, abandoning their prescribed habitation as spirit beings, the mystery of adverse effect will come into play by the Lord Jesus Christ, as described in *verse 9,* transforming the horde of the fallen angels into manlike appearance, giving them physical bodies in the likeness of sinful flesh to upset forevermore their subsistence and bring them under total destruction when fire comes down from heaven and devours them forever.

Unfortunately to a large extent, what is being taught and believed is that Jesus is coming back to reign for a thousand years in the earth during which time the people of all nations will for the first time live a peaceful and a satisfying life, with no sickness, no disease, no lack, and not even death. Total triumph over evil. But what a delusive imagery of the destructive power of sin. Although this imagination is somewhat evocative and solacing, we could not be more wrong with this fallacious anticipation of the facts on our part.

Imagine this preposterous setting for a moment:

During the millennium, those who remain in the earth will be given a **"thousand-year-long"** life with no sickness, no disease not even death.

Now let's look at the scenario. Jesus is back in the earth to reign for a thousand year. His holy angels and his "Saints" **(those chosen from before the world began)** who were resurrected and or raptured also came back as spirits to reign with him.

As anyone can see, the tone is explicitly formal.

How ludicrous it is to think that Jesus will come down to rule over the people who will have missed the Rapture and chosen Satan as their god in proud view of the mark of the beast, and bless them with a "thousand-year-long" life without sickness, without disease and best of all without death is totally missing the essence of the word of God.

All things considered, the mere thought that Jesus is back in the earth and reigning for a thousand years and not a single soul will be saved should trigger that more is at issue than simply what is being veneered. The answer, I think, resides in the stiffness of our own nature to understand and believe the scripture and the devastating power of sin.

Let me recapitulate a few things that perhaps will help our thinking straight. The Bible teaches that during the millennium, the earth will have lost all the elements necessary to sustain any physical life **(natural man born of woman)**. The sun, the moon, the ocean, and the rivers will have ceased to exist or will have dematerialized. How then can anyone teach or believe that humankind **(natural humans)** is still part of the earth habitat?

Furthermore, what is profoundly deceiving with this picture is the obvious gratification associated with this epigrammatic view, granting those left behind the most peaceful life never known before in the history of humankind.

If that were the case, I myself would definitely want to be left behind. But the question is, "What interests would such a scenario advance?" Or "What purposes would that serve?" One thing that will be difficult to explain in a reasonable and convincing manner with this fatuous concept is the fact that at the end of the thousand years, all who have lived during the millennium are burned to ashes and destroyed forever by Jesus himself according to *Revelation 20:9-10*.

The true approach in brief is as follows: At the end of the thousand years, Satan is released from his prison and goes out to deceive the "nations" in the four corners of the earth, Gog, and Magog (all inclusive) to gather them for battle. (**"Nations" here do not refer to the countries of the earth**) In number they are like the sand of the sea. They march across the breadth of the earth and surrounded the camp of God's people in the city he loves. Some versions of scriptures have them as coming up to the surface of the earth. *(Revelation 20:7-10)*

Let's pause here for a moment and remind ourselves that the history of the world had culminated a thousand years earlier. This is not only post- tribulation, we are in the post-millennium era, and the Antichrist and the false prophet have already been in hell for a thousand years and counting. Nations as individual countries no longer exist. The expression "breadth of the earth" signifies "To and Fro" on the surface without restrictions, without boundaries, covering the entire earth. Can any human being travel the entire earth without automobiles, ferry-boats, airplanes, or trains? What is even more striking is they encircle the camp of the holy saints of God in the beloved city. The beloved city is Christ himself (**Christ is Zion and *Psalm 48* teaches that Zion is the city of God**) and certainly not a physical geographical location in the earth. This is spirituality at its peak.

As anyone with a faith like a mustard seed can see, there is nothing metaphorical about these images. It is clear that the earth, during the millennium, will be comprised of two antagonistic groups of people or should I say "spirits". On the one hand we have one cognate group, the fallen angels numbered in zillion, in connivance with Satan; on the other hand, we have the Lord Jesus Christ, his holy angels, and the saints of God, ruling over the earth and judging these wicked angels as taught by the apostle Paul in 1 Corinthians 6:3, which judgment will last a thousand years.

The battle is clearly between spirits, between two kingdoms, "Darkness vs Light". According to *Zephaniah 3:8,* on one side we'll have the kingdoms of the earth also known as the "Nations", and on the other side the Kingdom of God with Jesus as King of kings with the fire of his jealous anger to consume the whole world and make a sudden end to this whole mess, as the earth is transformed into the eternal "Hell".

I don't know if you still want to call this "end-times" battle a "war". But as promised, these evil forces, having come to their appointed end, God will simply intervene and supernaturally put an end to their presence and their dominion in the universe.

In *Romans 8:3,* the Apostle Paul teaches that God has condemned sin in the flesh, but because of his incredible love for mankind, God gave his Son flesh of sin in the likeness of sinful men to free them from the law of sin and death. This transcendental law of God deals with all level or dimension of contingencies converting even the angels who abandoned their positions into manhood as a result of their sins, for their eternal destruction.

However, despite this obvious decrement, given they did come by water and blood, these fallen angels, though appearing humans are still spirit beings, capable of transitioning from one dimension to the next, maintaining a level of superiority over humankind and consequently having everlasting existence. However, when Jesus returns with his revisory power for the thousand-year reign, the unimaginable takes place; a reversal like only God can do is at hand.

While humankind reverts to their original pre-physical nature with Christ, Satan, the source of the power of evil, is bound and the annoying potencies of his demons are withdrawn as they are now being judged by God and men as a reprisal for the humiliating defeat mankind had suffered at the hands of the serpent in the Garden before the foundation of the world.

For the very first-time angels **(the fallen angels)** through the ringers of humankind (as men) will live beyond a thousand years in the earth, or or 1,260 days to be exact. The seven thousandth year or the true "Sabbath".

The enshrinement of the Sabbath, the seventh day, a holy day, a day chosen and set apart by God for his rest, a day being a thousand years, thus the seven thousandth year which is symbolic of the thousand-year reign of Christ and his Saints in the earth. Through this supernatural exploit **(the thousand-year reign)** God will ensure an extended life to these wicked spirits, a life that is symbolic of their everlasting existence lasting a full thousand years and a few days in addendum.

Were it not for Jesus, the Creator of heavens and earth, to intervene and enervate their spiritual capacities, their enigmatic representations would be everlasting. But again, as we read in *verse 9,* fire came down from heaven and devoured them. Lucifer, the great deceiver, was thrown into the lake of burning sulfur, where the beast and the false prophet had been thrown a thousand year earlier, and they will be tormented day and night forever and ever.

Now it's time for those who were skeptical or objected to the fact that the world was devoid of humankind since the end of *chapter 19* when the beast and the false prophet were removed from the earth, to draw the ultimate lines of demarcation, because beginning with the next verse is the threshold of the second resurrection, which will culminate with the second death. The second death and the second resurrection go hand in hand; they do not concern the living.

THE LAST JUDGMENT

Then John said he saw a great white throne and him who sat on it. The earth and the heaven were no more. The dead small and great were resurrected; and the books were opened. Another book was opened, which is the Book of Life, and the dead were judged according to what was written about them in these books.

The sea gave up the dead that were in it, and death and Hades gave up the dead that were in them, and all were judged based on what was written about them in the books. In *verse 14,* John says that death and Hades were thrown into the lake of fire, which is the second death. All whose names were not found written in the Book of Life were thrown into the lake of fire in communion with Lucifer, death, Hades, the beast and the false prophet.

CHAPTER 21

The New Heaven and the New Earth

According to the Apostle John, a new earth and a new heaven made their appearance. The sea was no more. The New Jerusalem, the Holy City, came down from God out of heaven, prepared as a bride for Christ, her husband.

A loud voice is heard from the throne saying, "Now the dwelling of God is with men as his people and he will live with them as their God. He will wipe every tear from their eyes, and there will be no more death, or mourning or crying or pain, for the former things have passed away."

After making everything new, he who was seated on the throne said, "Write this down: for these words are true and faithful." Then he said, "It is done. I am the Alpha and the Omega, the beginning and the end."

Then the Apostle John says that one of the seven angels who had the seven bowls full of the seven last plagues took him on a high and great mountain and gave him a tour of the Holy City, Jerusalem, which is the bride, the wife of the Lamb. The Apostle John describes its brilliance, clear as crystal, as it shone with the glory of God and comparing it to a very precious jewel, like jasper. The city had a high wall with twelve gates on which were written the twelve tribes of Israel, and twelve angels were securing them.

The wall also had twelve foundations, and on them were the names of the twelve apostles of Christ. The wall was made of jasper, and the city of pure Gold, like transparent glass.

The sun and the moon were no more, neither was there any temple in the city, for God is all-sufficient. Nothing impure will ever enter it, or anything that is shameful or deceitful, but only those whose names are written in the Lamb's Book of Life.

CHAPTER 22

The Kingdom of Heaven

After that the angel showed me the river of the water of life, says John. It is clear as crystal, flowing from the throne of God and of the Lamb down in the midst of the street of the city. The tree of life stands on each side of the river and bears twelve crops of fruits, yielding its fruit every month, and the leaves of the tree are for the healing of the nations. The nations will see God's face and his name will be on their foreheads. There shall be no darkness in the city and neither the need for candles or the light of the sun; for the Lord God will give them light and their kingdom is an everlasting kingdom.

Then Jesus said to John in *verse 7,* "Behold, I am coming soon! Blessed is he who keeps the words of the prophecy in this book."

In *verse 8,* John says, "I John saw these things and heard them." After having heard what was told to me and seen what was shown to me, I fell down to worship the angel who had shown me these things. But the angel said to me, "Don't do that! I am a fellow servant with you and with your brothers, the prophets, and of all who keep the words of this book! Worship God!"

Then the angel told me, says John, "Do not seal up the words of the prophecy of this book, for the time is at hand."

Again, Jesus said to John, "Behold I am coming soon and my rewards are with me to give to every man according to what he has done. I am the Alpha and the Omega, the Beginning and the End, the First and the Last." Jesus continues to say, "Blessed are those who wash their robes that they may have the right to the tree of life and may go through the gates into the city."

Then Jesus sadly added, **"Outside are the dogs, the sorcerers, the sexually immoral, the murderers, the idolaters and all who love and practice falsehood."**

Not that excellence is essential, but unfortunately what is refuted by many that could have promoted our spiritual interests unto salvation is the acknowledgment of our sinful nature and the blood of Christ as the cleansing agent.

These inconvenient sins described in the previous paragraph should be conspicuous enough to encourage the development of the ethos necessary to make the sojourn in the earth an enjoyable one, while making the invitation of Jesus described in the next two paragraphs an exciting prospect.

Then Jesus said to John, "I, Jesus, have sent my angel to give you this testimony for the churches. I am the root and the offspring of David, and the bright Morning Star."

In *verse 17,* "the spirit and the bride say, 'Come'. Let him who hears say, 'Come.' Whoever is thirsty, let him come. And whosoever will, let him take the water of life freely." In *verse 18,* Jesus gives this final warning through John: "I warn every man who hears the words of the prophecy of this book. If anyone adds anything to them, God will add to him the plagues described in this book. If anyone takes away from the words of the book of this prophecy, God shall take away his part out of the Book of Life and out of the holy city."

Verse 20 reads, He who testifies to these things says: "Yes, I am coming soon." Amen. "Come Lord Jesus."

The Apostle John concludes the book of Revelation in *verse 21* with these words:

The grace of our Lord Jesus Christ be with God's people. Amen.

I hope the contents of this book have been a blessing to your heart and soul, to the extent that if Jesus were to return in your lifetime you may experience the necessary spiritual metamorphosis and go from this caterpillar state you are in, to the promised butterfly dimensions, in readiness to meet the Lord in the air and forever be in his presence.

- God Bless You All -

www.ingramcontent.com/pod-product-compliance
Lightning Source LLC
Chambersburg PA
CBHW060900120626
46553CB00001B/158